Routledge Revivals

Monetary Reform in Theory and Practice

First published in 1936, this book gives the reader an insight into the tendencies and spirit of the monetary reform movement as a whole, as accomplished or proposed since the First World War. The author marks the consideration of the overall reform as being more important than specifically looking at the actual proposals and measures involved, and the views he attributes to the various monetary reform schools are therefore composite views of the various factions of those schools. As a comparatively recent convert to the idea of monetary reform, at the time of writing, the author offers a balanced view of the subject as he also has extensive experience of the ideas of the orthodox monetary system. However, he does not believe that monetary reform alone can achieve the desired end without considerable economic planning. Indeed, he suggests that the monetary reform movement he discusses desperately needs to adopt a broader perspective and thus, he suggests a compromise.

Monetary Reform in Theory and Practice

Paul Einzig

Routledge
Taylor & Francis Group

First published in 1936
by Kegan Paul, Trench, Trubner & Co., LTD.

This edition first published in 2013 by Routledge
2 Park Square, Milton Park, Abingdon, Oxon, OX14 4RN

Simultaneously published in the USA and Canada
by Routledge
711 Third Avenue, New York, NY 10017

Routledge is an imprint of the Taylor & Francis Group, an informa business

Publisher's Note

The publisher has gone to great lengths to ensure the quality of this reprint but points out that some imperfections in the original copies may be apparent.

Disclaimer

The publisher has made every effort to trace copyright holders and welcomes correspondence from those they have been unable to contact.

A Library of Congress record exists under ISBN: 36018670

ISBN 13: 978-0-415-81936-7 (hbk)
ISBN 13: 978-0-203-37456-6 (ebk)
ISBN 13: 978-0-415-81940-4 (pbk)

MONETARY REFORM IN THEORY AND PRACTICE

By

PAUL EINZIG

LONDON
KEGAN PAUL, TRENCH, TRUBNER & CO., LTD.
BROADWAY HOUSE: 68–74 CARTER LANE, E.C.
1936

Printed in Great Britain by Butler & Tanner Ltd., Frome and London

PREFACE

During the past few years an immense number of books have been published on various monetary reform proposals, groups of proposals, or selections of proposals. As far as the author knows, however, no book has as yet been published on the monetary reform movement as a whole. It is in order to fill this gap that this book has been written. Its object is not merely to give a bird's-eye view of monetary reform measures which have been proposed or adopted. That task in itself is well worth undertaking, for the man in the street is apt to become confused by the multitude of monetary reform measures and proposals. To enumerate the most important reform proposals and measures, classify them into categories, describe their essential characteristics and analyse them critically is in itself necessary and desirable. The author, however, has undertaken a more ambitious task than that of merely providing the public with a guide-book to the mazes of monetary reform. His object has been to give his readers an insight into the tendencies and spirit of the monetary reform movement as a whole.

The various monetary reform measures and proposals differ from one another widely in many essential respects. Their advocates disagree with one another, and fight one another. Nevertheless, their proposals, whether they exist only in theory or whether they have been put into practice, are like so many streams which swell the main river of the monetary reform movement. They have all one common object—they seek to make the monetary system more suited than it has been in the past to the advancement of the material progress of mankind. To attain their end they have to overcome the resistance of the common enemy: orthodox monetary conception, which is too deeply engrained in official opinion, in expert opinion, and perhaps also in large sections of public opinion, to be dislodged without a hard struggle.

The fact that there is an immense variety of reform proposals —this book attempts to deal only with some of the best known among them—does not alter the fundamental unity of the reform movement. After all, a major movement in history has hardly ever been initiated and carried out on uniform principles. Every broad movement is supported by a vast number of schools which agree on nothing but the necessity of achieving a certain end, and of overcoming the resistance of those opposed to the change. Indeed, in most historical instances, there have hardly ever been two outstanding personalities within the same movement who have held exactly the same opinion as to the means by which their desired end could and should be achieved. The French Revolution, for instance, was no more a uniform movement than is the monetary reform movement of our day. Every leader sought to attain the supreme end of *liberté, égalité, fraternité* by different means, just as the leaders of the monetary reform movement differ upon the methods by which the monetary system can be made more efficiently to perform its function. From the very outset until the very end there was a desperate fight between the conflicting revolutionary currents in France. Although the leaders of the monetary reform movement do not literally send each other to the guillotine as the French revolutionary leaders did, in many cases this is not for lack of wishing to do so. For the fight between the various schools, and even between the various factions within the same schools, is at times at least as bitter as it is between monetary reformers in general and their arch-enemies, the orthodox school. The fact that there was a similar internal fight within the French revolutionary movement did not prevent the Revolution from producing fundamental and lasting effects. These effects were not the work of any one of the revolutionary leaders but of the movement as a whole. Similarly, if and when the balance sheet of the present monetary reform movement is compiled, it will be found that the net result will differ from the proposals of any one reformer or any one school of reformers. It will be the outcome of the joint efforts of those who wanted to change the system, and the chances are that it will assume the form of some kind of compromise between the various reform proposals.

The fact that the author attaches more importance to the

reform movement as a whole than to the actual proposals and measures which it comprises has determined his treatment of the subject. He does not enter into detailed discussion of any individual reform as such, except in so far as it characterises a certain tendency in the reform movement. With relatively few exceptions, the views he attributes to the various monetary reform schools are composite views of the various factions of those schools. It is only when a certain school of thought is prominently associated with one name that the actual proposals of the reformer in question are discussed.

In pursuing this method the author exposes himself to criticism on the part of reformers who may conceivably feel that their proposals are misrepresented. In particular, the moderate wing of each school will probably object to the emphasis laid by the author upon the views of the extremist wing of the same school. It is often necessary, however, to exaggerate to draw attention to anomalies which would otherwise pass unnoticed. It was in any case impossible to deal within the limit of this volume with all the differences that exist within particular schools. Nor did the author consider it expedient to overburden the memory of the general reader, to whom this book is primarily addressed, by producing an intimidating array of names, quotations, and a detailed account of the endless polemics raging between the factions.

There is another source of possible criticism to which the author felt he must risk exposing himself. In practically every instance he has followed up his chapter dealing with the various schools of monetary reform proposals with chapters dealing with the practical application of the suggestions made by the respective schools or with the application of measures resembling those suggestions. Possibly some theoretical reformers will be indignant at the association of their ideas with certain practical measures which, perhaps, they may emphatically disown. Conversely, some of the practical reformers may be annoyed that their measures are classed with theoretical proposals which they are the first to denounce as unsound, doctrinaire, or Utopian. In this instance, too, as in regard to the differences within the same schools, the author's treatment of the subject has been determined by his view that the reform movement as a whole is more important than the individual measures and proposals of which it consists.

Above all, the author expects much criticism on the part of the members of various reform schools on the ground that he has not done justice to this or that reform measure, or that the space devoted to it or the emphasis laid on it is not in proportion to its relative importance among the other monetary reform proposals. The author had such an experience in 1931 when, in his book *The World Economic Crisis*, he sought to reconcile apparently conflicting explanations of the origin of the crisis. The rôle of the arbitrator or conciliator is more often than not a thankless one. Also it may well be objected that the author had no right to assume such a rôle, since he himself is an interested party, having associated himself with several reform proposals. In this respect, it is for the reader to judge whether the author has succeeded in attaining the degree of impartiality essential for performing his task.

The author is a comparatively recent convert to monetary reform. Until a few years ago he was in favour of the orthodox monetary system with only minor modifications of detail. For this very reason, he feels he is in a better position to see both sides of the problem than those who have always been either in the orthodox camp or in the radical camp. While he attacks the resistance of the orthodox school to the reforms that are essential for the welfare of mankind, he also attacks the reformers for their exaggeration. As a result, he fully expects to be condemned for heresy by the orthodox school, and at the same time criticised by radicals on the ground of having retained too much of his orthodox past. Although the author whole-heartedly supports some of the advanced radical proposals, he nevertheless believes in retaining a limited gold standard. He also realises the danger of proceeding too fast towards the desired end, and emphasises that the pace of monetary expansion should be limited by the necessity of safeguarding confidence in the monetary system. For confidence, after all, is the basis of credit. In the author's view, the object of monetary reform should be to carry monetary expansion up to the safety limit, and to create circumstances in which the safety limit can be extended.

Throughout the volume the author has emphasised that he does not believe that monetary reform in itself can achieve the desired end unless it is accompanied by economic planning. In the absence of a planned production and distribution, no monetary reform can possibly safeguard the community against shocks and setbacks. He considers it a matter for regret that some of the best brains in the monetary reform movement do not realise how one-sided and inadequate even the most comprehensive monetary reform would be if management is confined to the monetary sphere while anarchy continues in other spheres of the economic system. From this point of view, as well as from the point of view of the interrelation between the various reform schemes, the monetary reform movement is badly in need of a broader outlook.

The author does not in the least imagine that his proposal of a compromise between the various monetary reform schemes, and between monetary reform and economic planning, is the last word on the subject. He sincerely hopes that his attempt at suggesting a compromise will be followed by other similar attempts, and that as a result some basis will sooner or later be found on which the apparently conflicting proposals—or at any rate the moderate ones among them—can be reconciled with one another and with the general scheme of economic planning.

P. E.

THE WHITE COTTAGE,
SOUTH BOLTON GARDENS,
LONDON, S.W.5.
April, 1936.

CONTENTS

MONETARY REFORM
IN THEORY AND PRACTICE

CHAPTER I
INTRODUCTORY

(1) Money in the Melting-pot

The international economic crisis has thrown the world's monetary systems into the melting-pot. Until 1931 most people took it for granted that the gold standard had been adopted definitely as the permanent monetary system of the civilised world. Even during the war, when the operation of the gold standard was suspended, it was considered beyond doubt that the suspension would be purely temporary and that once the abnormal situation had come to an end the world would revert to the pre-war system. Developments between 1925 and 1931 apparently justified this assumption. The gold standard was restored. Indeed, its supremacy appeared to be even more safely established than before the war, for the system was adopted by a number of countries which before 1914 were on a silver or inconvertible paper basis.

Admittedly, the exact form which the gold standard should assume became the subject of much controversy during the period of post-war stability. While before the war it was accepted without question that the then existing form of the gold standard would be permanent, after the war the principles and technique of the gold standard became a matter for detailed examination and discussion. Various changes, whether in legal form or in practical technique, brought noteworthy departures from the pre-war system. It became evident that the rules of the post-war system were subject to an evolutionary change, although the trend of this movement was somewhat obscure. Nevertheless, while important questions of detail were considered open to modification, the fundamental principle, that of maintaining the various monetary units stable in relation to a fixed weight of gold, was not in practice called in question. It is true that there was no lack of proposals for reforms of fundamental importance, but the chance that any one of these might be adopted was infinitely remote.

(2) The Landmark of 1931

The suspension of the gold standard in Great Britain in 1931 marked the beginning of a vital change. That suspension, indeed, constitutes a landmark of fundamental importance in the evolution of the world's attitude towards its monetary system. From 1931 onwards, the predominant majority of those concerned with monetary matters ceased to take it for granted that after the termination of the crisis the world would return once more to the pre-war monetary system, with such modifications of detail as might prove necessary. It became evident that the results which the pre-war system had produced in post-war conditions had been highly unsatisfactory. In a number of countries, especially in Great Britain, the country of origin of the gold standard, strong opposition developed to a return to that system. Even circles which until 1931 had been decidedly orthodox began to flirt with the idea of a permanent inconvertible currency, and with other reform proposals. More recently, the fact that the countries of the Sterling Bloc have been relatively prosperous, while those of the Gold Bloc have suffered intensely through deflationary depression, has strengthened the movement against a return to gold.

In the United States, President Roosevelt's progressive economic and financial policy brought forth a crop of monetary reform proposals, many of which in present circumstances stand a good chance of being adopted permanently. Schemes which prior to 1931 were dismissed as Utopian have become the subject of serious consideration in official circles in various countries. Even extreme radical would-be reformers have succeeded in gaining considerable political influence in various parts of the world, and some countries bid fair to become experimental laboratories for the testing of radical projects.

The number of monetary reform schemes put forward during the last fifteen years or so is very large. Indeed, it is hardly possible to discover two monetary reformers whose schemes are identical. There are innumerable shades of reform proposals, ranging from mere modifications of the pre-crisis system on points of detail to fundamental changes of a revolutionary character.

(3) Extreme Schools

While the would-be reformers are quarrelling among themselves as to which scheme should be adopted, there are two extreme schools which are opposed to any kind of reform. There is the extreme orthodox school, which holds that what is required is not fresh reforms, but the cancellation of the reforms of detail which were adopted after the war, so as to restore the gold standard to its pre-war " purity ". Nothing short of an unrestricted and unmanaged automatic gold standard would satisfy this school. The other extreme opponents of monetary reform are the adherents of pure Communism. To the Communistic mind the monetary system should not be reformed but abolished altogether. The number of adherents to either of these extreme schools is, however, limited. The majority of orthodox economists are prepared up to a point to make concessions to progress. They are prepared to accept the reforms adopted after the war as definite changes in the monetary system, and many of them are prepared to go even further. In the orthodox camp there are few of those uncompromising diehards who insist upon a thorough-going return to the pre-war system. Similarly, the predominant majority of Communists do not regard the abolition of money as an integral part of their programme. Indeed, those who are engaged in putting practical Communism into operation in Russia have rejected the idea. It is only in countries where Communism is still no more than abstract theory that some of its adherents, more Royalist than the King, scorn the compromising attitude of Russian Communism and regard the abolition of the monetary system as one of the corner-stones of real Communism.

Between the two extremes there are scores of intermediate stages represented by those in favour of monetary reform either as a matter of conviction or as a matter of opportunism. For a large number of those advocating monetary reform are far from enthusiastic about their own proposals. They realise that there are insurmountable practical obstacles to the establishment of what they consider an ideal state of affairs, and so are prepared to accept a compromise in order to approach that ideal as far as practicable in existing circumstances. There are, on the other hand, a number of reformers who have a fanatical faith in the all-curing effect of the remedy they advocate, and who in their way are just as uncompromising as diehard orthodox economists or purist Communists are in theirs.

(4) What is Monetary Reform ?

Monetary reform in the narrower sense of the term means a fundamental change in the monetary system. In its broader sense, however, monetary reform includes also changes of detail, and changes in the method of operation of the old system. In this sense even the Bank of England, in spite of its ultra-orthodox character, has been responsible for a number of monetary reform measures, such as the adoption of the gold bullion standard and of the managed gold standard. Indeed, viewed through pre-war eyes, these reforms would have appeared almost revolutionary. Many economists who claim to be orthodox in the extreme are prepared to take it for granted that the physical use of gold coins represents an obsolete system. In the monetary sphere, as in many other spheres, yesterday's bold reformers are to-day's diehards; who knows whether in some future period the boldest of our present-day monetary radicals will not be regarded as conservative ? In John Law's time, the issue of paper currency was a revolutionary innovation. To-day, even the most reactionary of orthodox diehards would not dare to advocate a return to full metallic currency.

It is not our object to give an historical survey of the reforms adopted at various stages of the development of the monetary system, but it is well to bear in mind that monetary reform is as old as money itself. The prince who minted the first coin was a monetary reformer in his day, and the princes who debased their coinage to finance their deficits were also monetary reformers. According to some historians, managed currency was not entirely unknown to the ancient Egyptians, Greeks, and Chinese, who shifted bullion to and from the shrines of their temples in order to counteract movements in the price level. To anyone qualified to perform it, the task of collecting data about the early history of monetary reform would be fascinating indeed. We propose to confine ourselves to an examination of monetary reform accomplished or proposed since the war, using as a basis the monetary system as it existed during the last decade or two before 1914.

(5) Pre-War and Post-War System

Compared with the orthodox pre-war system, the post-war system of the gold standard embraces a number of important reforms. One of the most important of these, as we have already pointed out, was the change from the full gold standard to the gold bullion standard. The adoption of the gold exchange standard in a large number of countries constituted another important post-war reform. Above all, the establishment of a managed gold standard represents an almost revolutionary change from the automatic pre-war system. Indeed, it might be argued that in principle the transition from the automatic gold standard to the managed gold standard represents nearly as great a progress as the further step from the managed gold to a managed paper currency would be. The practice of preventing certain gold movements from producing their normal effect constituted a highly important reform. International co-operation between Central Banks and the establishment of a super-Central Bank at Basle also appear to be very advanced innovations if viewed through pre-war eyes.

All these reform measures failed, however, to satisfy a large number of radicals, and, since the proof of the pudding is in the eating, they also failed to satisfy the general public. Before the crisis, additional and much more radical reform measures had already been urged upon various Governments. According to one school, it was essential that money should be made cheaper. According to another school, what mattered was not so much that money should be cheaper but that it should be more plentiful. Yet another school urged that the quantity of money should be regulated not in accordance with gold movements but in accordance with the tendency of commodity prices or with the extent of legitimate trade requirements or social requirements. Some reformers proposed to rule out the gold standard altogether, while others advocated the reduction of its rôle to the settlement of international balances. Others again wanted to retain gold as a basis for currency but to make the gold parities subject to fluctuation.

(6) The Crisis and Monetary Reform

With the advent of the crisis both the number of reform proposals and the number of their supporters increased rapidly. To the schemes advocated before the crisis—some of these schemes, such as the policy of cheap money, were actually put into practice—innumerable new suggestions were added. There was the "spending school", which maintained that the stimulation of spending, public and private, could provide the only solution of the economic difficulties. There were various proposals for a system of negative interest rates, and proposals for a dual system of a stable external currency coupled with an elastic internal currency.

When the economic depression developed into a financial crisis, another group of reform proposals appeared. There was a revival of bimetallism. There were a number of drastic inflationary proposals, especially in the United States, and there was a proposal to replace the international gold standard by international exchange clearing. In practice many of the proposed reform schemes have been adopted. President Roosevelt, after showing some inclination to adopt the elastic gold currency, reverted to limited bimetallism. The formation of monetary groups, such as the Gold Bloc and the Sterling Bloc, constituted yet another reform. Last, but by no means least, exchange clearing has been widely adopted. To a large extent, practice has preceded theory and those who were responsible for adopting the various reform measures did not realise the full implications of what they were doing. Indeed, it is very difficult to draw a line between temporary emergency measures and reform measures. Many measures intended as palliatives may actually become permanent reform measures; conversely, some measures aiming at reform of the monetary system may be discarded after the emergency is over.

(7) "Currency Cranks"

Those who advocate or carry out monetary reform measures may be divided into three categories; practical reformers, scientific reformers and pseudo-scientific reformers. The latter are usually referred to as " currency cranks ", but the author's definition of that term differs considerably from its popular meaning. He is not in agreement with the view of the orthodox economists that all radical would-be reformers, and these would-be reformers alone, are currency cranks. There are, indeed, two classes of currency cranks: the radical currency cranks who propose to bring about the millennium with the aid of monetary conjurors' tricks, and the orthodox currency cranks who are prepared to sacrifice everything for the sake of maintaining monetary parities.

However widely these two classes may differ, they have one thing in common: their extreme exaggeration of the rôle of monetary policy in the economic system. The radical currency cranks think they are able to manage the economic system with the aid of their monetary policy alone, while the orthodox currency cranks demand that the whole economic system should be managed to suit the convenience of their own favourite monetary policy. While the eccentricity of radical currency cranks is obvious to everybody—the clown's bells on their revolutionary Phrygian caps are audible to all but themselves—that of orthodox currency cranks is carefully camouflaged behind a screen of time-honoured economic principles, which on the strength of their frequent repetition in text-books have come to be widely regarded as fundamental laws of nature. Yet it is just as eccentric to demand that a nation should bleed to death economically and financially for the sake of a monetary doctrine as to profess to be able to cure all the world's troubles overnight by replacing that doctrine by another monetary doctrine.

(8) Heresy-hunting

Until a few years ago the stronghold of orthodox economics was regarded as unassailable. Everybody outside the orthodox camp was stigmatised as a heretic and anyone in favour of monetary reform was branded as a currency crank. The orthodox school had a very strong hold over public opinion, and heresy-hunting was its favourite indoor sport. Indeed, since its members occupied practically all key positions in Universities and in the financial Press, there appeared to be little chance of influencing public opinion in favour of monetary reform. That progress was nevertheless made towards reform must be attributed rather to the inexorable pressure of facts than to the influence of public opinion. Faced with the fact that reform measures had been carried out after the war, the orthodox school either denounced them or minimised their importance, and sought to convey the impression that the system had not materially departed from its pre-war principles.

With the advent of the crisis practical developments went ahead of theory. Public opinion in many countries realised how costly it was to adhere to the pre-war monetary conception, even in its modified post-war form. Events and developments thus prepared the ground for the proposals of monetary reformers. Their arguments became more convincing, thanks to the experience of the previous few years. Needless to say, the inclination of the public to be more receptive to monetary reform assisted pseudo-scientific or frankly unscientific demagogues at least to the same extent as scientific reformers. A number of utterly irresponsible schemes gained adherents on an entirely unexpected scale.

It is of great importance that the public should learn to discriminate between serious monetary reform schemes and crazy "wildcat" schemes, between the feasible and the Utopian, between the scientific and the pseudo-scientific. Otherwise, the world might become the scene of mad experiments, the failure of which would intensify our economic difficulties and lead to a relapse into the bondage of ultra-orthodox doctrinairism.

In the following chapters we propose to analyse the various monetary reform schemes and to classify them according to their objects and methods. We shall enumerate the alternative solutions between which various countries will have to choose, and we shall indicate the temporary solutions which have been, or are likely to be, adopted pending the evolution of the new monetary doctrines.

CHAPTER II

THE AUTOMATIC SYSTEM

(1) The Pre-War Gold Standard

Before proceeding to the description of monetary reform measures adopted in practice since the war and those proposed during recent years, it is necessary to describe the system that existed before the war. The pre-war gold standard has been described and analysed innumerable times, and it is difficult to add anything to what has been said on the subject. Our object in the present chapter, however, is not to try to discover any new aspects of the pre-war system, but to explain those of its features which enabled it to work satisfactorily before the war and those features which prevented it from working satisfactorily after the war.

The principal feature of the pre-war gold standard was its essentially automatic character. The generation which has grown up since the war does not as a rule realise adequately the extent to which the monetary system was allowed to take care of itself before 1914, especially in Great Britain but also in other countries. The fact that the Governorship of the Bank of England was a part-time job held by each of the Directors of the Bank in turn is in itself characteristic of the extent to which the system was running itself with the minimum of intervention. It is true that about once in a decade the advent of the usual cyclic crisis put the qualifications of the Governor who happened to be in office to a somewhat severe test, but the steps to be taken on such occasions were determined by tradition and text-books. During the intervals between two cyclic crises, the function of a Central Bank was largely one of supervision rather than of management and intervention. It is true that from time to time the Central Bank had to take an active part by changing its bank rate. In the majority of cases, however, these movements were the consequences of previous developments in the open market, and merely confirmed the existing state of affairs and did not aim at changing it.

(2) Automatic Readjustment

Under the pre-war system of the gold standard such abnormal movements as occurred from time to time tended to correct themselves automatically. Any excessive change in the trade balance, in price levels, or in internal or international lending was cancelled out by the tendencies it provoked through its effect on interest rates, exchanges and gold movements. Whenever a country imported too much, lent too much abroad, or expanded credit too much internally, the result was a weaker exchange, higher interest rates and an outflow of gold. This again tended automatically to discourage the excessive imports, over-lending or credit expansion. The free flow of gold from centre to centre tended to maintain an equilibrium between prices in various countries and to secure a correct international distribution of monetary gold supplies. It is true that the gold standard was not everywhere as automatic as in Great Britain, but viewed through post-war eyes such interference with its free working as existed in various countries before the war was for practical purposes negligible.

From this description the pre-war gold standard may appear to be the ideal system. It is no wonder that so many people would like to return to it. Their wishes, like the wishes of those who would like to return to the period of Victorian prosperity and stability, in general are, however, impossible to realise. To put the clock back to 1913 is beyond our power. The conditions in which the pre-war gold standard worked exist no longer: they are as dead as the conditions in which nineteenth-century prosperity and stability existed.

(3) Why Pre-War System Worked

What were the conditions which made the working of the automatic gold standard possible prior to 1914? In the first place, there was a high degree of equilibrium, economic and financial, internal and international. There was equilibrium between the volume of fictitious capital and real wealth; between prices, wages and costs in the leading modern countries; between the international flow of capital and the international flow of goods. Moreover, development in many directions before the war was relatively gradual. There were no sudden changes in the price level, in capital requirements, in production, in consumption, in the relative position of the leading countries, in trade balances, in indebtedness, internal and international, etc. Changes were going on incessantly—the idea that before the war conditions were static is absurd—but they were so gradual as to reduce their unsettling effect to a minimum. Apart from this, there was a high degree of stability and confidence in the political and economic spheres before the war. It is true that from time to time political and economic crises occurred; they were not, however, on a sufficient scale to disturb confidence to a very large extent. In such circumstances, the high degree of freedom for international trade and complete freedom for the international movements of capital provided in pre-war days effective shock-absorbers. Lastly, London's position as the world's banking centre was unassailable and she was, therefore, able to fulfil the functions of international regulator of the gold standard. The technical superiority and elasticity of the London market, the absence of any spirit of hoarding and the essentially international mentality of the banking community and of the British investor qualified London to be the centre of the international monetary system.

(4) Post-War Changes

A glance at this list of conditions in which the pre-war gold standard was able to work satisfactorily is sufficient to make us realise how absurd it was to expect that the mere restoration of the gold standard after the war would be sufficient to restore the pre-war state of affairs. None of the conditions which secured the smooth working of the pre-war gold standard existed after the war. The state of equilibrium on which the pre-war system was based had disappeared. The abnormal increase of fictitious wealth after 1914 created a state of fundamental disequilibrium; there were wide discrepancies between the level of prices, wages and costs in various countries; the international flow of goods failed to keep pace with the requirements of the international flow of capital. The world's economic system had to face sudden and substantial changes. The price level in general, and especially in some countries, was subject to much more rapid changes than before the war. Methods of production were progressing rapidly, and the capacity of consumption became most unstable. The economic and financial balance of power between the leading countries was subject to kaleidoscopic changes. The trade balance of various countries became liable to fluctuations within a wide range. Indebtedness, internal and international, was changing to a much larger degree than was conceivable before the war.

In one word, the world was exposed to sudden shocks with the maximum of unsettling effect. Stability and confidence had disappeared. Both politically and economically, conditions were much less stable than before the war. Even though during the six years between 1925 and 1931 a feeling of security —a false security—began to develop, there were evident undercurrents which sooner or later had to disturb the apparently smooth surface.

International trade was subjected to much more interference in the form of tariffs than before the war, and international capital movements were also subjected to embargoes on foreign lending in certain centres. Finally, London was unable to recover her pre-war position as the world's banking centre. The lead was captured after the war by New York, even though she was not qualified to fulfil the functions required of the centre of the international monetary system. Subsequently, Paris made a bid for supremacy, and financial rivalry between the leading centres provided yet another source of instability.

(5) Gold Standard no longer Automatic

In the circumstances, it is not surprising that the attempt to restore the pre-war monetary system, even in a modified form, resulted in a failure. What is surprising is that it took six years for the attempt to break down. The reason why the post-war gold standard succeeded in resisting adverse circumstances until 1931 was that various reform measures had been put into practice, thanks to which the system was better equipped to withstand the new disturbances. These reform measures will be discussed in detail in Chapter V. For the present it is sufficient to note that the substance of the change compared with the pre-war system was that the gold standard after 1925 was less automatic in its working. Monetary management played a more important part in it. In addition, the political necessity of paying greater attention to the general economic interest when determining the nature of monetary policy became increasingly recognised in various countries.

What would have happened if after the war the world's monetary authorities had attempted to run the gold standard on strictly orthodox lines ? It would have meant the raising of the British bank rate in 1925 and subsequent years to a level so prohibitive that it would have resulted in a considerable increase of unemployment. It is easy to imagine what the political consequences of such a policy would have been. If, by 1926, unemployment had risen to, say, two millions in addition to those unemployed through the coal strike, it is more than probable that the general strike would have led to grave political upheavals.

(6) Big Figures

The political factor was by no means the only one which precluded a restoration of the automatic gold standard. From a purely economic point of view the automatic working of the system would have involved much more violent fluctuations than occurred before the war. As we have already pointed out, the actual and potential disturbing factors had become a multiple of their pre-war magnitude, and their number had increased considerably. Where before the war the magnitude of disequilibrium—in so far as it is capable of expression in figures—ran into millions, after the war it ran into tens of millions and perhaps hundreds of millions. Fractional bank rate changes would have been unable to readjust such disparities. The strong tendencies towards disequilibrium would have required drastic readjustment measures, and more often than not the remedy would have been worse than the disease.

Moreover, the automatic tendencies of readjustment would not, in any case, have operated so freely as they did before the war. Apart from the increased resistance they would have had to meet, their efficiency compared unfavourably with that of pre-war days. Wages, costs of production and costs of living were not nearly as elastic as before the war. Owing to the increased political power of trade unions and the establishment of a system of unemployment benefits in Great Britain and in a number of other countries, it was not nearly as easy as it was before the war to cause a fall in commodity prices through a high bank rate. Other things being equal, the rise in bank rate would have had to be much more considerable and its effect upon trade much more destructive than before the war if it were to produce the same effect on prices. If we take this fact into consideration, together with the fact that readjustments which the automatic working of the gold standard would have had to bring about would have been on a much larger scale than in pre-war days, we cannot escape the conclusion that the restoration of the automatic gold standard after the war was impossible.

(7) Orthodox Purists' Claim

It is easy for orthodox purists of the reactionary type to preach that the world crisis would have been avoided if only the purity of the gold standard after the war had not been adulterated by various reform schemes which interfered with the automatic working of the system. Such theorists can triumphantly point out that the gold standard in its modified form did not work, while their opponents are not in a position to prove by facts that, had the automatic gold standard been restored, the result would have been even more disastrous. What the orthodox purists do not realise is that, apart altogether from the important changes in the situation since the war, even in pre-war days the gold standard did not aim at counteracting fundamental tendencies. The automatic working of the gold standard did not prevent a steady fall of commodity prices between 1873 and 1896, when the index number of wholesale prices in the United Kingdom fell by some 40 per cent. Nor did it prevent a rise of some 25 per cent. between 1896 and 1913. The difference between the last few pre-war decades and the post-war years to 1931 was that during the latter period changes tended to be much more rapid than before the war. If the automatic gold standard was unable to prevent long-range movements during the forty years that preceded the war, there is no reason to believe that it would have been able to prevent similar movements, compressed within a much shorter space of time, during the fifteen years that followed the termination of hostilities. All that the automatic gold standard was capable of doing before the war was to regulate the international financial and economic situation on the basis of the fundamental trends over which it had no control.

(8) Cry for "Good Old Days"

It is easy to achieve cheap popularity in certain quarters by crying for the return of the "good old days". The fact that it is impossible to put the clock back, and that it is not human will but the force of circumstances which prevents the return to pre-war conditions, is often overlooked by those who advocate the return to the pre-war gold standard. After the war these advocates were a minority even in the orthodox camp. Those in charge of the official monetary policy in various countries between 1925 and 1931 can hardly be accused of monetary radicalism. They were ultra-conservative bankers, Treasury officials and statesmen brought up in the orthodox school. As they were burdened with the responsibility for the consequences of their acts, they realised they could not afford to experiment with the restoration of the automatic gold standard. They were aware of the necessity for compromise, and accordingly adopted a gold standard which was largely managed, and which differed in many essential details from the pre-war system. Their policy met with approval even in academic orthodox quarters. With few exceptions, academic economists approved the post-war monetary reforms, and the majority of those who opposed them did so on the ground that the reforms did not go far enough. It is safe to say, therefore, that no really serious effort was made after the war to enforce a policy aiming at a return to the automatic monetary system.

In a later chapter we shall raise the question whether the pre-war monetary system was really as ideal as even in pre-war conditions it appeared on the surface. We shall also examine how far the changes brought about by the crisis increased or further reduced the chances of returning to the automatic system. The present chapter has sought merely to indicate the reasons why the pre-war system was not integrally restored during the period of post-war stabilisation. In Chapter V we shall discuss in detail the difference between the pre-war and post-war gold standard, and shall indicate the actual reforms which have been put into practice. Before that, however, we must examine—as we shall do in Chapter III—the attempt made after the war to abolish money altogether. While the orthodox extremists, opposed to every kind of reform, comprised only a few academic economists whose influence was negligible, the radical extremists succeeded in assuming power in two countries—in Russia and Hungary. The next chapter will show how far they succeeded in carrying out their desire to abolish currency.

CHAPTER III

CAN MONEY BE ABOLISHED ?

(1) Communism and Monetary System

In our preceding chapter, which dealt with the pre-war system of the gold standard, we covered well-explored ground. By contrast, the subject of the present chapter is almost entirely unknown to the predominant majority of the English-speaking public. In a book dealing with monetary reform, there is, indeed, no need to apologise for including a chapter on the monetary system of Communism, for, judging by the extent of the general knowledge of Soviet Russia outside its borders, the country might be situated on some other planet. Such information as is available is either highly biased or is viewed with suspicion and thus is discounted as being biased. We are not concerned here with the controversy which surrounds Communism, and shall not enter into its general merits and demerits : we shall confine ourselves to an examination of one of its aspects, from a purely technical point of view.

It is a well-known principle of orthodox Communism that money is an essentially capitalistic institution and is bound to disappear with the abolition of capitalism. During the early period of the Bolshevik régime, this principle was fully endorsed by authorities on Communism, both in Russia and elsewhere. Opinions were divided, however, as to how the change would come about. One school argued that it would have to be brought about by deliberate measures following upon the nationalisation of private property. Another contended that there was no need to take any specific measures since money in a Communist State would in any case become an anomalous survival which sooner or later would reduce itself *ad absurdum*. This latter view was expressed by Bela Kun, head of the Hungarian Communist movement, during the brief period of his régime in Hungary in 1919.

(2) Abolishing Money through Inflation

Other authorities who advocated the deliberate abolition of money maintained that the best means to that end was to reduce the value of money to nothing by means of inflation. In any case, whatever may have been the views of the various Communist leaders in Russia and Hungary on the methods of abolishing money, in both countries inflation was actively pursued. The purchasing power of the currency issued by the Russian and Hungarian Soviet Governments declined rapidly. Although the Hungarian Soviet Government did not remain in existence long enough to see the complete demonetisation of its currency, during the brief period of four months it made remarkable progress to that end. In Soviet Russia the paper rouble had become entirely worthless by 1922, so that it would have been correct to state that by that time money had ceased to play any part in the economic system of the country. The Romanoff roubles and Kerensky roubles still commanded a certain purchasing power, and gold, silver and even copper coins remained, to some extent, the media of exchange, but the main circulating media, the Soviet roubles, were no longer in a position to fulfil the functions of money.

The theory on which those in favour of abolishing money worked is that in a Communist State everybody is a Government employee, and since the Government is the source of all production it is in a position to pay wages in kind. The idea is by no means new. It already existed in pre-Marxian Socialism. In Great Britain Robert Owen's proposal to issue labour tickets instead of money may be regarded as an early attempt to abolish money. Marx himself was not keen on the idea, and considered it Utopian. It is only because of the misinterpretation of his theory of labour values that the proposal to abolish money and replace it by labour tickets is attributed to him.

(3) Making Virtue out of Necessity

In reality, the developments which resulted in the almost complete abolition of money in Soviet Russia, and through which Hungary quickly approached a similar stage, were not due to any deliberate policy but to sheer necessity. Both in Hungary in 1919 and in Soviet Russia during the period between 1917 and 1922 production and trade were hopelessly disorganised. By their nationalisation of private enterprise, the Soviet Governments had killed the goose that laid the golden eggs; and they soon found that they were not in a position to meet their financial requirements out of taxation. Of course, in the chaotic conditions that prevailed in Central and Eastern Europe after the war, extreme inflation would have been inevitable in any case, as is shown by the experience of Germany, Poland and Austria. All that happened in the Hungarian and Russian Soviet republics was that the process became accentuated and accelerated through the disappearance of revenue and the increase of expenditure that inevitably accompany Communism during the early stages of its establishment.

Having no other sources of revenue, the Russian and Hungarian Soviet Governments simply had to fall back upon the Printing Press. They would have had to do so even if they had been opposed to the abolition of money. Nor is there any reason whatsoever to suppose that, because they were in favour of the abolition of money, they deliberately accelerated the pace at which the inflationary process was going on. On the contrary, it is reasonable to assume that they regarded the rapid depreciation of their note issue with dismay, since it increased the difficulty of financing their deficit. In public they may have comforted themselves with the idea that the depreciation of their currency was in reality in accordance with the Communist plan, but in doing so they merely made a virtue out of necessity.

(4) Premature Demonetisation of Rouble

Indeed, from the point of view of the orthodox Communist plan of abolishing money, the demonetisation of Soviet notes through their complete depreciation by 1922 was decidedly premature. During the first five years of the Bolshevik régime, the establishment of a Communist State in Russia did not reach a sufficiently advanced stage to make it possible to dispense with money. It is true that large industrial enterprises were nationalised almost immediately, and that by 1922 commerce, mining, etc., were entirely in the hands of the State. On the other hand, agriculture remained almost exclusively in private hands. The large estates having been divided among the peasants during the Kerensky régime, it was impossible to collectivise land until the system had been sufficiently firmly established to enable it to defy the opposition of farmers. Considering that in Russia agriculture is by far the most important industry, it may be said that in 1922 private ownership was still predominant. The number of State employees was only about 10 per cent of the total population. They received about 80 per cent of their wages in kind, since money had ceased to have any purchasing power; but as the predominant majority of the population were not State employees, they needed money as a medium of exchange. When money practically ceased to exist they had to revert to barter, a retrograde development which was hardly in accordance with the theory of Communism.

From the point of view of the Soviet Government itself, the demonetisation of the Soviet rouble was a highly undesirable development. Owing to the initial difficulties of the system, coupled with the devastations of civil war, nationalised production was in a deplorable state in 1922, and the Government was not in a position to reward services to an adequate degree by paying in kind. As the credit system had been destroyed completely, the only possible way of financing deficits was through the issue of a new currency. Accordingly, in October 1922 steps were taken to this end. New rouble notes were issued to withdraw the old issues from circulation at the rate of fifty milliard old roubles for one new rouble. The issue of new currency served the purpose of covering new Government expenditure. In order to inspire confidence in the new unit, the Soviet Government had to disown the idea of abolishing money. Indeed, it had to go so far as to revert to orthodox monetary principles. The rule was established that the tchervonetz notes should have a 25 per cent metallic cover. Even though they were not convertible into gold, it was the Government's declared intention to resume their convertibility at a later date. The fact that the notes have remained inconvertible up to this very day, and that the increasing gold production of the Soviet Union was used for financing imports rather than for making the notes convertible, does not alter the fact that the Soviet Government adopted orthodox monetary doctrines. The moment its currency was reduced *ad absurdum* through depreciation it became necessary to establish a new currency on orthodox lines.

(5) Ration Tickets *v.* Money

The fact that in 1922 the Soviet Government felt compelled to revert to the capitalistic monetary system does not in itself prove, however, that the idea of the abolition of money is dead and buried. Indeed, with the progress of the establishment of the Communist State, considerable headway has actually been made in that direction. This time the intention to abolish money was not broadcast. Indeed, it is doubtful whether the Soviet Government consciously had that end in view. What happened was that, with the gradual acquisition of control over agricultural production, the greater part of the population of the Soviet Union became Government employees, and as such were entitled to ration tickets.

For all practical purposes, it is these ration tickets that at present constitute the bulk of the currency in Soviet Russia. It is true that money wages continue to be paid, but, owing to the limitation of the possible use of money without ration tickets, the latter are far more important as media of exchange. As practically all commerce is in the hands of the Government, all the necessities have to be bought with the aid of ration tickets. There is, it is true, a market where sundry things are bought and sold against money, but the relative importance of this market is small. The fact that prices in the open market are ten and even twenty times higher than those paid by the possessors of ration tickets duly indicates the relative importance of ration tickets and money.

(6) A Necessary Evil

Does this necessarily mean that in Soviet Russia money will eventually disappear completely, and be replaced entirely by ration tickets? That seems most unlikely. As it is, there are certain legitimate uses for money, such as payment of tram fares and similar expenses, and from time to time certain goods of which a surplus is produced are obtainable without ration tickets. Indeed, the ultimate aim is to abolish ration tickets, which are simply a necessary evil that has resulted from the inadequate production of goods in relation to requirements. If the Soviet Government is successful in carrying out its second five-year plan and production is increased considerably, a stage may be reached at which there will be a sufficient volume of primary necessities to cover everybody's requirements. Rationing will then become superfluous.

Similarly, if and when production is able to supply secondary goods, as well as the primary necessities, in sufficient quantities, the Soviet Union will be able to afford the luxury of allowing its population to make their own choice as to the ways they spend their earnings. As rationing means the compulsory consumption of certain goods with no alternative, the progress of production will be accompanied by the gradual abolition of ration tickets. It is only if the Communist system fails to achieve its end of increasing production that ration tickets will remain all-important as the principal medium of exchange—indeed in that event their importance might well increase. As things are, however, it is reasonable to assume that this will not necessarily be the case.

At present it is only in international relations that the abolition of money by Soviet Russia is nearly complete, and only in this sphere is the virtual absence of money likely to continue. There is indeed no need whatsoever for a Communist State to maintain financial links with the rest of the world except through official channels. And for that purpose there is no need to maintain the exchange rate which converts the currency of one country into that of another country. As we shall see in Chapter XXXIX, the monetary isolation of the Soviet Union is practically complete. Since production as well as foreign trade is a State monopoly, considerations of cost of production or of inland prices do not influence the imports and exports of Soviet Russia. From that point of view, money is practically non-existent.

(7) Internal Rôle of Money

From an internal point of view, however, money is likely to play an increasing rôle. Apart from the limitations of the use of ration tickets when production is expanding and the variety of the goods is extending, the increase in the production of gold in the Soviet Union must also tend to rehabilitate money. It is claimed that the Soviet Union will soon become the largest gold producer in the world. If this proves to be true, there will sooner or later be enough gold not only to cover requirements for imports and for the repayment of foreign credits, but also for increasing the reserve ratio of Soviet notes. Efforts are being made to unify the official price level and the unofficial price level, and even though it is doubtful whether the unofficial market can ever be completely abolished, its significance can be reduced considerably. It is reasonable to suppose, therefore, that, if all goes well in the Soviet Union, before many years are past the currency system for internal purposes will be similar to that of capitalist countries.

It is, therefore, safe to conclude that post-war extremist experiments in the abolition of currency, as an alternative to its reform, have produced negative results. In the previous chapter we showed that it was impossible after the war to revert to the pre-war monetary system. Since it is equally impossible, even in Communist States, to go to the other extreme by abolishing money altogether, the solution must be found between the two extremes.

CHAPTER IV

DEMAND FOR MONETARY REFORM

(1) Pre-War Movements

As we pointed out in Chapter I, monetary reform is by no means a post-war invention. The monetary system has always been subject to evolutionary and sometimes revolutionary changes, and there have always been people urging such changes. During the decades preceding the war, there was, however, no pronounced pressure in favour of monetary reform. The last powerful movement favouring a change in the monetary system was the bimetallist movement of the 'nineties which demanded not a reform but the restoration of a state of affairs that existed in days gone by. During the decades that preceded the war, the leading economists discussed the possibility from a purely academic point of view, but few of them took any definite line to that end. There was no lack of enthusiastic reformers, such as Gesell or Kitson, but the public in general took no notice of them and economists could well afford to ignore such heretics. On the whole, it may be said that before the war the world was satisfied with the existing monetary system. To be exact, that part of the world whose word carried weight in the Universities, Parliaments and in the Press showed no sign of any considerable dissatisfaction with the pre-war monetary system.

And yet our monetary system before the war was far from ideal. Although it secured a relatively high degree of international and internal financial stability, this result was achieved at the expense of progress. There can be no doubt that the orthodox monetary principles that reigned supreme from the time of the liquidation of the Napoleonic Wars until the Great War handicapped progress in the welfare of mankind. There were no possibilities of rapid expansion, owing not only to the material restrictions imposed by the slow pace at which gold stocks increased before the war, but also because of the over-cautious mentality bred by generations of ultra-orthodox finance. There was no strong demand for credit expansion to finance an increase of production, no urgent pressure for a substantial improvement in the standard of living with the aid of capital expenditure under the auspices of the Government. It may be said that the absence of pressure from public opinion in favour of a more radical monetary policy was at least as much responsible for the inadequate progress before the war as was the rigidity of the pre-war gold standard.

(2) Pre-War System suited Nineteenth-Century Conditions

Was it an accident that strong movements in favour of monetary reform became evident after the war? Such an assumption is hardly acceptable. Conditions before the war were such as to make the then existing monetary system appear at its best. Indeed, to a very large extent the pre-war gold standard suited the conditions which existed during the nineteenth century. The whole mentality of economic optimism on which the belief in the automatic gold standard was based—"all will work out for the best so long as natural tendencies are allowed to take care of themselves"—fitted in remarkably well with the general atmosphere of Victorian smug self-satisfaction. The system secured a high degree of prosperity to the classes whose voice then carried weight, and even permitted a very slow improvement in the standard of living of the working classes. The latter had every reason to be dissatisfied with the system, for it held out absolutely no hope for them of any material improvement in their welfare during the lifetime of any one generation. Their influence was, however, relatively small during the nineteenth century (which for all practical purposes ended not in 1900 but in 1914). Labour movements in various countries were barely beginning to feel their feet during the last few pre-war years, and very few labour leaders were then qualified to form any definite opinion on highly technical monetary questions.

In any case, it would have been difficult to arouse public opinion in favour of proposals which might have been denounced as a danger to the stability that the world enjoyed before the war. When things are going tolerably well, proposals for changes find no fertile soil. Most people are afraid that if a change comes about it may be for the worse. It is only during periods of acute distress that the mind of the public is receptive of reform proposals, when the situation is considered so bad that the chances are that reforms will not change it for the worse.

(3) Historical Rôle of Orthodox System

Radical would-be reformers usually go out of their way to expose those responsible for the pre-war monetary system to contempt and ridicule. According to these critics, they were either knaves who deliberately enslaved the world in golden chains for the sake of their individual gains, or fools who knew no better. In reality, the automatic gold standard, like *laissez-faire* in general, fulfilled a useful rôle in its time. During the period of its existence it was well adapted to the stage of world economic and financial development of the time. The development of the modern financial system was bound to be a long process. Mankind had to learn through trial and error how to work the financial machinery which has assumed such a predominant rôle in our day. *Laissez-faire* in general suited the then existing stage of technical development remarkably well, and the time when the world could afford to discard it was a long way ahead.

Where both radical reformers and their orthodox opponents go hopelessly wrong is in their belief that any one particular monetary system is the best in all circumstances and in all ages. Radical reformers who regard the nineteenth-century statesmen and economists with contempt because they did not realise the blessing of a more radical monetary policy are just as wrong as those orthodox economists who believe that the system which worked reasonably well in the nineteenth century is bound to be the one satisfactory system to-day and for all terrestrial time in the future, until the collision of the Globe with some other planet puts an end to monetary problems. It was because the situation had changed that various important monetary reform measures were adopted in practice after the war, and it is for the same reason that the preachings of would-be reformers have found incomparably more response during the post-war period than they did in pre-war days.

(4) Socialism and Monetary Reform

Before the war the nations were prepared to put up with the disadvantages of a monetary system which obviously handicapped progress, for the sake of the stability that system secured. After the war it was found that this great advantage no longer existed. It was found that the system, in spite of the various reforms adopted, continued to handicap progress without providing security and stability in return. It is no wonder that the reform movements increased in strength.

Another factor that prepared the ground for their proposals was the increased influence of the working classes. Those who possess little or nothing are always inclined to favour a change since they have little or nothing to lose through it. On the other hand, those who have much to lose always prefer to retain the existing state of affairs, with all its deficiencies, rather than risk a "leap in the dark" which may or may not affect them adversely. Thus the progress of Socialism all over Europe should in itself be sufficient reason for the development of a stronger reform movement. In reality, whenever before the crisis Socialists assumed the responsibility of Government they proved to be practically as orthodox as the Governments representing the wealthier classes. Such radical tendencies as existed in their financial policy were tempered by their desire to conduct their monetary policy on strictly orthodox lines. The only difference between the monetary policy of the British Labour Government and that of the Conservative Government that preceded it was that pressure in favour of lower money rates was, if anything, stronger under the Labour Government. Or perhaps it is more correct to say that the Bank of England, anxious to avoid antagonising the ruling party, showed somewhat more inclination to yield to pressure than under the Conservative Government. The difference in practice was so slight that it is hardly possible to regard it as a change in the monetary policy, much less as a reform of the system. Until 1931 the Labour Party as such kept aloof from monetary reform proposals in England and also in other countries. It was only after the financial crisis that the British Labour Party began to flirt with monetary reform—in connection with their scheme for nationalising the banks. Even now many Socialists view monetary reforms with distrust and denounce them as "Fascist" methods of saving capitalism from its doom.

(5) Changed Mentality

One of the reasons why public opinion was more prepared to yield to reformist influences after the war than before 1914 was the change in mentality brought about by war-time experience. As we have pointed out, the lack of enterprising spirit in the monetary sphere before the war was at least as important a cause of the absence of any expansion as was the technical rigidity of the gold standard system. Generations of orthodox monetary policy could not help leaving its mark on the mind of the public, which had come to take it for granted that no other system was possible. Even the most discontented sections of society regarded purchasing power as something inelastic, and concentrated their efforts on a demand for its more equitable distribution without even thinking of demanding its expansion. During the war it became apparent that immense possibilities existed for the expansion of purchasing power. In fact, in every belligerent country the war was largely financed by this means, for newly created credit made possible the production of the war material required for national defence. The fact that in emergencies it was possible to add many milliards to the total purchasing power of the nations, thereby increasing the volume of material production, was bound to create a profound impression upon the minds of the public.

It is true that the final result of war inflation was a reduction of the purchasing power of important classes of the population, for the creation of artificial purchasing power was accompanied by a rise in commodity prices, which, belated as it was, took place eventually. To the minds of many people, however, this fact did not in itself discredit the idea of monetary expansion. It was argued that the only reason why the process had such destructive results during the war was that the additional goods produced were not available for normal consumption but were used for destructive purposes. It was argued that, if the same amount of artificial purchasing power and labour as was expended during the war for the purpose of national defence had been employed for productive purposes, the result would have been an immense increase in the standard of living. This argument found widespread response, especially in countries which escaped the destructive effects of advanced inflation. It is not surprising, therefore, that the war experience gave a strong stimulus to the movement which favoured monetary radicalism.

(6) Deterrent Inflation

The reason why this movement did not develop to any noteworthy extent during the years that followed the war was that it was discouraged by the abuse of monetary expansion in a number of countries. The disastrous consequences of inflation in Central and Eastern Europe deterred many people from favouring monetary expansion. The belief gained ground that such expansion was necessarily a dangerous experiment which might easily lead to results similar to those experienced in Germany and Russia. Indeed, in the countries which after the war suffered most through inflation, monetary reform schemes have remained extremely unpopular ever since. Even in countries such as France, which on balance benefited by the depreciation of her currency, the memories of the inflationary years have been sufficient to prevent any monetary reform movement from gaining ground.

It is almost exclusively in the countries that had no direct experience of advanced inflation that the demand for monetary reform has found ready followers. In the countries with inflationary experience, the extreme exaggeration of monetary expansion led to a natural reaction in public opinion, which reverted to extreme orthodoxy, and to a large extent was prepared to put up with the inconveniences of deflation rather than take any risk of a recurrence of inflation through the adoption of even moderately radical reforms. It is not, therefore, a mere accident that monetary reform movements after the war made more progress in the Anglo-Saxon and Scandinavian countries than in any other part of the world.

Even after the war, notwithstanding the experience of financial expansion during the war—or perhaps because of it—the monetary reform movements thus had but limited chances of success. The predominant majority of the public were anxious that pre-war conditions should return. They had become so accustomed to regarding the pre-war state of affairs as ideal that anybody who suggested that our aim should be to depart from the pre-war system instead of trying to return to it was bound to have a limited following. They regarded the monetary reforms introduced after the war as necessary evils and put up with them as a compromise in the absence of the possibility of restoring pre-war conditions in full.

(7) Discontent with Monetary System

At the same time, discontent with the existing monetary system increased materially, especially in Great Britain, where the difficulties caused by the circumstances in which the gold standard was restored became obvious long before the collapse of sterling in 1931. The deflationary policy that preceded the return to the gold standard in 1925 and the difficulties of the defence of sterling between 1925 and 1931 brought the shortcomings of the monetary system to the fore. In the United States, where monetary conditions were comfortable, monetary reform proposals such as Professor Irving Fisher's compensated dollar aroused no enthusiasm. In countries where the weak fundamental position was allowed to produce its effect on the exchange there was no persistent adverse pressure which called in question the existing monetary system. In Great Britain, however, the monetary reform movements had already established themselves long before the crisis, and the number of those who favoured reform had increased. After the war leading economists like Mr. J. M. Keynes and prominent bankers like Mr. Reginald McKenna launched criticisms against the orthodox monetary policy pursued by the authorities. It is true that, with the return to the gold standard in 1925, the reformers suffered a severe reverse. During the following years, however, when the difficulties of maintaining sterling at its overvalued level became increasingly obvious, their influence increased.

At the same time, pseudo-scientific critics of the orthodox system grew up like mushrooms. The work begun by Mr. Arthur Kitson was taken up by Major Douglas and Professor Soddy. They and a legion of lesser critics succeeded in recruiting a substantial following, strangely enough not among the working classes who stood to gain by a more radical monetary policy, but largely among retired colonels who took up monetary reform schemes as their hobby. The impoverished middle classes, which in Germany became the backbone of the National Socialist movement, in England gave vent to their wrath against society in this considerably less harmful way. In addition, industrial interests, who had been adversely affected by the overvaluation of the pound and who felt that the Bank of England had turned deaf ears to their complaints, sought their salvation in the support of some fanciful monetary reform scheme such as Mr. Taylor Peddie's dual system of stabilisation. And such movements did not gain only moral support, for considerable amounts have been raised for the purpose of research and propaganda. Notwithstanding all these efforts, monetary reform movements even in Great Britain made only slow headway before the crisis. It was not until the old system reduced itself *ad absurdum*, through the destructive deflation which its maintenance necessitated, that the movement in favour of reform began to grow rapidly.

CHAPTER V

POST-WAR REFORMS

(1) Lack of Uniformity

According to a popular conception, the gold standard is a well-defined system with identical rules all over the world. Indeed, one of the arguments in favour of the gold standard is that it secures a uniform monetary system for all civilised countries. Nevertheless, while the fundamental principles of the system are doubtless generally accepted, their application varies from country to country. This lack of uniformity in important details is by no means a post-war development. Before the war, there were already about as many systems of gold standard in operation as there were countries on a gold basis. Great Britain was the only country where the gold standard was practically automatic in the true sense of the term. In most other countries, its working was subject to various devices which impaired its automatic character. There was, for instance, the system of premiums by which the Reichsbank and other Central Banks encouraged from time to time the influx of gold. There was the option of the Bank of France to pay out silver coin whenever it sought to avoid an excessive drain on its gold stock. There was the Devisenpolitik of the Austro-Hungarian Bank, a forerunner of the intervention for exchange control in our days. In several countries the gold standard existed in law but not in practice. In other countries, such as Austria-Hungary, it existed in practice—since coins were in circulation and there was no disparity with the notes—but not in law.

Considering the diversity of conditions prevailing after the war, it is not surprising that the form in which the gold standard was restored also varied from country to country. It is true that, for the first time, an attempt was made to establish a certain degree of uniformity. The statutes of

Central Banks and the monetary laws adopted by countries whose currencies were stabilised under the auspices of the League of Nations were almost identical. A similar tendency towards uniformity was also noticeable among the Latin American States whose currencies were stabilised on the basis of recommendations made by Professor Kemmerer. In most cases, however, the practical application of monetary legislation varied to such a degree as to reduce the progress towards uniformity.

(2) The Post-War Gold Standard

The United States was the first country to restore the gold standard after the war. Being in possession of a huge gold reserve far in excess of her requirements, she could have well afforded to restore the automatic gold standard in the pre-war sense of the term. Nevertheless, she did not do so, but supplemented the system by the practice of open market operations. Although their object was primarily internal, these operations were bound to produce an international effect, thus influencing the working of the international gold standard. Apart from this, however, the working of the gold standard in the United States was free.

In Great Britain it was considered expedient to restore the gold standard in a limited form. The issue of sovereigns to the public was discontinued, and the conversion of notes into gold for internal purposes was discouraged by legal provisions authorising the Bank of England to call in gold held by British residents if in excess of £10,000. The system adopted was called the gold bullion standard, an official recognition of the difference between that system and the pre-war system. Most countries returning to the gold standard followed the British example by adopting the gold bullion standard. Some of them introduced additional limitations to the free working of the system. This was especially necessary for small countries, which were exposed to heavy drains to a particular degree. In Holland, for example, for a long time the Netherlands Bank paid out gold only for the purpose of genuine arbitrage. Those desirous of withdrawing gold had to prove that the transaction was profitable, and had to produce evidence subsequently of the way in which the gold had been disposed of. Denmark and other countries based the working of the gold standard on the principle of reciprocity. It was stipulated that the export of gold was free, but only to countries which allowed gold to be exported to Denmark. Subsequently, this same principle was adopted, in practice though not in law, also in Great Britain. In 1927, when the Bank of France, although not working on the gold standard, withdrew a certain amount of gold from the Bank of England, the transactions gave rise to official British protests, and had the French authorities not eventually agreed to discontinue withdrawals, legislation would in all probability have been passed embodying the principle of reciprocity.

(3) Gold Exchange Standard

Gold movements to and from the majority of countries which returned to the gold standard after the war were anything but automatic. In Germany, Italy, Switzerland, Belgium, etc., there was no free withdrawal of gold for arbitrage. While the Central Banks accepted gold offered for sale by arbitrageurs, they themselves performed the function of exporting gold whenever the exchange tended to depreciate below gold export point. In practice, the notes in these countries were convertible not into gold, but into foreign exchange. Moreover, they were not converted at a fixed rate but at the daily rate of exchange, which varied between the gold points. This was really a form of gold exchange standard, although strictly speaking that system implies the conversion of notes into a currency on a gold basis at a fixed rate. This was the system adopted by Czechoslovakia, whose exchange was pegged in relation to the dollar.

The post-war system of the gold standard differed in many substantial ways from the pre-war system. In most respects it represented a more radical conception, and the scientific element had much more scope in its elaboration. The pre-war gold standard was an entirely natural growth, while in the post-war gold standard the elements of national and even international planning began to manifest themselves. This was inevitable, for as we pointed out in Chapter II, in the conditions prevailing after the war the automatic system would have stood even less chance of succeeding than did the semi-managed system elaborated by a number of countries.

The following are the essential reforms in the gold standard system introduced after the war:

1. The use of gold coins was discontinued.
2. The use of bar gold for internal purposes was discouraged.
3. Gold reserves were supplemented by foreign exchange reserves.
4. The gold exchange standard was adopted in place of the gold standard by a number of countries.
5. To a large extent the gold standard lost its automatic character owing to internal management and international co-operation.

(4) Withdrawal of Coins

The withdrawal of gold coins from circulation was a reform of first-rate importance. Like so many essential reforms, it came about almost imperceptibly in the form of a temporary emergency measure. During the war all belligerent countries were anxious to increase their gold reserves, and appealed successfully to the patriotism of the public. Many people, failing to foresee the coming depreciation of the paper currencies in terms of gold, willingly surrendered their gold coins against notes. It was taken for granted that, once hostilities were over, gold coins, just as white bread and other luxuries of life which disappeared during the war, would reappear. Owing to the circumstances prevailing during the first few post-war years, however, none of the countries had a chance, for some years, of reintroducing gold coinage. Even the United States, with its immense gold stock, preferred to issue gold certificates.

In Europe it was believed that when the various countries returned to the gold standard they would reissue the coins withdrawn from the public. There was, however, no keen demand for a gold coinage, for in the course of ten years the public had realised that it was easier to do without gold coins than to do without any of the other things which they had to forgo during the war. There was no pressure upon the Governments to resume the issue of gold coins. When in 1925 the gold standard was restored in Great Britain, the absence of a provision for the issue of sovereigns barely caused surprise and provoked practically no criticism. All the other European countries which returned to gold followed the British example. Even though some monetary authorities considered it advisable to have their gold minted into coins, they were in no hurry to issue them to the public. Holland provided an exception, for in 1926 the Dutch Government began to issue gold coins. It was found, however, that as soon as the coins were issued they promptly disappeared, either through hoarding or through export. The Dutch authorities first sought to limit the issue by fixing the maximum amount of gold coins each person was entitled to withdraw, but subsequently they prudently discontinued the experiment altogether. The French stabilisation law made provisions for the possibility of issuing coins, but it was not until 1935 that the authorities began to take steps to that end. Even then the decision to put the law into operation was a mere gesture to strengthen confidence. The actual issue of coins was indefinitely postponed.

(5) Importance of the Change

The importance of the reform of the monetary system by the elimination of gold coins from circulation cannot be over-estimated. In a way, between 1914 and 1925 more progress was made towards monetary radicalism than was made between some several thousand years B.C., the time when the first metallic coin appeared, and 1914. As a result of the reform, the notes assumed an essentially fiduciary character. The idea that they represented a certain weight of gold of a certain fineness became reduced to a fiction. For internal purposes the gold content of the monetary unit became a mere symbol devoid of practical meaning. This highly important reform was carried out entirely by practical men. There was hardly any movement, scientific or pseudo-scientific, which demanded the adoption of such a reform. While there was a certain amount of opposition to the restoration of the gold standard, both the theoretical economists and the pseudo-economists who began to appear after the war regarded the question of the issue of coins as a minor detail which was barely worthy of their attention. The gold standard was attacked as a whole, but few special attacks were directed on the system of gold coins. It was only after the abolition was accomplished that a theoretical background was created for it. The use of coins was then denounced as a primitive arrangement, a barbarous relic which was not worthy of our advanced civilisation.

In reality, it may well be asked whether that famous civilisation of ours really made such immense progress during the eleven years that passed after 1914. How was it that before the war it did not occur to anybody that the use of gold coins was an indication of inferiority, worthy of savage tribes but not of civilised communities? The explanation is simple. Before the war there was no scarcity of gold or, at any rate, the scarcity of gold that may have existed did not threaten to upset the equilibrium and did not interfere with normal routine. After the war, for reasons which will be discussed in the next chapter, an acute scarcity of gold developed. Its adverse consequences were accentuated by the maldistribution of the existing monetary supply of gold. Thus, while before the war the world could afford the waste involved in issuing into circulation huge amounts of gold coins, after the war a gold coinage would have been too expensive a luxury. Most countries, moreover, endeavoured to increase their gold stock, or at any rate to prevent it from falling. To encourage the withdrawal of gold for internal circulation, and even to take the initiative to that end by resuming the issue of gold coins, was therefore unthinkable. It is true that by reissuing gold the authorities would have reduced the note circulation, the increase of which was largely due to the withdrawal of gold coins. In most countries, however, a certain unit of gold was used as a basis for the issue of two and a half or three times as many units of notes, so that the issue of coins into circulation would have had to be accompanied by a much more than corresponding reduction of the note issue.

Gradually, it has become recognised that gold should serve for settling international balances rather than for internal purposes. This conception was another consequence of the relative scarcity of gold. Before the war there was enough in the leading countries both for internal and for international purposes. After the war the use of gold for internal purposes on the pre-1914 scale would have depleted the monetary stocks to such an extent as to make it extremely difficult to provide for international requirements.

(6) Discouraging Internal Use of Gold

The monetary authorities of various countries sought to discourage the internal use of gold also by other means. Hoarding of gold on a small scale was discouraged by fixing the minimum weight of gold bars, the smallest unit into which notes were convertible, at a relatively high figure. In Great Britain the weight of a gold bar was 400 ounces, which means that anyone desirous of withdrawing gold had to possess at least £1,700, compared with 10*s*. before the war. This practice, which was adopted by most countries after their return to gold, was in itself sufficient to reduce considerably the number of those capable of withdrawing gold for internal purposes. The British authorities, however, went even further. While the general mechanism of the gold bullion standard was designed to prevent internal withdrawals on a small scale, the provision in the Currency and Bank Notes Act of 1928 which empowered the Bank of England to call in any gold holding in excess of £10,000 if it was not owned by foreigners or was not meant for export, was directed against withdrawals on a large scale.

Although this example was not followed by most countries on a gold basis, various countries adopted other methods of discouraging the withdrawal of gold for internal purposes, mostly by means of moral pressure. Together with the discontinuation of the issue of gold coins, the various measures taken to discourage the internal use of gold constituted a most important measure of monetary reform. Unquestionably, the post-war system was much more advanced and scientific than the pre-war system. It was not, however, any advance of civilisation but considerations of sheer practical necessity that induced the world to adopt a more civilised form of currency.

(7) Foreign Exchange Reserves

Similar considerations were also responsible for the extended use of foreign exchange reserves by Central Banks. Although before the war some Central Banks pursued the practice of keeping a foreign exchange reserve in addition to their gold reserves, after the war this practice became almost universal among Central Banks on a gold basis. In many cases, the statutes provided for the inclusion of the foreign exchange reserves in the note cover; in other cases, foreign exchange reserves were not included in the official reserves, but served none the less as a " second line of defence ". The difference was for the most part more apparent than real, since even those Central Banks which were entitled to keep part of their note cover in the form of foreign exchange holdings endeavoured to hold the full legal minimum reserve in the form of gold and only the surplus in the form of exchange.

The object of keeping part of the international resources of Central Banks in the form of foreign exchange was to reduce the scramble for gold which was brought about by the sudden restoration of the gold standard in a number of countries with inadequate gold reserves. The League of Nations, under whose auspices a number of countries returned to gold, encouraged the use of foreign exchange reserves by inducing the countries concerned to incorporate provisions to that end in the new statutes of their Central Banks.

(8) Open Market Operations

The automatic character of the gold standard received a much more severe blow from the increasing adoption of the practice of open market operations for the purpose of neutralising unwanted tendencies. The adoption of this practice probably constituted the most important monetary reform measure introduced after the war. It was a deliberate effort to interfere with the automatic working of the system. With the aid of open market operations, a Central Bank was in a position to sterilise an influx of gold and thus to prevent it from producing a corresponding degree of credit expansion, or, indeed, from producing any expansion at all. Similarly, Central Banks were in a position to prevent an embarrassing outflow of gold from causing a corresponding contraction of credit. Through the adoption of this practice, the post-war gold standard has become to a large extent a managed monetary system.

Needless to say, this reform failed to satisfy either the orthodox school or the radical school. Orthodox currency cranks, who consider the automatic working of the monetary system as an end in itself, and not a means to an end, were indignant about such artificial interference with the operation of the supreme laws which in their opinion ought to be allowed to work without let or hindrance. The adherents of the radical school, on the other hand, still considered the new system too orthodox. While it was possible to neutralise temporary movements, the volume of credit in the long run continued to depend very largely upon the amount of the gold reserve.

The scope for monetary management even under the new system of the gold standard was rather limited. That is, while the power of Central Banks to sterilise a surplus gold influx was for practical purposes almost unlimited, their power to offset an efflux of gold was limited by the necessity of maintaining a minimum reserve ratio. In this respect, legislation in various countries made some concessions to practical requirements. In given circumstances, Central Banks were authorised to lower their minimum reserve ratio or, in the case of Great Britain, it was possible to raise the amount of the fiduciary issue. These measures were not used, however, as part of the normal routine. They were applied only in extreme emergency. Thus, this new device in the system could be regarded only as a safety-valve, and not as a normal part of its functioning.

(9) International Co-operation

Another important reform in the practical application of the monetary system was international co-operation. The basic idea of this is the very negation of the principle of the automatic gold standard. Its object was to bolster up weak positions, instead of allowing them to be corrected by the normal functioning of the gold standard. Under an automatic gold standard, agreements between Central Banks affecting the normal flow of gold were unthinkable. To change the bank rate or to abstain from changing it to suit the convenience of another Central Bank was in glaring contradiction of the principle of the automatic gold standard. In a sense, however, Central Bank agreements to co-operate tended to restore the pre-war state of affairs. Reciprocal agreements between Central Banks, whereby one would abstain from withdrawing gold by direct purchases from the other except with the other's consent, tended to reduce the scope of official initiative in gold movements, and to increase the scope of private initiative. In such a case, Central Banks agreed to depend for the increase of their gold reserve, as before the war, upon an influx through arbitrage transactions. This came to be regarded as the rule, and an increase of the gold reserve through purchases on official initiative became the exception.

It is highly probable that, but for the intervention of the crisis, the progress towards a more advanced monetary system would have continued. The establishment of the Bank for International Settlements was an important step in the right direction, even though that institution did not live up to expectations by a sufficiently active and enterprising policy. Between the establishment of the Bank for International Settlements in May 1930 and the beginning of the international financial crisis about twelve months later, a number of interesting monetary reform schemes were, however, under consideration, and probably some of them at any rate would have been adopted sooner or later.

In all probability, even those reforms in addition to the ones which were put into practice before 1931 would have failed to prevent the international crisis. The efforts to adapt the gold standard to the changed circumstances were bound to fail because of the existence of fundamental disequilibrium. In face of the disequilibrium between fictitious wealth and real wealth and in face of disequilibrium between prices and costs in various countries, together with many other disturbing circumstances, the post-war reforms were mere palliatives which did not tackle the fundamental problem. They aimed at counteracting symptoms and surface tendencies. Their application merely postponed the breakdown of the gold standard which was bound to take place.

CHAPTER VI

REFORM MOVEMENTS AND THE CRISIS

(1) Orthodox System Discredited

The monetary reform movement, which had been of almost negligible extent in the immediate pre-war years, began to make itself felt during the post-war period. Its progress was, however, slow. But for the advent of the world crisis, both public opinion and the majority of expert opinion would have continued to regard most would-be reformers as essentially eccentric creatures, and the number of their following would never have risen sufficiently to have made them a factor in public opinion. The development of a strong movement in favour of monetary reform was due largely, if not exclusively, to the world crisis. The experience of 1931 and subsequent years threw discredit on the orthodox monetary conception. It aroused strong dissatisfaction with the monetary system which, it was considered, had been responsible for our difficulties.

While the monetary chaos that followed the war was attributed to *forces majeures* such as unbalanced budgets, political disturbances and to the war itself, this second currency chaos within the same generation was generally regarded as evidence of the unsuitability of the monetary system to existing conditions. The author is not amongst those who regard the monetary factor as the sole cause of the crisis. It is, however, difficult to deny that monetary difficulties had by far the largest share in the responsibility for it. Not only was the gold standard unable to act as shock-absorber, but it actually tended to accentuate the shock. It became only too painfully evident that the gold standard was unsuited to post-war conditions.

(2) Attitude of the Public

It is true that in conditions of fundamental disequilibrium, no monetary system, however perfect, could in itself have given satisfactory results. It is equally true that there were innumerable disturbing factors which prevented the modified post-war gold standard from securing a fair chance. These considerations, however, are of no consequence from the point of view of the development of public opinion towards monetary reform. The general public is always inclined to judge by results, and prefers accidental success to any failure, no matter whether or not there were mitigating and justifying circumstances. All that the public realised was that under the post-war gold standard things were going badly. Rightly or wrongly, it inferred that the fault lay with the monetary system. This explains the relief with which the suspension of the gold standard was received by the public in Great Britain and other countries. This also explains the facility with which monetary reformers succeeded in gaining ground from 1931 onwards. The fact that the monetary system in several leading countries and in a number of smaller countries was thrown into the melting-pot provided the reformers with a unique opportunity for attack, but this fact would not in itself be sufficient to account for the increased popularity of monetary reform movements. After all, during the inflationary crisis of post-war years, the public was longing to get back to the pre-war system. On the other hand, during the deflationary crisis the same public was longing to get away from the system which at best had not mitigated the difficulties, even if it had not actually caused them. After the experience of 1931, the ground was well prepared for a monetary reform movement.

Unfortunately, many of the most ardent of the post-1931 would-be reformers have belonged to the camp of unscientific currency conjurers. The names of some of them had been known for some years, but others like Dr. Eisler appeared on the horizon only with the acute crisis, and disappeared with its passing. Well-established extremist reformers such as Professor Soddy, Major Douglas and the minor figures of the movement, had, of course, the chance of their lives. In particular, Major Douglas increased his popularity to no slight degree. In various parts of the British Empire his adherents have run candidates for parliamentary elections, and in the Province of Alberta they actually succeeded in obtaining a majority. Even in the motherland the number of his adherents has grown rapidly, especially in the discontented north. Although the two candidates who stood for social credit at the general election of 1935 forfeited their deposits, in the country as a whole there must be hundreds of thousands of supporters of radical currency schemes.

At the same time, the monetary reform movement gained millions of adherents as a result of the change of the Labour Party's attitude towards monetary policy. The change was to a large extent due to the resentment caused in the Labour Party by the rôle bankers were alleged to have played in connection with the political landslide of 1931. In addition, Lord Snowden, who represented monetary orthodoxy in the Labour Party, resigned from it. Moreover, it was evident that, amidst the dissatisfaction caused by orthodox monetary policy, it was practical wisdom to advocate an unorthodox policy.

(3) Reform Movement in the U.S.A.

Simultaneously with the progress of the monetary reform movement in Great Britain, progress was also made in the United States. The economic depression there assumed much larger dimensions even than in Great Britain, and the contrast between the immense productive capacity of the nation and its reduced purchasing power was even more striking. Since the crisis was largely attributed to the inability of the monetary system to adjust itself to technical progress, the movement for monetary reform received considerable support from quarters concerned with the technical side of production. Engineers, having come to the conclusion that they would be in a position to increase the production of wealth almost indefinitely but for the defects of the financial structure, considered it their task to point out these defects and propose remedies. Hence the birth of Technocracy in the United States, and hence, too, the speedy popularity which it gained during its brief career. These advocates of bold monetary reform found the public ready to listen to their advice, notwithstanding the fact that until then they had specialised in problems, not of economics, but of mechanics. There appeared for a while a tendency towards the revival of a form of St. Simonism, that rudimentary form of French Socialism in which engineers were to be kings of the Universe. But the revival was short-lived. With the advent of President Roosevelt, the legion of economists, with their manifold monetary reform proposals, pushed the dilettantes well into the background.

Unquestionably, President Roosevelt introduced a record number of important practical monetary reform measures. At the same time, his inspiration to the reform movement far surpassed the extent to which he himself actually contributed to the progress of monetary reform. His message which very nearly blew up the Economic Conference referred to the gold standard as an " old-fashioned fetish "—a statement entirely without precedent on the part of a responsible statesman in office. Roosevelt's leaning towards monetary reform caused a revival among the advocates of the elastic gold dollar, such as Professors Irving Fisher, Warren and Pearson, who succeeded in persuading him to undertake the experiment of gold price fixing at the end of 1933 and the beginning of 1934. But those who expected Roosevelt to pursue this policy as a permanent system were disappointed when in January 1934 he decided to stabilise the dollar at a fixed parity. The experiment of gold price fixing nevertheless gave a strong stimulus to the stable money movement in the United States. Hopes are still entertained in many quarters that sooner or later President Roosevelt will revert to the system of the elastic dollar.

(4) Various Reform Schools during Depression

The most active of all the many reform movements was that of bimetallism in the United States. Although the actual importance of the silver producing industry is negligible, by skilful political manœuvring Senator Key Pittman succeeded in securing considerable support for the remonetisation of silver both from Congress and from public opinion. To some extent President Roosevelt yielded to his pressure, but the ultimate aims of the silver group are still far from being realised. Outside the United States, especially in England, the influential quarters which have been working in favour of the remonetisation of silver have failed to achieve any progress whatever. In face of the negative results of their efforts, their campaign slackened down considerably just at the time when it was making progress in the United States.

One school of monetary reformers, the one which advocates cheap money as the remedy for the world's ailments, to a very large extent attained its end in the course of the crisis, at least as far as short money rates are concerned. The decline of short-term interest rates went beyond all anticipations. The low records created during the 'nineties were easily beaten. This fact disarmed many reformers, who ceased to take any further part in the movement against monetary orthodoxy. Their only concern was that cheap money should be maintained. As is often the case with those whose radical claims become reality, they adopted a conservative attitude towards other radical claims, such as the abolition of the gold standard, or inflation. Some adherents of the cheap money school were, however, far from satisfied with what had been done. While they could hardly expect the decline in short-money rates to go any further, they were disappointed by the inadequate response of long-term money rates to the downward trend of short-money rates. Amongst them the view gained ground that it was useless to await the establishment of equilibrium through an automatic process, and they began to demand that the Government should intervene to hasten the reduction of long-term rates.

Another school of monetary reformers whose attack has weakened during the advanced stages of the crisis is that which seeks credit expansion. These contestants were forced to realise that in spite of the ample resources available, credit could not expand for lack of demand. They consequently confined their activities to demanding measures to secure an adequate credit supply after the revival of demand had begun through the increase of trade activity.

(5) Expansionism and Gold Standard

The school of monetary reformers which has gained in strength more than any other is the one advocating not an expansion of credit but an expansion of purchasing power. It is to the various schemes to this end that the strongest popular support has gone. An immense variety of schemes have been put forward by all sorts of reformers, ranging from essentially practical statesmen of the Lloyd George type to hopelessly impractical doctrinaires of the Douglas type. In many cases the proposals have not involved monetary reform in the true sense of the term, for schemes aiming at the creation of employment and purchasing power propose their financing through the mechanism of the existing monetary system. In substance, none the less, they represent a change of monetary conception.

A reform movement which has been pushed forward with great vigour and persistence by various schools of reformers is that which demands the abolition of the gold standard. Although various radical reformers may disagree about the means by which they claim to be able to restore prosperity, the majority of them agree that the definite demonetisation of gold is a preliminary condition to success. The view has taken root in the camp of monetary reformers that a return to the gold standard would preclude the possibility of continuous cheap money, would necessitate credit restriction, and would thus involve contraction of purchasing power. While a minority of monetary reformers would countenance a return to gold in the distant future, subject to a series of conditions, the majority rejects unconditionally the very idea of it. Indeed, most reformers are convinced that their respective monetary reform movement will succeed or fail according to whether or not it proves possible to prevent Great Britain from returning to gold, and thus to prevent the re-establishment of an international gold standard.

In addition to the recognised currents of the monetary reform movement, there is an immense variety of other schemes proposed from various quarters. Gesell's scheme of "free money", subject to deduction of interest, gained new popularity during the crisis. It was put forward in a different form by Dr. Robert Eisler and Mr. Isidore Ostrer; the latter proposed that banks, instead of allowing interest on deposits, should charge interest thereon. Another exotic monetary reform scheme, which has also been put forward in various forms during recent years, is that for divorcing the internal and international functions of money. Yet another new scheme, put forward by the London Chamber of Commerce, and belonging to a different class from that of the schemes mentioned above, advocates the substitution of international exchange clearing for the international gold standard.

(6) Drifting towards Radicalism

In many countries, but especially in the United States, entirely reckless and irresponsible monetary reform schemes have been advanced by demagogic politicians or well-meaning fanatics. The late Senator Huey Long, Father Coughlin and Dr. Townsend are the representative examples of this type. They are the " wild men " of the monetary reform movement, and are viewed with strong disapproval by the more sober monetary reformers, who are afraid that the reckless exaggeration in which these extremists indulge may throw discredit even on moderate and well-founded reform schemes. Indeed, fear of the extremists has been an important source of discouragement to practical monetary reform in the United States and elsewhere. Various members of President Roosevelt's " Brain Trust ", who at the beginning threw themselves with enthusiasm into the monetary reform movement, withdrew one by one for fear that the movement might go too far.

On the whole it may be said that as a result of the crisis the monetary reform movement lost some of its responsible elements and drifted towards a higher degree of radicalism. Indeed, experience has shown that the more radical the monetary reform proposals were, the more ready the general public was to follow them. The masses were unmoved by the scientific theories of a Hawtrey or a Keynes, but plunged with enthusiasm to the support of pseudo-scientific or frankly unscientific reform movements. Moreover, the fact that the scientific theories of recognised economists have for the most part been too involved for the man in the street does not by any means account for the lack of popular support for their proposals. After all, Major Douglas is no less involved, and a good deal more obscure, than Mr. Keynes. It is the method of their approach to the public that wins support for the pseudo-scientific and unscientific reformers. Scientific reformers cannot possibly operate with the same weapons.

Hitherto we have given a survey of the general development of the monetary reform movement in theory and practice since the war. In the following chapters we propose to examine the various monetary reform schemes individually, to follow their evolution, and to forecast their prospects.

CHAPTER VII

MONETARY REFORM DURING THE CRISIS

(1) Breakdown of Post-War System

The question whether the world crisis of 1931 was due to the deficiency of the monetary system has been one of heated controversy. Volumes could be, and indeed have been, written about it. Its detailed examination is outside the scope of this book; those interested in the author's views on that subject are referred to his book on *World Finance since 1914*. We are concerned here only with the effect of the crisis upon the practical application of monetary reform. Rightly or wrongly, the predominant majority of expert and inexpert opinion concluded—whether under the inescapable logic of facts or merely on the basis of the principle that the proof of the pudding is in the eating—that the monetary system as it operated after the war was inadequate. Some of the critics of the monetary system objected that it was too orthodox, while others objected that it was not nearly orthodox enough. According to the extent of the one conception or the other in a country, so its Government resorted either to reform measures or to an increasingly orthodox policy.

Even in the countries inclined to orthodoxy, it was realised that in the changed circumstances there could be no question of increasing the automatic character of the system. While applying the orthodox devices of monetary defence, they resorted at the same time to innovations which were in a sense as unorthodox and revolutionary as those applied by the countries which proceeded on definitely unorthodox lines.

(2) Currency Depreciation *v.* Default on Debt

The first and most important of all the monetary reforms adopted during the crisis was a changed conception towards the defence of existing parities. This changed conception manifested itself in two extreme ways. In some countries, such as Germany, Austria and Hungary, etc., the Government was determined to defend the parities even at the cost of suspending the transfer of the service of foreign debts. In other countries, such as Sweden, Japan and the United States, etc., the view adopted was that it is admissible to abandon the defence of the parity as a matter of expediency in face of prolonged adverse pressure, even if that pressure would not in itself have caused an immediate collapse of the currencies concerned. Both conceptions are essentially new. In former times, default on liabilities—which is what the suspension of transfer on foreign debt services amounts to—was considered a greater evil than the depreciation of the currency, and no country would have sacrificed its reputation as a debtor for the sake of avoiding the depreciation of its exchange. The reason why countries of the standing of Germany were prepared to default rather than to allow their exchanges to depreciate was probably that they realised that abandonment of their parities would not save them from the necessity of wholesale default on their external debts. For this reason they did not hesitate to adopt transfer moratoria as an unorthodox means of defending their stability.

The other extreme is represented by countries which considered it futile to put up a desperate resistance to adverse tendencies, and abandoned their parities at a time when they were still technically in a position to continue the defence of their monetary stability. The suggestion that their decision constitutes an important monetary reform would doubtless come as a surprise to those responsible for that policy. They simply decided to suspend the gold standard, or in some cases to devalue their currency, because they realised that sooner or later they would have to take that course, no matter what sacrifices were made in the meantime in order to postpone the inevitable end. Yet that attitude constitutes the very essence of vital monetary reform.

(3) Defence of Parity

Technically the monetary system has remained the same, but our conception of it has undergone a change. Up to 1931, it was understood that once a first-rate country had adopted a parity it was its duty to defend that parity no matter what it cost. The examples provided by Sweden and many other countries between 1931 and 1935 proved that this was not necessarily the case, and that it is possible for a country of high standing to abandon the gold standard or devalue its currency without being technically forced to do so. While Great Britain considered it her duty to spend the equivalent of her total gold reserve in defence of sterling, the Scandinavian countries adopted a more rational attitude and followed Great Britain in suspending the gold standard before they were actually driven off it.

Other countries, such as Japan, Greece and the Union of South Africa, put up a fight, but did not wait until they were technically defeated. They surrendered when they found that the fight was too costly. The same may be said of countries, such as the United States, Estonia, Czechoslovakia and Belgium, which abandoned their parities at a later stage. It remains to be seen whether the conception adopted between 1931 and 1935 will endure. If so, it will constitute one of the most important monetary reforms that are compatible with the maintenance of a metallic currency.

(4) Exchange Control

Another set of monetary reform measures adopted during the crisis comprises the various forms of exchange control which have been introduced. Transfer moratoria, mentioned above as a means of supplementing the orthodox defence of parities, are but one of the many forms of exchange restriction which serve the same end. Doubtless, exchange restrictions are not innovations. They were adopted during the war and maintained after it, in many cases with increased stringency. Those measures were, however, always regarded as essentially temporary in character. On the other hand, exchange restrictions adopted during the crisis are beginning to be regarded as being in harmony with the general tendency towards a higher degree of Government intervention.

When exchange control was practised before the period of post-war stabilisation everybody without exception looked forward to the moment when such irksome restrictions could be abolished, but now the number of those who believe that some form of exchange restriction is bound to be retained even after the period of depression is over is increasing steadily.

Various political parties have made it an essential part of their programmes to devise means by which to prevent a flight of capital in future, and to regulate the inflow and outflow of capital whether in the form of short-term or long-term commitments. It is widely believed that under the pressure of public opinion the complete freedom of exchanges that existed before the war, and also during the period of post-war stability, will never be entirely restored.

Government intervention in the foreign exchange market constituted another important monetary reform measure which was adopted during the crisis. Official operations in support of the national exchange, like exchange restrictions, are not altogether new. They were undertaken by a number of countries during and after the war. Like exchange restrictions, however, they were considered an essentially temporary interference. At present, nevertheless, the arrangements made in Great Britain by the establishment of the Exchange Equalisation Account, and similar arrangements in other countries, have the characteristics of lasting reform. It may be taken for granted that, even if Great Britain and other countries which "manage" their exchange were to return to the gold standard to-morrow, Government intervention would continue to play an important part in regulating the exchanges.

(5) Orthodox Reformers

It is not only countries with depreciated currencies that have adopted measures which depart from the principles of the automatic standard. Even countries with an orthodox monetary policy have been forced by circumstances to give up the idea that they would be able to maintain the stability of their currencies under the automatic system, or even under the semi-automatic system that existed after the war. France and the other countries of the Gold Bloc have had to adopt drastic measures of exchange restriction to supplement the traditional devices of the orthodox system. They introduced prohibitive customs duties, tariffs and quotas as measures to defend the exchange against an adverse trend caused by over-valuation in terms of other currencies. Strictly speaking, such measures do not belong to the monetary sphere, but since they were dictated by monetary considerations it is justifiable to regard them as measures of monetary reform.

It is highly probable that the tariff policy of the nations will in future be governed to a large extent by considerations of monetary stability. While, before the crisis, customs barriers were used either to protect home trade or to secure a revenue for the exchequer, in future they will also have for their object the defence of the currency.

(6) Exchange Clearing and Compensation

Another set of measures adopted by countries with stable currencies comprises a variety of clearing and compensation agreements. During the earlier stages of the crisis these agreements were concluded for monetary purposes mainly by financially weak countries, most of which had depreciated exchanges. While countries with gold currencies became parties to such agreements, their object was to secure a market for their products and to secure payment for their exports. It was only in 1934 that countries with stable currencies began to regard clearing and compensation agreements as a means of monetary defence. Germany was the first to recognise the use of compensation and clearing agreements for the purpose of defending the parities of her currency. Her example was followed by Italy, and there was a distinct tendency for the countries of the Gold Bloc to supplement their existing system of monetary defence by the conclusion of such agreements. Here, again, the monetary reforms represented by these measures are largely of a permanent character, even if they may temporarily be suspended sooner or later.

The fact that even the most ultra-orthodox countries considered it necessary to adopt such utterly unorthodox methods for the defence of their monetary stability is in itself a sufficient proof that the days of the automatic monetary system are past. Even countries with huge gold reserves have not cared to trust the process of natural readjustment to secure the stability of their currency. These countries decided to intervene on a hitherto unprecedented scale. It remains to be seen whether the methods they have adopted will remain in force, but the author is convinced that, even if the new measures were to be suspended after the end of the abnormal situation in which they were adopted, sooner or later they will have to be adopted once more.

(7) Monetary Reform and Trade Recovery

In many ways the countries with stable currencies have gone much further towards the adoption of monetary reform in the form of tariffs, quotas, exchange clearing and compensation agreements than the countries with depreciated currencies have done. There was, indeed, much more need for the former group to resort to drastic measures for the defence of their currencies. Pressure on the depreciated currencies was naturally not so strong as on the gold currencies, and in any case the countries concerned were not so particular in resisting the pressure whenever it arose. The monetary reform measures adopted by countries with depreciated currencies have been of a different nature from the measures of the Gold Bloc. As there was no need for them to concentrate their monetary policy on the defence of their exchange against depreciation, they were able to afford to employ monetary policy as a means of improving trade conditions.

The great variety of reflationary measures adopted in various countries in itself constitutes an important method of monetary reform. The adoption of the view that monetary policy can be made a means to an end and that it is not an end in itself, is clearly an important step towards monetary radicalism. In practice, it assumed different forms and different degrees in various countries. In Great Britain it chiefly took the form of a cheap money policy which was pursued by the Government irrespective of the tendency of sterling. In accordance with the orthodox rules, the policy of cheap money ought to have been reversed every time sterling became strongly adverse. In reality, money rates have been maintained at a low level even when sterling has been subject to selling pressure. It may be argued that the British Government could afford to pursue this policy only because sterling was not on a gold basis. This is doubtless true if we assume that the only conceivable method by which a currency can be stabilised on a gold basis is the one which was in force before the war and which was restored in a modified form after the war. Upon this question more will be said in a later chapter.

(8) Monetary Management

The methods of monetary management adopted in Great Britain, and to a still larger extent in Sweden, represent another type of monetary reform. Even if these countries returned to the gold standard, it is certain that, after the experience of recent years, they would retain a much higher degree of management than they employed before 1931. Meanwhile, these currencies and, in general, all the currencies of the Sterling Bloc, provide an interesting example of the monetary reform advocated by many experts, according to which the external stability of a currency should be sacrificed for the sake of its internal stability.

The very existence of the Sterling Bloc is in itself an interesting piece of monetary reform. Here we have a large number of countries whose inconvertible paper currencies have been maintained practically stable in relation to one another for several years. Although in official circles in Great Britain as well as in other countries of the Sterling Bloc, the solution which has been adopted is regarded as essentially provisional, many quarters are inclined to regard it as the forerunner of the future system which will sooner or later be definitely adopted. The very fact that the British Government is so reluctant to consider a return to the gold standard is interpreted by many people as an indication that there is a possibility that the existing state of affairs may be made permanent. It is argued that, even though the British authorities would not think of admitting any such intentions, once the Sterling Bloc arrangement has worked satisfactorily for a series of years, it will be adopted definitely and its legal status will be regulated. Whether or not this view can be accepted as being within the realm of probability, the working of the system of Sterling Bloc can certainly be considered as monetary reform in an experimental stage.

(9) President Roosevelt's Reforms

With the advent of President Roosevelt, a series of monetary reform measures were put into operation. In the first place, the departure from the gold standard by the United States as a matter of expediency in face of persistent pressure, constituted a reform measure of first-rate importance. We pointed out at the beginning of this chapter that there were already, from 1931 onwards, indications of a changed attitude towards the defence of existing parities. This development was nowhere more pronounced than in the United States.

In the case of countries which suspended the gold standard during 1931 and 1932 without having been actually swept off it, it was evident that the defence of their old parities would break down within a few weeks or a few months. The United States, on the other hand, with her huge gold reserve, was technically well able to continue to defend the dollar at its old parity for at least another year. In spite of this, President Roosevelt decided to devalue—because he realised that the further defence of the dollar, even if possible, was not worth the sacrifice it would have required. The United States thus provided the only clear case of abandonment of the existing parity as a matter of expediency.

This all-important monetary reform was followed almost immediately by another, that of the deliberate reduction of the internal and external value of the dollar. Until 1933, such a policy was considered unthinkable. A rise in commodity prices and a depreciation of the national exchange were always regarded in the light of a calamity whose avoidance was the supreme duty of the authorities. While the degree of expected resistance was a matter of opinion, it was taken for granted that Governments had to resist the tendency of the national currency to depreciate. The United States, however, provided an example of a country which, far from resisting the depreciating tendency, deliberately provoked it and accentuated it. President Roosevelt has initiated active reflation as part of the monetary policy of the United States.

The next important monetary reform measure introduced was the attempt to regulate the exchange by means of fixing and varying the official " internal " price of gold. In practice, this reform proved short-lived, but its significance must not be underestimated.

Lastly, President Roosevelt resorted to a kind of bimetallism, authorising the holding of silver as 25 per cent of the total metallic cover. From an historical point of view, this was a retrograde step rather than a reform, but from a technical point of view it was an important reform, calculated to broaden the basis of currency and credit, and thus to secure a wider scope for credit expansion.

All these reform measures of the crisis period will be discussed in detail in later chapters. This preliminary survey is designed simply to give the reader an idea of the extent to which monetary reform was adopted in practice during the brief period between 1931 and 1935. While at the present stage it is difficult to form an opinion as to how many of the reform measures will be cancelled and reversed once the depression is over, it is certain that the world cannot return to the system which existed before 1931, let alone to the pre-1914 system.

CHAPTER VIII

POLICY OF CHEAP MONEY

(1) Pre-War Tendencies

Proposals aiming at a reduction of the cost of borrowing probably constitute the least radical and most innocuous form of monetary reform scheme. It is a matter of opinion whether such proposals are compatible with the maintenance of an otherwise orthodox monetary system. Much depends upon the degree to which the adherents of the cheap money school are prepared to proceed, and upon the methods by which they propose to achieve their end. Being themselves borrowers, Governments are naturally in favour of cheaper money, though their desire to maintain the stability of their currency by means of high interest rates often silences the arguments in favour of cheaper borrowing.

The first and most extreme advocate of the cheap money school was St. Thomas Aquinas, whose doctrine, " money breeds no money ", might well be chosen as the *motto* of the cheap money school. The other extreme is represented by the ultra-orthodox economists who, far from considering dear money a necessary evil, regard it as desirable for its own sake. This is not the place to discuss the controversial question whether, from an ethical point of view, lenders are justified in charging interest over and above the cost of the labour involved in their operations. Under the existing economic and social system owners of capital in practice can and do charge interest which includes, in addition to the reward of clerical labour and the compensation for the risk involved, a certain indefinable surplus for the hire of the funds. Before the war, whenever there was a tendency towards the decline of interest rates as a result of a trade depression, such as was experienced in the 'nineties, suggestions were put forward every time that interest might disappear altogether or at any rate might be reduced to compensation for the clerical labour involved. From time to time debtors complained about the excessive interest burden, but before the war there was no definite movement for a reduction of interest rates from a general economic point of view.

(2) War and Interest Rates

The origin of the post-war movement in favour of lower money rates was the spectacular rise in money rates after 1914. It is worth while to examine the causes of this rise, in order to be able to form an opinion of the extent to which the maintenance of interest rates at a high level was justified after the war.

The urgent and enormous requirements of the Governments to finance national defence were mainly responsible for the rise in interest rates between 1914 and 1918. It is true that simultaneously with heavy Government borrowing there was also an expansion of the amount available for lending. As, however, the borrowers were keener to borrow than the owners of the capital were to lend, the former had to pay the price at which they were able to induce the latter to part with their funds. But for considerations of patriotism, moral pressure, and a certain degree of official intervention, the cost of borrowing during the war would have risen even higher. To some extent the rise was due to the feeling of insecurity. The gigantic dimensions of war expenditure could not fail in some measure to undermine confidence in the solvency of any Government, especially while the outcome of the war was uncertain. Another consideration was the decline in the purchasing power of the monetary unit, especially during the advanced stages of the war. By 1917 or 1918 the owners of capital were beginning to realise that, even if they received twenty shillings in the pound, they received less in terms of commodities than the amount they had lent. To some extent they wished to be compensated for such losses through higher interest rates. This may not have been a conscious attitude in the majority of cases; in practice, the problem presented itself in a different form. The exceptional profit made during the war by most producers attracted capital towards industrial investment. The rising trend of prices induced capitalists to acquire commodities, real property, etc., so as to benefit by the upward trend. Borrowers had to compete with the rivalry of higher yield for capital appreciation offered by other forms of employment of funds. Indeed, in the circumstances it is remarkable that the rise in interest rates was not even more substantial. The view that the abnormal conditions prevailing during the war were essentially temporary was probably largely responsible for the absence of a much more pronounced rise.

(3) Post-War Inflation and Stabilisation

During the period of post-war inflation the credit of Governments further declined, and borrowing rates further increased in consequence. The rates of Government borrowing determined to a large degree the tendency of borrowing costs for private borrowers. In countries where inflation reached extreme stages, interest rates rose to a fantastic level, but even then they failed to compensate lenders for the decline in the commodity value of their capital.

The stabilisation of currencies was not followed by a sudden and substantial decline of interest rates. The newly established stability of the currencies was defended to a large degree by means of high interest rates. Confidence was also rather slow to return; it was a matter of years before the public began to realise that inflation was over. In addition, there was strong demand for capital in countries whose financial resources had been destroyed by inflation. Countries such as Germany, with a highly developed industrial system and commanding a high degree of confidence abroad, borrowed huge amounts in the international capital market. Owing to the extreme scarcity of capital in the home market, borrowers were prepared to pay abnormally high interest rates in general. Last, but by no means least, there was the enormous dead-weight indebtedness inherited from the war and post-war inflation. While the purchasing power created at the time of the issue of the war loans disappeared through taxation or through the post-war slump, the debt itself remained. In Great Britain it amounted to over ten times its pre-war figure. Its immense volume made the task of conversion extremely difficult, especially as a large part of it consisted of one single type of security. The other former belligerent countries, and to a less extent even neutral countries, were confronted with a similar situation. In countries where inflation wiped out or reduced public debt, it wiped out or reduced at the same time the volume of savings, so that a scarcity of capital developed. In countries where inflation did not adequately reduce the commodity value of public debt, its immense size prevented an adequate decline of interest rates.

(4) Burden of High Interest Rates

Thus, not only did the capital amount of fictitious wealth increase enormously after 1914, but, in addition, the total interest burden increased more than proportionately. The result was that the deadweight debt absorbed an excessive proportion of the result of productive activity. The productive section of the population had to carry this huge burden in the form of crushing taxation. In the author's opinion, the disequilibrium between fictitious wealth and real wealth created since 1914 has been the main cause of all our economic troubles since the war. For detailed argument on this point, he must, however, refer readers to his book *World Finance since 1914*.

The desirability of reducing interest rates after the war was duly realised by many prominent economists, bankers and business men. They urged the Governments to effect a reduction for the sake of stimulating trade. Indeed, one of the reasons why the orthodox monetary policy pursued by the British Government and other Governments met with strong opposition was that it necessitated high interest rates. The demand for low rates, however, was strongly opposed not only by those representing the interests of creditors, who benefited by the high rates, but also by orthodox economists. The latter argued that high interest rates were necessary in order to defend the currencies of certain countries. This argument did not sound convincing, for the same result could have been achieved by a reduction of interest rates in the financially strong countries. When on one single occasion this was done, in the United States in 1927, there was an outcry of indignation in the orthodox camp, whose protests have not subsided to this very day. Another favourite argument in favour of high interest rates was that they were necessary in order to prevent a boom. The experience of 1929 proved, however, that high interest rates are unable to prevent a boom.

An ultra-orthodox American economist, Mr. Benjamin Anderson, came forward with the argument that interest rates after the war were not nearly high enough, and that they ought to have been much higher so as to stimulate saving and thus to enable the world to reconstruct the capital destroyed during the war. He remained conveniently vague as to what kind of capital he had in mind. If he meant the fictitious capital which can be reconstructed by means of savings, that has increased to a very large extent since 1914, in fact its increase is one of our principal troubles. If he meant the real wealth which was destroyed in the course of hostilities, high interest rates are a most effective way of preventing its reconstruction since they discourage the production of real wealth.

(5) Creditors *v.* Debtors

Those who point out that a reduction of interest rates means a contraction of the purchasing power of the creditor classes overlook the fact that what the creditor classes stand to lose through the reduction, the debtor classes, or taxpayers, stand to gain. From a moral point of view, creditors have a very weak case indeed for claiming that they are entitled to the high yields which they have received during the past twenty years. In fact, the higher interest rates they have been receiving constitute a windfall, an unearned surplus. While the increase was justifiable during the period of heavy Government borrowing, once this expenditure came to an end high interest rates had no longer the same *raison d'être.* While during the war and during the period of inflation it was justifiable to regard the security of Government bonds as inferior to what it was before the war, this justification was removed once war and inflation were over.

It is true that the Governments had a larger public debt than before the war, but in the case of the first-rate countries this fact did not in the least impair their solvency. During a period of falling prices, however, they were not entitled to claim the maintenance of interest rates at the level to which they had risen during the period of increasing prices. From 1920 onwards—or in the case of a number of countries from the time of the stabilisation of their currencies between 1922 and 1927—commodity prices had a persistent falling tendency, and creditors benefited by it. Although in some countries conversion operations were carried out and interest rates tended to fall, they remained none the less considerably above their level of 1914.

(6) Limitations of Cheap Money

There was unquestionably a strong case to be made for a drastic reduction of interest rates after the war. Those who advocated such a reduction throughout the period between 1920 and 1931 were doubtless theoretically right. There is, however, another aspect of the picture. It may well be asked what the result would have been if their advice had been followed and if before 1929 there had been a world-wide reduction of interest rates not only on short-term credits but also on long-term loans. In all probability the result would have been a further accentuation of the speculative boom, and the slump that followed it would have been, if possible, even more disastrous than it actually proved to be. Cheap money would have encouraged speculation and also over-production. It is true that the reduction of interest rates would have resulted in a better distribution of purchasing power, but the improvement in itself would have been barely sufficient to counteract the consequence of the disequilibria that, in the absence of economic planning, would inevitably have arisen from over-stimulation of trade activity.

Cheap money is doubtless highly desirable from more than one point of view. In the absence of economic planning, however, it may easily lead to over-production, over-speculation and profit inflation, and may easily end in a crisis. In order that cheap money may produce constructive results, it is essential that the encouragement to trade which it generates should be diverted into proper channels and should be organised. In any case, even in ideal conditions of economic planning there is a limit beyond which a reduction of money rates ceases to be desirable. Even the extreme adherents of the spending school must admit that a certain degree of saving is necessary and advantageous. The decline of interest rates to a nominal figure might discourage saving to an unduly high degree. At the same time, such a decline inevitably increases the age limit at which those holding responsible positions can afford to retire from business. This tends to slow down promotion for the younger generation and would be detrimental to economic progress.

In any case, it is easy to over-estimate the good effects of cheap money upon progress. In itself cheap money does not go very far towards stimulating trade if general conditions are otherwise unfavourable to revival. The mere fact that a producer or a business man can borrow at a low interest rate does not induce him to increase his stocks of commodities if he expects to encounter difficulties in their sale. This is a point which has not been adequately appreciated by the enthusiasts of cheap money. While low interest rates unquestionably assist a trade revival, and may indeed be indispensable to it, they can produce satisfactory results only in conjunction with other factors working in the same direction. The rôle of a policy of cheap money is largely confined to removing an obstacle to trade revival rather than to creating trade revival. Some of the more advanced supporters of the cheap money policy duly realise the necessity of supplementing that policy by Government intervention to enforce an all-round reduction of interest rates. The more conservative advocates of that policy believe that all that the authorities have to do is to reduce the bank rate and await results. According to classical principles, cheap money must work itself from the short-term loan market into the long-term loan market, automatically adjust all interest rates, and also the yield of securities with variable dividends, to the lower level. The experience of the last few years has proved that in the existing circumstances that process is bound to be extremely slow, and may never go far enough. It is indeed possible that a trade revival would reverse the trend of interest rates altogether, so that money would become dear exactly at the moment when its cheapness was beginning to be really beneficial to production and trade. While it is inevitable that a trade revival at its advanced stage should tend to produce higher money rates, it is important that in the meantime the basic figures from which the rates rise should be consolidated at a low level. Radical reformers such as Mr. J. M. Keynes realise that to that end it is necessary to depart from the " wait and see " policy which has hitherto been advocated by the cheap money school. The Government, it is urged, must take active steps to enforce an all-round reduction of interest rates. The method suggested is that of "de-funding", or the conversion of long-term loans into low interest-bearing short-term loans until the discrepancy between long and short money rates is reduced to normal proportions.

Adherents of orthodox financial principles shrink in horror at the very idea. And yet, as we shall see in the next chapter, some Governments, actuated by orthodox motives of currency defence, have actually resorted to much more drastic action, in the form of direct cuts of interest rates by legislative measures, or by ill-disguised forced conversions. Government interference with private contract rights has not been confined to countries with dictatorial régimes. The abolition of the gold clause in the United States, Belgium, Poland, and a number of other countries shows that such interference can be effected also under the ægis of parliamentary democracy. The example of France in cutting interest rates by 10 per cent is particularly remarkable.

In itself a reduction of money rates in order to relieve the burden of debtors, or in order to provoke a trade revival, does not constitute a monetary reform. For a policy of cheap money to be entitled to be regarded as a reform measure, it must be pursued systematically. The fundamental principle of such a reform is that cheapness of money should take precedence over other considerations, such as the international stability of the currency. The adoption of the principle of cheap money as a basis of monetary policy means that if the choice lies between a depreciation of the currency and higher money rates, the former will without hesitation be chosen. In such an extreme form, the cheap money principle is just as much in conflict with the orthodox school as are the more radical reformers of the expansionist school of the opponents of the gold standard. Indeed, in practice, a cheap money policy in an extreme form implies both expansion and the abolition of the gold standard. Even its systematic application to a moderate degree would constitute a substantial departure from the gold standard system as it operated before the war and before the crisis, and as it still operates in some countries. It is conceivable that a gold standard can be maintained in spite of the adoption of a policy of cheap money, provided that cheap money is adopted universally, or, if it is not, then provided that ex-

F

change restrictions prevent the difference in money rates from causing disturbing international movements of funds. In the minds of most monetary reformers, however, cheap money is associated either with a policy of credit expansion or with a managed currency. It is a general belief that under the gold standard money rates cannot be maintained on a low basis for any length of time, since the defence of the gold reserves necessitates high rates. This objection is based on the pre-war and post-war experience of the working of the gold standard, when the margins of gold reserves were relatively narrow in most countries. If, however, a drastic devaluation of all currencies were achieved, and were not followed by a rise in commodity prices to anything like a corresponding extent, it would increase the margins of gold reserves very largely, and would thus enable the monetary authorities to maintain cheap money for some length of time, even though such a policy involved a substantial outflow of gold. On such a basis the gold standard could be worked on entirely unorthodox principles. According to the classical rules, it is only through the effect of gold movements upon interest rates that the gold standard can bring about the desired readjustment in countries which are out of equilibrium with the rest of the world. The existence of abnormally large margins of gold reserves, however, could obviate the necessity for such an automatic process of readjustment, and the authorities could thus avoid it should they deem it against the general interest. It is true that, in the absence of the process of readjustment, the degree of disequilibrium might tend to widen, with the result that the outflow of gold would be accentuated. This, of course, would be the case if the world returned to the comparative freedom of international trade that existed before the crisis. If, on the other hand, the system of regulating foreign trade by exchange clearing is adopted, it may become possible to avoid a deterioration of the trade balance in the absence of automatic readjustment.

CHAPTER IX

CHEAP MONEY AND THE CRISIS

(1) Opposition to High Interest Rates

Even before 1931 the pressure in favour of cheap money was considerable, especially in Great Britain where trade since the post-war slump had been in a permanent state of semi-depression. British public opinion began to attach considerable importance to the level of interest rates, which consequently had to be kept much lower than appeared desirable from the point of view of the defence of sterling. It is open to argument whether sterling would have been less vulnerable if interest rates had been kept at a higher level. Possibly interest rates abroad would have been raised in sympathy; possibly high money rates in London would have further accentuated the influx of "bad money" which eventually proved to be the direct cause of the collapse of sterling. However it may be, it is certain that during 1929 the authorities showed some reluctance to raise the bank rate for fear of unduly antagonising public opinion. In fact, even during the crisis of the pound they were unwilling to follow the advice of orthodox quarters, which advocated the raising of the bank rate to a fantastic level in order to save the pound. Presumably, the authorities were aware that a high bank rate would not have saved the pound but would have resulted in unfavourable political consequences, in addition to adverse economic effects.

In the United States, too, there was a movement in favour of cheap money before the crisis, but there was no political pressure comparable with that experienced in Great Britain. To some extent debtor interests agitated for cheaper money, and they were supported by Wall Street. When the United States authorities endeavoured to check the speculative boom by means of a policy of dear money, they met with resistance from financial as well as from agricultural interests.

In France, after the stabilisation of the franc, the Government adopted an orthodox monetary policy, in pursuance of which money rates were maintained at an unnecessarily high level. The object was to prevent the rise in the French price level which would have been necessary to readjust it to the world price level. When it was suggested that the French authorities might relieve the pressure on sterling by lowering their bank rate, the answer was invariably that the right way to counteract the pressure on sterling was to raise interest rates in London and not to lower them in Paris. In France, essentially a *rentier* nation, the number of those favouring high interest rates was necessarily considerable and their political influence was substantial.

In Germany and various other countries which suffered a great deal through inflation, and where interest rates after stabilisation remained intolerably high, there was a strong feeling in favour of lower rates. The promise of the National Socialist Party programme to release the nation from "the thraldom of interest" was one of the causes of its growing popularity. The Government itself was torn between the desire to limit the influx of foreign capital and the desire to lower the interest rates in the internal capital market.

(2) Depression and Falling Money Rates

The economic depression resulted in a world-wide decline of interest rates. The decline was, however, interrupted by the financial crisis of 1931. Great Britain, Germany and a number of other European countries raised their bank rates in order to defend their currencies. Even in the United States the rediscount rates had to be raised in the autumn of 1931, in face of the pressure caused by the withdrawal of French balances. The reaction was, however, purely temporary. From 1932 onwards the world-wide declining trend of interest rates was resumed, though from time to time it was interrupted in various countries which resorted to a high bank rate as a means of defending their currencies.

In Great Britain the Government adopted a policy of cheap money early in 1932, and has pursued it even since. Within a few months the bank rate was lowered from 6 per cent to 2 per cent, at which rate it has since remained. The conversion of the 5 per cent War Loan removed the main obstacle to the decline of long-term money rates, which at last began to adjust themselves slowly to the fall in short-term rates. The yield on Government securities declined to below 3 per cent, and 2½ per cent Consols early in 1935 were well on their way towards parity. Adherents of the cheap money school in Great Britain had indeed every reason to rejoice. Their dreams were becoming reality. With market discount rates under ½ per cent and with the yield of long-term Government securities declining towards a 2½ per cent basis, they had little reason to complain.

The trouble was that other short-term and long-term interest rates were rather slow to adjust themselves to the lower level. As a rule the rate of interest charged on overdrafts was still 4½ per cent to 5 per cent. Competition between banks, savings banks and building societies kept deposit rates far too high. The standard rate for well-secured mortgages was still 5 per cent, and industrial debentures had also to offer a fairly attractive yield. The advocates of cheap money maintained that the Government did not take up a sufficiently active policy of intervention to force money rates down. Indeed, they doubted if the decline of money rates which had taken place since 1932 was the result of the Government's policy. In many quarters the decline was attributed mainly, if not exclusively, to the trade depression which reduced the demand for credit. It would, however, be a mistake to overlook the deliberate increase of the Bank's gold holding and security portfolio.

(3) British Government's Policy

The Government, on the other hand, claimed full credit for having lowered interest rates by means of a deliberate policy and also for having brought about a trade recovery by its policy of cheap money. It maintained that cheap money was the result of the balanced budget and the restoration of confidence brought about by the Government's sound financial methods. It also maintained that the encouragement to trade through the reduction of money rates was largely responsible for the reduction of unemployment. Neither of these two contentions can be accepted without much qualification. It is true that but for the balancing of the budget it would have been difficult to convert the 5 per cent War Loan in 1932. It is equally true that during the spring of 1932 the authorities took deliberate action to " pump " money into circulation. At the same time it must be admitted that cheap money was mainly the natural consequence of the prolonged depression, and that it was bound to come about as soon as the deliberate policy of defending the exchange by means of high money rates was abandoned. The fact that short money in the United States is at least as cheap as in Great Britain, notwithstanding the huge budgetary deficit, shows that a balanced budget is not an indispensable condition to cheap money.

As for the effect of cheap money upon trade, it is undoubtedly a commonplace of elementary text-books on economics that low money rates tend to stimulate business activity. The importance of this factor in the existing conditions must not, however, be overestimated. Cheap money in itself cannot create a trade revival to any large extent. It is true that the reduction of short-term and long-term interest rates tends to encourage borrowing. So long as the outlook is gloomy, however, it does not in itself lead to increased borrowing. Even a negative rate of interest would fail to induce a business man to borrow for the purpose of increasing his production or his stocks if he thought he had reason to doubt whether he would be able to dispose of them at a profit.

(4) Limited Effect of Cheap Money

When the Government adopted its cheap money policy in 1932 the advocates of cheap money were triumphant. They were convinced that, if only money were kept sufficiently cheap for a sufficiently long time, a trade revival was bound to set in. The adoption of their policy by a Government which was otherwise highly conservative and orthodox was highly gratifying to those who had advocated this policy for years. Their triumph, however, was short-lived, for the experience of the last three years has shown the limitations of the cheap money policy. The extent to which its adoption was followed by an increase of employment was relatively small. Even that increase was to a large extent due to protective tariffs, to the passing advantage of a depreciated and under-valued exchange, and to the rise in commodity prices that followed President Roosevelt's reflationary policy. If we allow for all these factors, the net positive result of the policy of cheap money upon trade in Great Britain has been very meagre indeed. Admittedly, in a negative sense cheap money played a very important part in making it possible for British trade to benefit by the other favourable factors at work. In the absence of cheap money, the extent to which trade would have benefited by protective tariffs, depreciation of sterling and the rise in the world prices of commodities, would have been much smaller. Dear money can effectively kill trade, and from this point of view the Government's cheap money policy was very useful indeed. The rôle that policy played in a negative sense was much more important than its rôle in directly creating additional trade.

If the experience of the last few years has proved one thing conclusively, it is that cheap money in itself is not sufficient to create prosperity. It is true that after past crises a prolonged period of cheap money has always been followed by trade recovery. Those, however, who infer from this that recovery was brought about by cheap money are guilty of the fallacy of *post hoc ergo propter hoc.* The mere fact that recovery followed cheap money in chronological order does not mean that there was the relation of cause and effect between them. The low money rates were the consequence of the cyclic depression and, when the cause of that depression ceased to operate, a gradual recovery ensued. Cheap money may have assisted the process, it may have made it possible, but it was certainly not the principal cause.

(5) Cheap Money Abroad

The British experience of cheap money repeated itself in the United States. There, low money rates were brought about largely by the same factor which operated in Great Britain, namely the absence of demand for credit for productive purposes. It is true that the authorities endeavoured to lower interest rates by pumping money into circulation, but this policy played a relatively subordinate part. In the absence of the possibility of employing funds, banks were keen buyers of Treasury bills and commercial bills, and the discount rate for the former declined even below that for British Treasury bills. At the same time, the banks bought long-term Government securities, the yield of which declined almost to the same extent as that of British Government securities. As in Great Britain, so in the United States, the extent to which cheap money worked itself into various forms of long-term loan rates was, however, inadequate. For this and other reasons, trade failed to benefit from it to a sufficient degree.

In several countries a deliberate policy of cheap money was enforced not only in the sphere of Government loans but in that of private loans. In Italy and Germany an all-round reduction of interest rates was effected by Government intervention. In both countries the existing political and economic system enabled the Government to take drastic action. Both in Italy and Germany a conversion "offer" was made to holders of mortgage loans to convert their holdings on a 3½ per cent basis. In theory they were at liberty to refuse, but in practice circumstances were such as to make it rather awkward for them to do so. In fact, both in Italy and in Germany the number of dissentients represented a fraction of 1 per cent of the amount involved. It is only by means of such semi-compulsory conversions that an all-round reduction of interest rates can be enforced, especially in countries like Italy and Germany, which are determined to defend their overvalued exchanges. In the ordinary course this determination would necessitate the maintenance of high interest rates, and would preclude the possibility of a cheap money policy. Both Italy and Germany, however, seem to have solved—temporarily at any rate—the problem of eating their cake and having it. They resorted to unorthodox methods of supporting their currencies at an overvalued level, and proceeded to reduce interest rates. The existence of strict exchange restrictions prevented the cheap money policy from producing its normal effect in stimulating the outflow of capital. In any case, during the last few years the international movement of capital has been determined not by considerations of yield but by considerations of security.

(6) Radical Intervention in France

The fact that a really effective cheap money policy necessitates drastic Government intervention is illustrated by the failure of a relatively moderate policy in France. Early in 1934 the French authorities defended their exchange by the orthodox method of raising the bank rate, but at the beginning of 1935 the Government declared itself in favour of a deliberate policy of cheap money. It was announced that, with the aid of new credit facilities to be granted by the Bank of France, interest rates would be reduced. This policy, however, was a complete failure, for the Government was unable to enforce it even in regard to the Bank of France. Although a new Governor was appointed who was in favour of the new policy, the passive resistance of the executive of the bank made it impossible for the Government to compel it to expand credit. In consequence, the cheap money policy produced absolutely no results and interest rates in France at the time of writing are higher than they were when the new policy was announced.

In the circumstances, the French Government felt compelled to resort to more drastic measures. M. Laval took a leaf out of the book of Signor Mussolini and Herr Hitler by enforcing an all-round cut in interest rates, on Government loans as well as on private loans. In fact, he even went a step further by abstaining from all efforts to make the reduction appear to be the result of voluntary conversion. Interest rates in France were reduced by 10 per cent by Government decree. This is by far the most radical method of initiating cheap money that we have encountered so far. It must be pointed out that while most advocates of cheap money regard their policy as serving the interest of expansion, the drastic measures applied in France, and also in Italy, Germany and Belgium, were designed for distinctly deflationary objects. Indeed, these measures formed part of the policy of "consistent deflation" which will be discussed in Chapter XXIX.

There is an essential difference between the cheap money policy pursued in countries with depreciated currencies where money tended to be naturally cheap, and in countries with overvalued currencies where the natural trend was towards high money rates. In countries where Government policy merely confirms a natural trend, the level to which interest rates are reduced by Government operations tends to be maintained after the Government operations are over. In Great Britain, for instance, the large conversion operation of the 5 per cent War Loan to $3\frac{1}{2}$ per cent was followed by a genuine and lasting decline of long-term interest rates. On the other hand, in countries where Government intervention was in conflict with the natural trend of interest rates, the effect proved purely temporary. It was impossible to borrow new money on the basis of the level to which interest ratés on existing loans were cut down. In Italy, Germany and France, the Government and other borrowers had subsequently to pay even higher rates for their new borrowing than those which prevailed before the compulsory reduction in interest rates. Unquestionably, the relief to private debtors through this compulsory conversion was a step in the right direction. Its effect on trade, however, was negligible.

(7) Prospects of Cheap Money Policy

Taking the world as a whole, the favourable results of the policy of cheap money pursued in various forms by various Governments have so far been relatively small. Nevertheless, the cheap money policy should not be under-rated as a means of improving general conditions. As we have already pointed out, in a negative sense cheap money eliminates a major obstacle to improvement of trade. Moreover, once the factors that make for trade revival begin to operate, the maintenance of cheap money will become increasingly helpful. It remains to be seen how far the various Governments will maintain their cheap money policy when, as a result of an increased demand for credit, there is a tendency towards a rise in interest rates. As far as Great Britain is concerned, Mr. Neville Chamberlain has made it plain that he means to continue to pursue a policy of cheap money even though trade conditions have improved. A suggestion to reverse that policy by means of raising the bank rate was rejected early in 1935. The chances are that trade recovery will have to go a long way before the Chancellor of the Exchequer will consent to put the brake on it by means of reversing the policy of cheap money.

In the United States, too, there is every reason to expect that the policy of cheap money will continue. Even though banking circles have become increasingly uneasy about the possibility that the large banking reserves may lead to credit inflation, the authorities are not likely to jeopardise the trade revival by reversing their cheap money policy. With unemployment still well over ten millions, the warnings against the dangers of an inflationary boom carry but little conviction.

As for the countries with overvalued currencies, they can adopt a consistent policy of cheap money with any chance of a lasting success only if they allow their currencies to find their natural levels, thereby removing the main factor that makes for higher money rates. As the devaluation of the gold currencies is inevitable sooner or later, it is safe to assume that the cheap money policy will eventually become world-wide.

What will happen, however, after the general currency stabilisation, which may presumably be expected within a few years? The answer depends upon the circumstances in which the currencies are stabilised. If stabilisation is followed by adverse pressure on certain currencies and if the margin of their gold reserves is not sufficiently large to enable the countries concerned to view a heavy efflux with equanimity, the result will be a reversal of the cheap money policy in those countries. From this point of view, it is of little use to make New Year's resolutions—in accordance with the suggestions made by some economists—that under the new gold standard a policy of dear money would not be used for the purpose of defending the stability of the currencies. Once the gold standard is restored, the decline of the margin of gold reserve to a very low level would inevitably lead to dear money. It is well to bear this in mind in deciding the time and circumstances of the return to the gold standard.

CHAPTER X

THE CREDIT EXPANSIONIST SCHOOL

(1) Cheap *v.* Plentiful Money

The term " expansionism " is used in general to indicate all the various proposals which seek to increase prosperity through an increase in the volume of the means of payment. It is necessary, however, to discriminate between those who propose to expand currency and credit for productive purposes and those who advocate the expansion of the consumer's purchasing power. The former may be termed the credit expansionist school, while the latter are adherents of either the income expansion school or the spending school. In this chapter we are concerned only with the monetary reformers who advocate an expansion of credit for the purposes of production.

It is a popular belief that money is cheap whenever it is plentiful and that it is plentiful whenever it is cheap. This is doubtless true in normal circumstances, especially in the market for short-term loans. The experience of the war has proved, however, that money can become very expensive even though it is manufactured by the milliard. At an advanced stage of inflation interest rates tend to rise to fantastic figures. It is a mistake, therefore, to assume that cheap money and plentiful money on the one hand, or high interest rates and scarcity of money on the other, are one and the same thing. It is true that, as a rule, the school of thought which is in favour of cheap money is also in favour of monetary expansion. Many adherents of this school, however, have a preference for the one or the other. Some of them, like Mr. Keynes, attach more importance to the fact that trade should obtain loans at low rates of interest, while others, like Mr. McKenna, consider it less important that the price of money should be low than that there should be enough of it.

The majority of monetary reformers, while favouring low interest rates, consider it infinitely more important that there should be enough money to cover the requirements of an expanding production coupled with an expanding consumption. The view is held that, during a period of prosperous and expanding trade, producers are in a position to stand the burden of relatively high interest rates. Indeed, they can better afford to pay high interest rates then than to pay the lower interest rates charged to them in times of depression. In spite of this, most monetary radicals attach importance to cheap money, because in practice high money rates are usually accompanied by a scarcity of money and also because high interest rates lead to a redistribution of purchasing power which may not favour an expansion of production and consumption.

(2) Creed of Scarcity

That there should be relative scarcity of money is one of the fundamental rules of the orthodox monetary system. According to the supporters of that system, it is necessary that money should be kept scarce so as to preserve its value. According to this school, it is the duty of Central Banks to maintain the volume of currency and credit slightly below the amount of normal requirements. Those who believe in this doctrine regard a moderate but perpetual deflationary policy as an indispensable condition for securing the stability of exchanges.

The policy which aims at a permanent scarcity of money is bound to be an obstacle to the expansion of production. The question is whether it is worth while to sacrifice progress for international stability. The answer of the radical school is an emphatic negative. By far the greater number of monetary reformers, faced with the alternative of maintaining the stability of the exchange at the cost of monetary stringency, or of allowing the exchange to find its level in order to avoid embarrassing trade by restricting the supply of money, would choose the second alternative without hesitation. This is the reason why most adherents of the expansionist school are enemies of the gold standard. In reality, monetary expansion is not incompatible with the gold standard, any more than is cheap money, provided that there is an adequate margin of gold reserve available as a basis of the expansion. Like the cheap money school, the expansionists condemn the gold standard as an insurmountable obstacle to their policy, basing their case on their experience before 1914 and from 1925 onwards.

From the point of view of the possibilities of monetary expansion, as from that of the possibilities of cheap money, it is not so much the gold standard as such that ought to be regarded as the obstacle, as the mentality that is associated with the operation of the gold standard. We have seen that in countries such as the United States or France, there was before 1931 an ample margin of gold reserve to enable the monetary authorities to expand money without running the least risk of suspending the gold standard. Instead, they preferred to hoard their surplus and sterilise it rather than to allow it to provide the basis for a corresponding monetary expansion.

(3) Various Kinds of Expansionism

The camp of monetary expansionists is a very mixed company. There are scientific expansionists like Mr. J. M. Keynes or Mr. R. G. Hawtrey, practical scientific expansionists like Mr. Reginald McKenna, and an infinite variety of pseudo-scientific or frankly unscientific expansionists. The object of their policies differs widely, and so do the methods by which they would like to achieve their ends, and the degree of expansion which they consider expedient. It is customary to discriminate between expansionists—meaning scientific supporters of moderate expansion—and inflationists—meaning unscientific advocates of a large dose of expansion—but such a crude division over-simplifies the real state of affairs.

The following are the best known relatively moderate proposals for credit expansion:

1. Expansion through an economical use of gold reserves.
2. Expansion through a reduction of cash ratios of banks.
3. Expansion through a reduction of reserve ratios of Central Banks.

The conservative wing of the expansionist school believes it possible to satisfy increased credit requirements on the basis of the gold standard by making the existing amount of monetary gold do more work. Economy in the use of gold, which was one of the popular slogans of the period of post-war stability, did in fact work towards this end. One of the objects of international co-operation between Central Banks was to enable countries with comparatively small gold reserves to maintain a relatively large volume of credit and even to expand it if this appeared expedient from the point of view of internal trade.

(4) Reduction of Cash Ratio

A more radical school of expansionists advocated expansion of credit on a gold basis by the reduction of the cash ratios of commercial banks from the level determined by custom and tradition. In various countries banks have come to observe unwritten laws which, while differing from one another in detail, have had the same practical result of limiting credit expansion. In British banking the ratio of cash to deposits is usually maintained above 10 per cent. On the Continent, more importance is attached as a rule to the ratio of the banks' own resources (capital and reserves) to their outside resources (deposits and other liabilities subject to withdrawal at sight or at short notice.) In most countries there is no legislation compelling banks to observe any minimum ratios, but in practice these ratios are usually observed, even though there is usually a certain amount of elasticity in the application of the self-imposed rule.

In times of depression the cash ratios usually rise well above the self-imposed minimum and do not constitute an obstacle to expansion simply because there is no demand for expansion. During periods of active trade, however, this self-imposed limit to the expansion of credit is subject to much complaint. Its existence prevents banks from financing new enterprise even if in itself it is considered sound. Thus, the banks often have to abstain from granting loans even though the security offered appears to be satisfactory, affording an ample margin to safeguard the lender, and the object of the loan is essentially constructive and commercially sound. It is no wonder that the system of a minimum cash ratio should be criticised by expansionists. Some of them suggest as a remedy the adoption of a greater elasticity in fixing the minimum cash ratio. It has been argued that in normal periods a low ratio meets requirements, while in times of a crisis even a very high cash ratio is no safeguard against a general run on the banks. Before the crisis these arguments did not sound any too convincing, but after 1931 the conception gained ground in radical quarters that, since banks always fall back upon their Governments in case of trouble, they should be forced to allow their cash ratios to decline in connection with credit expansion for approved purposes. From such a viewpoint, the proposal to nationalise the banks in the interest of credit expansion is but a short step. One of the favourite arguments in support of nationalisation is that, since the Government has to take the full risk of the liabilities of banks, it is entitled to expect the latter to use their resources as far as necessary in the interest of the improvement of the standard of living.

(5) Central Banks' Rôle

Another expansionist school maintains that the remedy for the limitation of credit expansion lies in the hands, not of the commercial banks, but of the monetary authorities. The latter are in a position to pave the way for expansion by increasing the basis of the credit structure. If the Bank of England buys securities in the open market, the proceeds find their way to the banks, and the result is a net increase in their balances with the Bank of England and those balances form part of their cash reserve. Such an operation obviates the necessity for a reduction of the cash ratio for the purpose of expanding credit. In other countries, whose credit structure is less developed than that of Great Britain, the Central Banks can contribute to credit expansion more directly by increasing their note circulation in connection with increasing their rediscounting facilities. Whichever method is chosen, the result is a decline of the reserve ratio of the Central Bank. To induce the monetary authorities to effect such a decline whenever necessary was one of the aims of many expansionists before the crisis.

It was argued, too, that the minimum ratio of gold reserve to sight liabilities—usually between 33 per cent and 40 per cent—was much too high and that the general adoption of a much lower reserve ratio would pave the way to legitimate expansion. In the case of Great Britain, with her peculiar segregation of note-issuing from banking functions, the movement assumed the form of a demand for an increase of the fiduciary issue, which amounts to the same thing as a reduction of the legal minimum reserve ratio by Central Banks of other countries.

No actual progress, however, was made in the desired direction before 1931. In fact, far from relaxing the anti-expansionary effect of the legal minimum reserve ratios, most countries reinforced it. While, before the war, the reserve ratio was reckoned only on the basis of the note circulation, after the war the principle was adopted almost universally that the basis should be note circulation *plus* other sight liabilities. Moreover, most Central Banks endeavoured to increase their gold and foreign exchange reserves far beyond the legal minimum. In consequence of this policy, even a reduction of the legal minimum would have made but little difference in practice. It would have merely increased the safety margins above the legal minimum.

(6) Object of Expansionism

Opinions of scientific expansionists are divided not only upon the means by which expansion should be achieved but also upon the object of expansion. Those concerned with practical banking, such as Mr. McKenna, favoured an expansionary monetary policy with the object of satisfying all legitimate requirements for credit. Theoretical expansionists, such as Mr. Hawtrey, are in favour of expansion as a means of maintaining the stability of employment. Other theoretical expansionists, such as Professor Cassel, advocate their policy for the sake of maintaining the stability of the price level in face of a declining trend. Most economists with Socialist leanings are in favour of expansion as a means of raising real wages and the purchasing power of consumers in general, necessarily at the expense of the purchasing power of the unproductive classes.

All these various shades of expansionists are in favour of a relatively moderate and gradual scientifically regulated expansion. Apart from these scientific expansionists, a number of would-be reformers advocate expansion either on pseudo-scientific grounds, or without any pretence of a scientific background. The difference between scientific expansionism and these pseudo-scientific or unscientific proposals lies partly in the degree of expansion proposed. In this respect it is justifiable to discriminate between expansionism and inflationism. Another essential difference is that while most scientific expansionists advocate monetary expansion within the framework of the existing economic system and social order, the pseudo-scientific and unscientific expansionists generally aim at the creation of an entirely new economic and social system, largely based upon their expansionary monetary principles. In some cases, expansion is merely an excuse for a redistribution of wealth.

The expansionist school has the same failing as the cheap money school. While the latter assumes that money would be used for constructive purposes if only it were cheap enough, the former bases its case on the belief that, once the limits to credit expansion are relaxed, there is nothing to prevent an increase of production and consumption. As we pointed out in Chapter VIII, the mere fact that money is cheap does not in itself induce producers to borrow. Similarly, the mere fact that money is available does not in itself induce producers to make use of it. This is a point which, obvious as it is, is very often overlooked by monetary reformers. In their zeal to overcome the resistance to their proposals, they are inclined to be one-sided and to exaggerate the results of the adoption of the reforms proposed. They fail to realise that the increase of the volume of money and credit actually or potentially available does not automatically induce producers to make use of the facilities offered to them. Producers are prepared to use new credit if they expect to be able to sell their products at a profit. During a period of boom the demand for credit is practically unlimited, but during periods of depression it is difficult to find borrowers.

(7) Expansionist Fallacies

Many economists who hope to regulate the price level and the volume of employment by means of regulating the volume of credit are inclined to overlook the elementary fact that plentiful money does not in itself create markets, any more than cheap money does. In a negative sense the restriction of the volume of credit can produce a very strong adverse influence both on prices and on the volume of trade. Unquestionably, it is possible by means of credit restrictions to reduce both. In a positive sense, however, the effect of the regulation of the volume of credit is not always dependable. Indeed, when it is most important that the credit policy should produce its maximum effect, its influence is invariably beneath expectations. A policy of credit expansion would be fully effective during a period of boom, when there is no need to stimulate business activity. It is, however, largely ineffective if applied during a period of slump or prolonged depression when it is most desirable that it should produce its effect. The credit expansion school is, therefore, unduly optimistic in believing that it would be able to regulate the economic system and maintain a reasonable degree of stability combined with progress simply by the manipulation of the volume of credit. Unfortunately, the problem of control and stability cannot be solved simply by turning the credit tap on and off at appropriate intervals.

Another great failing of the credit expansion school is that it attaches exaggerated importance to the general price level, and thus underestimates the importance of tendencies in the prices of individual commodities. This tendency to worship the average is one of the main shortcomings of modern economic science. Those addicted to it fail to realise that the average is composed of individual prices. According to the credit expansion school, a fall in the price of even such an important commodity as wheat is of no great importance provided that it is caused by over-production in that particular commodity and not by a contraction of credit. They firmly believe that, if only the volume of credit is maintained, the fall in the price of wheat will be offset by a rise in the price of other commodities so that the average price level will remain unchanged. In reality, far from causing a rise in other commodities, the fall in wheat is likely to cause an all-round fall, owing to the contraction in the purchasing power of an important class of consumers. It is useless to argue that the loss of wheat producers would be the gain of wheat consumers, and that the purchasing power thus released would be spent by the latter on other commodities. For one thing, it takes a long time for the benefit of a fall in wholesale prices to be passed on to the ultimate consumer. Before the process of adjustment is completed—if it is ever completed—there is a contraction in the total purchasing power of many millions of consumers—the wheat farmers—and this inevitably tends to force down prices in general. It is true that during the transition period the earnings of middlemen, who benefit by the time lag between wholesale and retail prices, will increase. The increased purchasing power of a few thousand middlemen or even a few hundred thousand shareholders does not, however, make up for the fall in the purchasing power of many millions of consumers. The result of the change is a maldistribution of purchasing power.

(8) Limitations of Expansionism

It is thus possible for a slump in general prices and in employment to be brought about by the fall in the price of one important commodity or group of commodities. Nor would it be possible to check such a slump by credit expansion. Even if the banks were willing to expand credit at a time of acute slump, it is doubtful whether there would be any demand for it. In the normal course, credit would automatically contract with the fall of prices and employment. The example of a fall in wheat is sufficient to indicate the limitations of credit expansion as a means of preventing a slump.

Let us now consider its limitations as a means of preventing a boom. Those who hope that by mere credit manipulations it would be possible to check over-speculation and over-production do not adequately allow for the human factor. If conditions are reasonably prosperous for some length of time, producers, business men, investors and speculators tend increasingly to take it for granted that rising prosperity will go on for ever. In consequence, producers increase their output to the maximum of their capacity, feeling certain that whatever they produce can be sold. For the same reason merchants will increase their stocks to an unreasonable degree and without due discrimination. By means of instalment buying consumers will anticipate their incomes, and will mortgage their earnings for years ahead. Investors will anticipate capital appreciation and buy securities at very high prices. Finally, speculators will take it for granted that all the markets can go only in one direction and will embark upon reckless gambling. The result will be gross over-production and a speculative boom. The experience of the United States during 1929 shows how little the authorities can do in face of such a sweeping movement. Credit restrictions are powerless to stop it unless they are applied to such a drastic extent as to provoke a slump. Thus, the manipulation of the volume of credit is unable to prevent either a boom or a slump.

Having said all this, it is necessary to add that, notwithstanding its shortcomings, the credit expansion school has its great merits. It has drawn attention to the necessity for a less timid credit policy and to the possibility of expanding production with the aid of credit expansion. Like every other school of monetary reformers, it is guilty of gross exaggeration, but then exaggeration is sometimes necessary to draw attention to facts which would otherwise be overlooked. Combined with adequate economic planning, which would prevent booms and slumps, credit expansion is certainly one of the principal means of achieving an improvement in the standard of living.

CHAPTER XI

CREDIT EXPANSION DURING THE CRISIS

(1) Expansionism before 1929

The idea of credit expansion became very popular during the period of stability that preceded the crisis. It has been advocated by some of the leading authorities on monetary questions, especially in Great Britain. At the same time, a number of enthusiastic reformers, such as Major Douglas and Professor Soddy, obtained the support of those sections of public opinion which were unable to follow the scientific reasonings of Mr. Keynes or Mr. Hawtrey. In practice, however, the movement achieved no noteworthy result. In a negative sense, it was possibly in part responsible for the reluctance of the authorities to restrict credit in order to re-adjust British prices to the world level. Even in this respect the determination of trade unions to oppose wage-cuts was a more important factor than the movement in favour of credit expansion.

By far the greater number of bankers in Great Britain, and more particularly in countries where inflationary experience had made a profound impression, were opposed to a policy of credit expansion. They were not prepared to take a hand in it by materially lowering their cash ratios. Their attitude was emphatically endorsed by the Central Banks which were unwilling to reduce their legal minimum reserve ratios; in fact, most Central Banks endeavoured to increase their actual ratios. The only direction in which official efforts were made to facilitate credit expansion was in the economy in the monetary use of gold. Nor was the general public keen on expansion. After the disastrous effect of post-war inflation, public opinion in most countries preferred to err if anything on the orthodox side, and did not as a rule press for an expansionary policy.

Notwithstanding this, there was undoubtedly a world-wide

credit expansion. This, however, was due not to any deliberate policy but mainly to the excessive confidence created by the stabilisation of most currencies, and to international over-lending on a large scale. To a very large extent expansion of credit was an effect and not a cause of the boom. The monetary authorities in various countries, especially in the United States, made an effort to check credit expansion in 1928 and 1929, but they were helpless in face of the sweeping movement.

(2) Credit Contraction after 1929

After the Wall Street slump there was an automatic contraction of credit brought about by the decline of security and commodity prices and by the economic depression in general. This contraction was accentuated by the deliberate action of banks, which sought to safeguard themselves against any possible losses arising from the slump. Most countries witnessed a ruthless cutting down of credits by the banks. This again was not brought about by any deliberate action on the part of the monetary authorities. On the contrary, the latter adopted a policy of easy money immediately after the Wall Street slump and by 1931 the bank rates had declined to low record figures in many countries. This policy of easy money did not, however, aim at any deliberate credit expansion. It was partly the reversal of the policy of dear money adopted in 1928–9 in face of the credit expansion during the boom. The need for contraction having passed, the restricting brakes were removed. The monetary authorities did not expect that their changed policy would lead to an early credit expansion; nor did they, with the memory of the Wall Street boom fresh in their minds, even want such an expansion. They reduced their bank rates on the assumption that the effect of easy money would gradually work itself through the economic system, and that, in accordance with experience of past crises, there would be a natural recovery after the depression had spent its force. Their policy at that stage was not one of deliberate credit expansion.

The financial crisis of 1931 brought about another reversal of the official policy. Confronted with the wholesale withdrawals of foreign deposits, the monetary authorities of Central European countries, Great Britain and the United States adopted deliberate measures to create monetary stringency.

At the same time, banks all over the world, confronted with the menace of a run, were cutting credits ruthlessly. There can be no doubt that this policy of credit restriction aggravated the crisis to no slight extent, without being able to save the currencies or the banks for whose defence it was adopted. At the risk of being accused of jobbing backwards, the author believes it would have been better to have abstained from reversing the easy money policy in 1931. A deliberate policy of credit expansion would have spared the world much of the losses inflicted upon it by the mismanagement of the crisis of 1931. Fortunately, the monetary authorities of Great Britain and other countries remained relatively moderate in their orthodoxy during the crisis. Had they followed the advice of the extreme orthodox school, the result of the wholesale credit restriction which this school advocated would have been a catastrophic financial and political crisis, leading to social upheaval and perhaps to the collapse of Western civilisation. Monetary fanaticism can indeed produce most disastrous consequences.

(3) Policy of Easy Money

In 1932 the improvement of sterling and of the British budgetary conditions enabled the Government to relax the deflationary measures which it took simultaneously with the suspension of the gold standard. In fact, a policy of cheap money was adopted. It was hoped that by such means it would be possible to bring about the credit expansion necessary for a revival of trade. The extent to which trade availed itself of the ample credit facilities was, however, very moderate. For over two years there was very little indication of any actual credit expansion. It was not until after a substantial depreciation of sterling and a rise in world prices, mainly through world-wide rearmament, that trade was stimulated to a sufficient degree to lead to a moderate actual expansion of bank advances, which was entirely the effect and not the cause of recovery.

In the United States, credit continued to contract until the suspension of the gold standard, with disastrous results too well-known to require description. President Roosevelt's reflationary policy consisted largely of spending on a large scale, of deliberately depreciating the dollar and of creating artificial purchasing power. Expansion of credit, however, also played a certain part, in the form of advances through various official organisations and open market operations. The banks themselves were frequently called upon to do their share by expanding credit, but, owing to the absence of adequate demand, they were not for a long time in a position to do so even if they had been willing to act as the executive hand of a policy of credit expansion. It was not until 1935 that signs of actual expansion of credit began to show themselves. There was an outcry in banking circles against the "danger" that this movement might assume an inflationary character owing to the large reserves of member banks of the Federal Reserve system. Notwithstanding the demand for restrictive measures, the monetary authorities declined to depart from their policy of expansion. Indeed, with unemployment still well over 10,000,000, it was, to say the least, premature to fear the dangers of excessive expansion.

(4) Policy of Gold Bloc Countries

In various parts of the Sterling Bloc there was a certain degree of credit expansion noticeable, but, as in Great Britain, it was the effect rather than the cause of the economic recovery. In the countries of the Gold Bloc, on the other hand, credit continued to contract, at first through deliberate deflationary efforts and subsequently in consequence of the general decline of trade and the fall of bank deposits through the flight of capital. At the beginning of 1935, however, the French Government decided to adopt a deliberate policy of credit expansion. Inspired by the example of Great Britain, M. Flandin hoped to be able to bring about a recovery by making money cheap and plentiful for trade. He overlooked the fact that in Great Britain it was not so much easy money that brought about the recovery as the depreciation of the pound, the confidence inspired by the balanced budget and the effect of the newly established customs tariff. Even though there could not have been a recovery without a policy of cheap money, the latter merely prepared the ground and was not the cause of it. In France the fundamental conditions for a recovery did not exist, and for this reason the policy of credit expansion could not possibly have produced much effect. It is a pity that, owing to resistance on the part of the Bank of France, this policy could not be put into operation, for it would have provided an interesting example to prove that in itself credit expansion is not a sufficient stimulus. After the crisis of May–June 1935, M. Laval's Government embarked upon wholesale deflation. Curiously enough, it endeavoured nevertheless to adopt a policy of easy money. Hence the rapid reduction of the bank rate. Owing to the chronic crisis of the Treasury and the frequent political and financial scares, however, this experiment of cheap money amidst deflation also failed.

In Germany economic recovery was brought about without any policy of credit expansion. Recovery there was the result of public works and rearmament, and public expenditure on a gigantic scale was succeeded in due course by an expansion of the volume of currency and credit. The initiative came from public expenditure, and credit expansion was the effect, not the cause.

It appears that credit expansion played but a subordinate part among the means by which various Governments succeeded in bringing about a recovery from the depression. In the absence of genuine commercial demand for credits, it was indeed difficult to bring about an actual expansion. Even though, during the more advanced phases of the depression, the banks had been only too willing to grant loans, there was no demand for them by eligible borrowers. In most countries the Governments had to supplement the policy of credit expansion by other reflationary methods, whose effect was stimulated by the existence of an adequate volume of credit at the disposal of trade.

(5) Preparing the Ground

While the actual part played by credit expansion during the depression has not been very important, conditions during the last few years have gone a long way towards preparing the ground for credit expansion during a period when credit will be in demand. During the boom that preceded the depression, the shortage of gold put a natural limit to possible credit expansion. The depreciation of the currencies since 1931, being unaccompanied by a corresponding rise in commodity prices, has gone a long way towards removing this obstacle to credit expansion. In the United States the revaluation of the gold reserve has opened wide possibilities for the increase of the volume of credit when trade revival results in an increase in credit requirements. In Great Britain the transfer of a substantial amount of gold from the Exchange Equalisation Account to the Bank of England increased the latter's note reserve and there are prospects of a further considerable increase when the gold reserve is revalued after the stabilisation of sterling, and when the whole gold stock of the Exchange Equalisation Account is transferred to the Bank. The credit resources of most countries of the Sterling Bloc are also reasonably wide. The British Dominions have accumulated a fair amount of reserves in recent years, while, among the Scandinavian countries, Norway and Sweden have also increased their reserves. Even though Japan was unable to recover most of the gold it lost prior to the suspension of the gold standard in 1931, the drastic depreciation of the yen has opened up immense possibilities for the broadening of the basis of the credit structure. The countries of the Gold Bloc have lost large amounts of gold. A great part of it will, however, be repatriated after the devaluation of their currencies. They, too, will thus be able through the revaluation of their gold reserves to broaden the basis of their credit structure to no slight degree. As for the countries whose gold stocks became depleted, they are not likely to stabilise on a gold basis unless and until there is a fair redistribution of gold in their favour.

Assuming that sterling and the dollar are definitely stabilised around the present level within a few years; that the currencies of the Gold Bloc are devalued in the vicinity of their economic parities with sterling and dollar; and that there is no spectacular rise in commodity prices, there will be a fair scope for comparatively moderate credit expansion. Should the leading currencies be depreciated further, and should they eventually be stabilised at a lower level, then the scope for credit expansion would widen accordingly. Opinions are divided as to whether on the existing basis the monetary gold stocks will be sufficient to meet all requirements. Many expansionists hold the view that, even at the existing level of currencies, the possibility of the recurrence of a gold shortage has been ruled out. In the author's opinion, however, it would be advisable to play for safety and to devalue all currencies to such an extent as to provide for every possible increase in credit requirements for a long time to come.

CHAPTER XII

PURCHASING POWER EXPANSION

(1) Credit Expansion *v.* Purchasing Power Expansion

While a number of expansionists claim to be able to create prosperity by increasing the volume of credit available to production, another group of the same school sees the salvation of mankind in the expansion of consumers' purchasing power. Even though members of the two groups of expansionists overlap, the difference between the two reforms is sufficiently marked to justify us in regarding them as being distinct from each other and to a large extent even opposed to each other. Needless to say, those advocating expansion of purchasing power constitute by far the more radical school, both from a financial and from a political point of view. The credit expansion school includes many industrialists and landowners who are politically conservative and who are, generally speaking, in favour of a conservative budgetary policy. Those in favour of expansion of purchasing power, on the other hand, are for the most part Socialists, even though many of them would not be described or describe themselves as such. They believe in the creation of purchasing power by the State, if necessary at the cost of an unbalanced budget and monetary inflation.

Those who favour an expansion of purchasing power believe that, ultimately, it is the purchasing power of consumers that determines the extent of trade activity and the degree of prosperity. They hold the view that in itself an increase of credits for production would not achieve that purpose. Apart from the generally known argument that a credit expansion in itself is effective only in times of boom, while in times of depression it is in itself useless, their attitude is based on the belief that credit expansion does not in itself necessarily lead to an increase in consumers' purchasing power on a scale commensurate with the increase of production. Consequently, the inevitable result is over-production, which is the cause of the cyclic crises.

(2) Consumption *v.* Production

The experience of the last decade or so has gone a long way towards confirming this theory. It is now widely accepted that one of the main causes of the slump was the maldistribution of purchasing power during the period of boom, especially in the United States. Since wages did not keep pace with the increase of profits, a large proportion of the newly created purchasing power became accumulated in the form of savings instead of being used for consumption. This meant that the counterpart of this newly created purchasing power, represented by the increase of industrial and agricultural production, became unsaleable.

In the view of the advocates of purchasing power expansion, the credit expansionists have caught hold of the wrong end of the stick. What is necessary, they say, is not to stimulate production, trusting to luck that the goods produced will be sold, but to stimulate consumption, for that will lead to increased production. It is argued that technical progress and efficient methods have eliminated the main obstacle to the expansion of production, provided that there is a sufficiently large and steady demand for the goods produced. It is pointed out that if a manufacturer has sufficient orders in hand, it is easy for him to obtain credit for financing his production. In the view of the purchasing power expansion school, the problem is, therefore, to enable consumers to stimulate production by buying up stocks and placing orders for future delivery.

Many adherents of this school realise, however, that under the existing system the expansion of consumers' purchasing power is in itself not sufficient to secure adequate financing of production unless it is accompanied by an expansion of producers' credit. The difference between these expansionists and those advocating a credit expansion as the sole means of improving world conditions, is that the former lay the emphasis upon the expansion of consumers' purchasing power and consider the expansion of producers' credit as a mere secondary necessity.

(3) Conservative Expansionists

It would be a mistake to suppose that all adherents of the policy of expanding purchasing power are extremists, politically or financially. Indeed, this school of thought includes a conservative wing which seeks to attain its object by the very moderate means of encouraging the instalment system. Among economists it has such conservative supporters as Professor E. R. A. Seligman, while among practical business men it is, needless to say, supported by all industries whose prosperity depends upon instalment selling. Before the crisis, the expansion of instalment business was considered one of the weakest spots in the situation in the United States. Since 1931, however, it has become amply evident that these fears were much exaggerated. The instalment system withstood the test of the crisis much better than even the most optimistic advocate of the system had anticipated. The proportion of defaults was remarkably low. It is surprising that notwithstanding this, so very little has been done in the United States or elsewhere towards encouraging instalment business as a means of achieving recovery, and that the supporters of the system do not make any noteworthy effort to that end.

Admittedly, instalment business can expand only when consumers are sufficiently optimistic to anticipate their future incomes. Amidst existing uncertainty many of them may hesitate to do so even though producers and merchants are willing to take the risk. In any case, the instalment system has its limitations, since it is bound to reach saturation point. Future incomes cannot be anticipated indefinitely. The experience of 1929 shows that the expansion of the instalment system cannot in itself prevent over-production due to inadequate purchasing power in the hands of consumers. It is essential that the purchasing power of consumers should keep pace with the increase of production.

(4) "Share the Wealth" Campaigns

To that end various radical politicians and monetary reformers have put forward a variety of remedies. The Social Credit scheme of Major Douglas, by which every member of a community is entitled to a share in the proceeds of the production of that community, is probably the most popular of the various reform schemes proposed to that end. It is gaining in popularity in the British Dominions, as is shown by the victory of the Social Credit Party in Alberta in 1935—and also in some other countries. In the United States, the " Share the Wealth " campaign of the late Senator Huey Long, Father Coughlin and Dr. Townsend bears some resemblance to the Douglas scheme, although it is more radical. Professor Soddy's ideas of monetary reform also move on lines similar to those of Major Douglas. Even ultra-orthodox France has her equivalent to Major Douglas, M. Dubois. The proposals of all these reformers go rather beyond the scope of monetary reform. They imply a fundamental change in the economic system and in the social order. Since such violent changes could be brought about only at the price of a collapse of the existing credit system, the only way in which the proposals could be financed would be by means of the printing-press. These radical reformers would treat the banking system as Public Enemy Number One and would destroy the degree of confidence which is the prerequisite of the creation of that intangible factor, credit. In practice, all their complicated proposals would boil down to the crudest form of currency inflation through the use of which the system would soon reduce itself to absurdity. Indeed, these fantastic schemes are calculated to do immense harm to the chances of progressive and realistic monetary reform, for they tend to discredit any departure, however reasonable and justified, from the canons of orthodox finance.

Between the conservative wing of the purchasing power expansion school and its radical wing there is an immense variety of shades of opinion. There are those who favour a radical extension of consumers' credits as an alternative to instalment selling. Others seek to obtain an increase of consumers' incomes by means of higher and still higher wages in face of a steady price level. Others again advocate a redistribution of purchasing power and of accumulated savings by means of more radical direct taxation. There are again those who want to create additional purchasing power by the extension of the existing social assistance to the unemployed, old age pensioners, etc. Many of these proposals do not come, strictly speaking, within the realm of monetary reform, though in their effect they certainly concern that sphere. They all aim at the redistribution of purchasing power so as to enable consumers to buy a larger proportion of the goods produced, thereby avoiding over-production and preparing the way for an expansion of production.

(5) Redistribution *v.* Net Increase of Purchasing Power

In so far as the increase in the purchasing power of consumers by any of the above methods amounts merely to a redistribution of the existing purchasing power, it inevitably constitutes an additional burden upon producers in their capacity of employers and taxpayers. The process merely robs Peter to pay Paul. While the purchasing power of consumers could be increased by such methods, if carried too far they would discourage production and increase unemployment. Thus, while one group of consumers would benefit by the policy, another group would suffer.

In order to make the increase in the purchasing power of consumers effective, it is necessary that there should be a net increase in the total purchasing power. In other words, the purchasing power given to one group of consumers should not be taken away from some other section of the community but should be added to the existing volume of purchasing power. In plain English, such a net expansion of purchasing power is called inflation, but there is no need to be afraid of names. A moderate, well-planned, and intelligently executed inflation can only be beneficial and its adverse effects can be reduced to a minimum if not eliminated altogether. If this expansion of purchasing power is applied only if and when there are signs of over-production and accumulation of commodity stocks, then there is no need to be afraid that it will lead to a disastrous rise in prices. On the contrary, it will prevent a disastrous fall in prices.

(6) Rules of Purchasing Power Expansion

The detailed examination of the circumstances in which an increase in consumers' purchasing power could and should be brought about is within the realm of economic planning and is, therefore, outside the scope of this book. It is possible, however, to lay down some obvious rules—

1. The expansion of consumers' purchasing power should be part of a broader scheme of economic planning and should

not pursue the interests of any one class but of the community as a whole. The principal shortcoming of Socialist proposals for the expansion of purchasing power is that they aim at the improvement of the standard of living of the working classes at the expense of the rest of the community.

2. During prosperous periods the expansion of consumers' purchasing power should be made to keep pace with the expansion of profits, so as to avoid profit inflation and maldistribution of purchasing power. If the experience of 1929 has taught the world only this lesson, the losses caused by the depression will not be a total waste.

3. It is only if the accumulation of commodity stocks and other symptoms indicate general over-production or under-consumption that an increase in purchasing power should be resorted to. To pump additional purchasing power into circulation when there is no sign of general over-production would merely lead to an unwanted rise in commodity prices.

4. The system should operate both ways: it should be possible to reduce purchasing power if its excessive volume produces unwanted inflationary effects or if a contraction in output, due to the failure of crops or other non-monetary causes, has to be met.

5. The management of the volume of purchasing power should be combined with the management of the volume of currency and credit and should thus serve the object of regulating the ratio between investment and the production of capital goods on the one hand, and consumption and the production of consumption goods on the other.

6. Above all, the management of consumers' purchasing power does not obviate the necessity for planning production in each individual branch so as to bring it in accordance with the demand by consumers, which in turn should itself be influenced and brought as far as possible in accordance with social requirements.

The detailed discussion of all these considerations would in itself require a volume. Here we must confine ourselves to the mere indication of a few points which are sufficient to show that the solution of an ideal economic system lies to a very large extent outside the monetary sphere. It is unfortunate that some of the best brains of our generation have devoted their attention almost exclusively to the monetary aspects of the economic problem and have developed a narrow conception of the remedies. The narrowest conception of all is the one which believes in the possibility of managing the course of the world by purely technical monetary means, in particular by the manipulation of bank rates. The bank rate worship is not confined to the orthodox school. As is shown by the example of Professor Cassel, some of the radical economists are also addicted to it. According to a somewhat broader conception, the economic system should be managed by changes in the volume of credit to producers. Most of the advocates of scientifically managed currency have this kind of management in mind. A still broader conception is represented by the school which aims at controlling the economic system by regulating both producers' credit and consumers' purchasing power. Even this conception is, however, narrow, and to a very large extent doctrinaire, for even if in theory the total volume of purchasing power corresponds to the total value of goods available, within these totals there may develop strong dislocations and a state of disequilibrium may easily arise. It is only a system which allows for the possibility of such disequilibria that can be regarded as adequate. Among the non-planner economists, Mr. Keynes realises the necessity for discrimination within the grand total of goods output on the one hand and purchasing power on the other. His policy is based on distinction between capital goods and consumption goods. There is, however, ample scope for discrimination also within these two major categories. All this, however, is outside the realm of monetary reform.

CHAPTER XIII

PURCHASING POWER EXPANSION DURING THE DEPRESSION

(1) The Socialist Attitude

Until quite recently purchasing power expansion as a system of monetary policy was unknown in practice. Even in theory its implications in the sphere of monetary policy were almost entirely unknown. It is true that Karl Marx, and other Socialist writers, and also economists such as Mr. J. A. Hobson, denounced the deficiency of the capitalist system on the ground that consumers do not obtain sufficient purchasing power to enable them to buy all the goods produced, and that consequently from time to time there is bound to be a breakdown owing to over-production. The conclusion of this group was that this inherent defect of capitalism could not be remedied, and was bound sooner or later to lead to the collapse of the system. In practice, the Socialist movement has done its utmost to remedy this particular shortcoming, even though its leaders were not aware that their efforts to obtain higher wages would tend to produce that result. The efforts of trade unions and of the Labour Party in Great Britain and of their counterparts in other countries, had no particularly profound theoretical background in the monetary sphere. Higher wages were demanded as a matter of practical politics, not as part of a general monetary policy, and certainly not in an effort to overcome the shortcomings of liberal capitalism.

The experience of Great Britain during the post-war period shows that in itself the expansion of purchasing power cannot produce adequate results in the absence of economic planning. Although to a large extent wages were left at their inflated level in spite of the fall of prices, the result was not an increase in the volume of consumption, for the simple reason that, in the absence of any adequate efforts to adjust the British system of production to changed requirements, a high degree of unemployment continued to exist throughout the post-war period. Under the system that developed in Great Britain as a result of free trade, the prosperity of the country depended upon its foreign market. Since wages abroad were lower than in Great Britain, British exporters were undersold by their foreign rivals. Thus, the relatively high wages prevailing in Great Britain led to a high degree of perpetual unemployment. The net result was a decline, instead of an increase, in the total purchasing power of consumers. This example shows that the simple method of demanding higher wages does not lead to an expansion of purchasing power, unless it is done as part of a general scheme of things.

(2) No Deliberate Policy

Neither the movement for higher wages, nor the tendency towards increasing social assistance, had for its aim an expansion of purchasing power for the purposes of monetary policy. It is true that in Great Britain the system of unemployment benefits has been adopted and that similar methods of transferring purchasing power to consumers have been applied in various forms in a number of countries. None of these measures, however, was a deliberate action taken for considerations of monetary policy. They were dictated by political necessity combined with humane motives, and those responsible for these measures had no considerations of monetary policy in their minds. The idea of deliberately influencing the volume of consumers' purchasing power with the object of influencing the price level or the volume of trade and employment was almost entirely unknown. It was not only in orthodox quarters, responsible for the monetary policy of most countries, that this theory was ignored: many even of their radical critics could not think in terms of consumers' purchasing power as a factor of monetary policy. They considered that the manipulation of the volume of producers' credit was adequate for their purpose. The world needed the lesson of the depression of 1929–35 to bring home the significance of the factor of consumers' purchasing power.

Even after the beginning of the depression there was for a long time no evidence of any deliberate policy aiming at the expansion of purchasing power. On the contrary, throughout the world there has been an orgy of deflation. In order to balance budgets and to adjust costs of production to the low price levels, Governments and private employers have made desperate efforts to reduce consumers' purchasing power. The high degree of unemployment in itself lowered the purchasing power of consumers to no slight extent. In addition, successful efforts have been made all over the world to reduce wages and salaries. Owing to the increase of unemployment, the resistance of the working classes to these efforts was weakened. Thus, at a time when the accumulation of huge commodity stocks and the decline of industrial production to a fraction of its capacity would have made it most desirable to expand purchasing power, instead of being expanded, it was considerably reduced.

(3) Contraction of Purchasing Power

Even in countries which abandoned their efforts to bolster up their currencies by deflationary means, the process of contraction in purchasing power continued. In Great Britain, simultaneously with the suspension of the gold standard, a series of drastic economy measures were adopted. During the last quarter of 1931 and the beginning of 1932 there was an almost universal cut in wages, salaries, pensions, unemployment benefits, etc. In countries which put up a desperate resistance to the adverse pressure on their currencies, these deflationary cuts assumed much larger dimensions, and have continued unabated up to the time of writing. In the United States, the degree of the fall in wages prior to the suspension of the gold standard was spectacular. On the Continent wages were tumbling everywhere. It is true that at the same time the cost of living was also declining ; but in most instances the fall in wages was more pronounced than that of the cost of living—even though it lagged far behind that of wholesale prices, so that it was not only nominal wages that declined but also real wages. Indeed, the system of liberal capitalism showed itself at its very worst. Never before in modern history was such a large percentage of the population of most countries reduced to starvation level, depending for their bare existence upon charity, public or private. Never before were producers compelled at the same time to destroy such huge quantities of unsaleable goods, or to allow them to deteriorate. Never before was there such a wholesale restriction of production and accumulation of unsaleable products —unsaleable not because they were not wanted, but because the wholesale cutting of purchasing power deprived consumers of the means of buying them. Never before was the shortsightedness of haphazard cutting of purchasing power so glaringly evident. The whole world during the years of depression presented one huge accusing example of "poverty amidst plenty". From cheap catchword of demagogues and cranks, that phrase has become undeniable reality.

It was not surprising, therefore, that at this stage a large and increasing number of adherents of various expansionist schools should raise their voices in protest against this orgy of deflation. Whereas before the crisis the Socialists were practically alone in protesting against wages cuts, since 1931 they have begun to receive support from essentially non-Socialistic quarters. The experience of the crisis has made many people realise that a cut in wages is inevitably accompanied by a fall in demand and is bound to aggravate the depression. In Great Britain and other countries there was, therefore, a strong and increasing movement which opposed further reduction of purchasing power and demanded the restoration of earlier cuts. Notwithstanding this, until 1933 practically nothing was done in that direction. In many countries—especially in the Gold Bloc—deflationary cuts are to this very day still regarded as the highest form of civic virtue. Even in countries where the depreciation of the currency obviated the necessity for any further deflation, some of the earlier cuts were restored only most reluctantly and with considerable delay.

(4) Roosevelt and Hitler

It was not until the advent of President Roosevelt in the United States and Herr Hitler in Germany that the expansion of purchasing power appeared as a method of monetary policy. One of the many ways in which President Roosevelt sought to reflate was by the distribution of purchasing power in various forms to consumers. He could well afford to do so on a generous scale, for the money was there, and Congress was only too willing to spend it. By far the greater part of

President Roosevelt's expenditure was covered by means of normal borrowing, so that the process amounted to the transfer of purchasing power from those who had sterilised it to those who were eager to use it.

The German National Socialist Government was in a much less favourable position. There was no money available, or obtainable in the ordinary course, for distribution among consumers. Purchasing power, therefore, had to be created artificially. To that end, the Government ordered employers to increase the number of their employees whether they required additional hands or not. To begin with, this method appeared to amount merely to the distribution of the scanty reserves of industrial undertakings among unwanted workmen. As, however, the process involved an all-round increase of purchasing power, it led to an increase of consumption which enabled most industrialists to find work for their additional employees. At the same time, the increase of consumers' demand contributed towards the accumulation of savings, thereby enabling the Government to finance its public expenditure.

To a very large extent, the creation of additional purchasing power both in the United States and in Germany assumed the form of public works. This method of expanding purchasing power will be dealt with in the next two chapters.

In the United States President Roosevelt made great efforts to increase purchasing power by means of impelling an increase of wages. The principal aim of the whole of the New Deal was to compel employers to raise wages. In this respect, Germany was not able to follow the example of the United States, as it was of vital importance for her to keep the cost of production down in order to be able to export. In the United States the partial success of President Roosevelt's efforts did not bring the result anticipated. It is true that the New Deal policy led to an increase in the total wages paid out, but at the same time the increased burden to industries discouraged a trade revival. The decline of unemployment was not as pronounced as it would have been had not Government intervention resulted in the "putting of the cart before the horse" by increasing the wages bills before there was any corresponding increase of industrial earning. Unquestionably, President Roosevelt did the right thing in the wrong way.

(5) Practical Results

Nevertheless, the American example of an effort to achieve trade revival by means of higher wages did not fail to produce its effect in other countries, especially in Great Britain, where it led to a practically complete all-round restoration of cuts. Indeed, in some instances the wages were actually raised above their level of 1931. In the countries of the Gold Bloc, on the other hand, the process of deflation continued unabated. Instead of endeavouring to break the vicious circle by pumping purchasing power into circulation, the Governments of the Gold Bloc continued to regard cuts and further cuts as the only possible way out.

The extent to which the policy of creating consumers' purchasing power has been used in practice during the last few years is thus on the whole moderate. Even in the United States it played but a subordinate part in bringing about a recovery. In Great Britain and the countries of the Sterling Bloc its importance among the factors responsible for the relative prosperity has been only moderate. As for the rest of the world, there has been no sign of any attempt to improve conditions by the expansion of purchasing power. Nor are future prospects too bright in this respect. While purchasing power will be created, it will be mainly through rearmament and not through any material increase in the amount spent in social assistance. The breakdown of the New Deal in the United States brought about a setback in the movement favouring the expansion of purchasing power as a method of monetary policy. There is not much to be expected, therefore, in this respect in the near future.

Looking further ahead, however, there is good reason to hope that when a higher degree of economic planning is adopted, the deliberate expansion of purchasing power for the purpose of increasing consumption will be one of the fundamental rules. Even in the absence of deliberate planning, President Roosevelt has certainly made the world realise that an expansion of purchasing power is an essential condition of prosperity. And even though his experiment was not allowed to be carried to its conclusion, it attracted attention to the immense possibilities, which are not likely to be forgotten altogether.

CHAPTER XIV

THE SPENDING SCHOOL

(1) Demand for Public Works

In the foregoing chapters we have been dealing with two schools of expansionists, those favouring an expansion of the means by which production can be financed and those advocating an expansion of consumers' purchasing power. There is a third school, which in a way occupies an intermediate stage between the advocates of credit expansion and those of purchasing power expansion. This school has come to be known under the name of the "spending school". Its underlying principle is that the Government should encourage production and consumption by means of carrying out public works on a large scale. Like those in favour of credit expansion, the spending school desires to tackle the problem at the production end. On the other hand, the execution of public works constitutes a direct Government intervention, in which respect it is to a large degree similar to the expansion of purchasing power by Government action.

The adherents of the spending school have duly realised that in times of depression it is idle to expect the mere expansion of the volume of potential credit to lead to an increase of trade activity. They believe that during such periods the Government should supplement private initiative. While they do not go so far as to suggest that the Government should put artificial purchasing power into the hands of consumers—whether directly or by forcing employers to raise wages—they claim that the execution of public works would achieve the same result by slightly less artificial means. Purchasing power would not be given away, but would be created in return for constructive work done. Instead of giving something for nothing, the Government, at the same time as creating purchasing power, would execute useful public works which would increase the national wealth and improve the standard of living.

(2) Effect on Purchasing Power

The adherents of the spending school claim that the purchasing power created by an increase of expenditure on public works is several times larger than the actual amount of additional Government spending. The amounts spent by the Government, it is said, enable the recipients to increase their own purchases, thereby increasing in turn the purchasing power of those engaged in the production and distribution of the goods they have bought. The money spent goes round and round, creating at each turn additional purchasing power. According to Mr. Keynes, who is generally regarded as the leader of the moderate scientific spending school, the total purchasing power created may be estimated at two and a half times the amount originally spent by the Government. In the author's opinion, this figure probably errs, if anything, on the conservative side. It is impossible to estimate how many times the money spent will be re-spent again and again before it settles down in the form of savings. Part of it probably disappears from circulation at the beginning of the process, for the chances are that part of the profit paid by public works will not actually be spent again by large shareholders and industrial undertakings. Part of it, on the other hand, probably circulates almost indefinitely. Much depends upon the extent to which the public works initiated tend to increase optimism regarding a future improvement of trade.

Another important consideration is whether public works are financed by means of loans or by means of inflation. If the funds are raised out of existing savings, then the process amounts to the conversion of potential expansion into actual expansion which would not otherwise have taken place. At the same time, it uses up the potential source of credit expansion, whereas if the public works are financed by means of inflation proper, the already existing resources available for private enterprise remain untapped.

(3) Reaction from Cult of Saving

The spending school has arisen as a reaction against the cult of saving which existed until the war. As Mr. Keynes remarked in his *Tract on Monetary Reform*, according to the nineteenth-century conception even the rich man might after all enter the kingdom of heaven if he only saved. The believers in this theory have, however, remained numerous and influential, in spite of the increasing popularity of the spending school which has made rapid headway, particularly since the crisis. A desperate struggle is going on between those who want to balance the budget at all costs, and those who demand that budgets should be deliberately unbalanced in times of depression. The orthodox school, which is opposed to the expansion of credit and the expansion of purchasing power, is also opposed to any spending beyond the limits to which it can be covered by current revenue. It refuses to recognise any difference between current expenditure and capital expenditure and insists that even the latter should be undertaken only if it can be financed out of taxation receipts.

Against this, the spending school maintains that the deliberate unbalancing of budgets by public works should become an integral part of our economic system. It holds the view that, by means of well-timed and judiciously selected public works, the Government would be in a position to smooth out cyclic trade fluctuations, and thereby would eliminate one of the main defects of the capitalist system. It is argued that in times of depression public expenditure is practically the only method by which the deflationary vicious circle can be broken and an early recovery achieved. In addition, it is argued, an increase of the national wealth can be attained which would otherwise be unattainable, as the works in question would never be carried out by private initiative. The spending school thus claims to kill two birds with one stone.

(4) Attitude towards Public Debt

The attitude of the spending school towards the inevitable increase of the public debt as a result of public works is also essentially unorthodox. In reply to criticisms that the counterpart of the public works will be represented by a deadweight debt, it is argued that an increase of Government indebtedness is a natural phenomenon that accompanies the progress of civilisation and the improvement of the standard of living. The spending school refuses to be alarmed by the growth of public debt. Its adherents point out that the amount of public debt at the end of the Napoleonic Wars was considered unbearable, but was regarded as trifling by 1914; that the amount of public debt which constituted a substantial burden in 1914 is now viewed as having been negligible; that even our staggering burden of over seven milliards of Government indebtedness will be regarded as a moderate amount a hundred years hence. They also argue that, far from being a dead burden, public debt is a source of wealth, since it provides a basis for an expansion of constructive credits.

In this respect, the attitude of the extremist wing of the spending school is unquestionably one-sided and exaggerated. The increase of public debt that accompanies spending on public works can be regarded only as a necessary evil, and it is idle to try to make a virtue of a necessity. The increase of the fictitious wealth in proportion to the real wealth of mankind since 1914 has been the main cause of all our economic troubles in recent years. This question was discussed in detail in the author's book *World Finance since 1914*. Here let it be sufficient to point out that the increase of fictitious wealth leads to an increase of the proportion which unproductive classes can claim from the wealth produced. It means an increase of the burden upon the shoulders of productive classes, a burden which may become so excessive as to paralyse production.

The existence of a huge volume of fictitious wealth, the counterpart of which does not exist in the form of real wealth, is moreover a constant source of instability and leads to the development of disequilibria. It is true that in this respect there is a difference between public debt created through constructive works and public debt created as the result of a war or rearmament. But even though the former adds to real wealth, the chances are that a stage will be reached when it handicaps the increase of real wealth by discouraging normal production. The indifference of the spending school towards the increase of public debt is doubtless one of its weakest points. Many of the moderate "spenders" are fully aware of this, and dissociate themselves from the exaggerations of the extremist wing.

(5) Need for Discrimination

There are other points open to criticism. First and foremost, a large section of the spending school advocates the use of public works as a means of reducing unemployment without duly discriminating as to its cause. While a temporary increase of unemployment due to deflationary depression can and should be cured partly by means of public works, it is entirely unjustifiable to use the same remedy when the symptoms indicate a need for a fundamental reorganisation of industries. These symptoms have been present in the case of unemployment in Great Britain since the war. By 1929 it had become only too glaringly obvious that the reason why unemployment remained around the million figure, while other countries were enjoying a boom, was largely the permanent loss of foreign markets for Great Britain's main exporting industries. The fact that the depreciation of sterling since 1931 has failed to lead to an adequate recovery of these basic industries is in itself sufficient to show that to a high degree they are redundant. What was wanted, and what is still wanted, is the adjustment of the British system of production to changed requirements.

Instead, the spending school even before the depression advocated a reduction of unemployment by means of gigantic public works. This was the substance of the programme with which Mr. Lloyd George and the Liberal Party went to the country in 1929. The fact that some of the prominent leaders of the spending school had already advocated spending before the crisis rather weakened the force of their argument when they advocated spending as the way out of the crisis. While certain works of national importance—such as, for instance, slum clearance in the case of Great Britain or the planting of a forest belt in the United States—should be carried out irrespective of considerations of monetary policy, apart from such works the Governments should confine their extraordinary public works expenditure to periods of depression. After all, the public debt cannot be increased indefinitely, and it is wasteful to increase it during periods when private initiative can be relied upon for credit expansion, provided that the system of production is organised in accordance with the changing requirements.

(6) Budget and Confidence

Nor can the enthusiasm of the spending school for unbalanced budgets be accepted without reservations. Admittedly, the maniacs of the sound budget, who would cheerfully raise income-tax to 20s. in the pound in order to avoid a deficit, are largely responsible for the swing of the pendulum in the other direction. The unbalancing of the budget is not, however, a desirable end in itself. Like the increase of public debt, it may be a necessary evil, the disadvantages of which may be more than offset by the benefit derived from the effects of additional expenditure. If carried too far, however, this policy may become dangerous.

One of the reasons why the troubles of 1931 and following years were in many ways not as grave as those following the post-war slump was that in the meantime the Governments had to a very large extent recovered their credit, which was badly affected by war and post-war finance. While immediately after the war the Governments in many countries depended upon the banks for their financial equilibrium, during the recent crisis it was the banks that had to fall back upon the Governments. It is because budgetary deficits have been reduced to manageable proportions that Governments have come to be regarded once more as the ultimate source of credit and support. While it may be necessary and desirable at times to unbalance the budget, care should be taken to ensure that the deficit remains manageable, and that it does not undermine the Government's credit. The Government should always be in a position to call a halt to spending policy, and to restore budgetary equilibrium should this be necessary to prevent the development of a wave of distrust. Otherwise a situation might arise in which the public works undertaken would have to be discontinued at the wrong moment, simply because the Governments were no longer in a position to raise the capital required for the financing of these works.

(7) Merits of Spending School

Notwithstanding these shortcomings, the spending school, like other schools of monetary reform, has performed the great service of attracting attention to the increase of expenditure as a means of fighting depression and of improving the standard of living. If we discount its exaggerations, there remains a valuable contribution to the monetary reform movement. What is essential is that the Government should not depend exclusively, or even to a very high degree, upon public works programmes. As we pointed out above, an excessive increase of expenditure on the public debt in connection with public works might discourage normal trade, and this would cancel out the beneficial effects of the spending policy.

Combined with various other measures of monetary reform and as part of a general scheme of economic planning, the spending policy can play a highly beneficial rôle. In reality, most of the advocates of the policy of spending are also advocates of various monetary reforms. They are usually in favour of credit expansion and frequently of purchasing power expansion. While Mr. Keynes is the recognised leader of the scientific spending school, at the same time he is equally prominent in the cheap money school and among the advocates of managed currency. For the most part, adherents of the spending school are opposed to the gold standard, owing to the assumption that the need for defending gold parities would lead to the discouragement of spending. Thus, most supporters of the policy of spending cannot be accused of wanting to bring about the millennium exclusively by means of public works. If they are liable to criticism it is on the ground that they lay too much stress upon that particular aspect of monetary reform.

CHAPTER XV

SPENDING POLICY DURING THE DEPRESSION

(1) Public Works and Monetary Policy

Of the various expansionist theories, that of spending was adopted to the largest degree during the depression. Needless to say, public works are almost as old as man himself. Nor is there anything new in the execution of public works for the sake of reducing unemployment. Such a policy was adopted towards the middle of the nineteenth century in France and in other countries when adverse conditions threw too many hands out of work. There is, however, a considerable difference between such haphazard public works schemes as have been undertaken on rare occasions in the past for the purpose of reducing unemployment, and the systematic and deliberate policy adopted by a number of countries during the depression. It is the first time that spending on public works has come to be regarded as a means of monetary policy.

During the past four years public works have for two different reasons been undertaken partly or wholly in connection with monetary policy. In some countries, especially in the United States, the object of Government spending on public works was to stimulate reflation. In other countries, such as France and Italy, the object was to counteract the effects of deflation. The monetary aspects of public works are more evident in the case of reflationary countries than in that of deflationary countries.

The first country to undertake public works in conjunction with a reflationary monetary policy was the United States under President Roosevelt. Before 1933 the efforts of the spending school to induce the British and several other Governments to embark upon public works met with no response. Indeed, the suspension of the gold standard in Great Britain was followed by an all-round cutting down of even the normal public works undertaken by the Government and local authorities. In order to avoid an excessive depreciation of sterling, rigid orthodoxy was practised in this respect. Nor did any other countries of the Sterling Bloc attempt to reflate by means of public works.

(2) President Roosevelt's Spending Policy

With the advent of President Roosevelt, the spending school had the satisfaction of witnessing the adoption of its principles by the most important of all economic units. And since the United States is the country of gigantic figures—it seems to be the American national ambition to produce the largest figures regarding every sphere of human activity—the public works policy has been adopted on an immense scale. Where other countries thought hesitatingly in terms of millions, the United States acted without hesitation in terms of milliards. Enormous amounts have been spent since the second quarter of 1933 upon various kinds of public works. The amounts allocated by Congress for that purpose run into almost astronomic figures. Apart from the war expenditure during 1914–18, never in history has public expenditure been embarked upon on such a gigantic scale. In fact, since war expenditure was forced upon the belligerent countries it may be said that never before has public expenditure been deliberately adopted on a scale comparable with that of public works under President Roosevelt.

The object of this policy was twofold. In the first place, President Roosevelt was anxious to reduce unemployment and to revive trade. At the same time, he was equally anxious to raise the price level, and thus to relieve the burden of private indebtedness. The reduction of unemployment by means of public works is not, strictly speaking, a matter of monetary policy. On the other hand, the deliberate effort to raise commodity prices through Government spending definitely comes within the realm of monetary policy. Whether or not President Roosevelt's spending programme can be regarded largely or mainly as a monetary reform scheme depends not so much upon its object as upon its results.

Public works can produce monetary effects either by bringing about credit expansion or by bringing about an expansion of purchasing power. In the United States, they cannot be said to have produced a credit expansion comparable in extent to the enormous amounts involved. This was because to a very large extent these public works were financed by means of borrowing which meant merely a redistribution of credit resources and not their actual expansion. On the other hand, there can be no doubt that President Roosevelt's public works did lead to an expansion of purchasing power. What is uncertain is how far normal productive activity was discouraged by the fears of heavy taxation as a result of the rapid growth of public debt.

(3) American Spending as World Factor

The spending policy was only one of the many means by which President Roosevelt endeavoured to reflate. From time to time he concentrated upon other methods of reflation, and although public works were continued, for months they faded into the background among the means of monetary policy. After a while, however, they invariably came once more to the forefront. In particular, at the beginning of 1935 the newly adopted public works schemes were considered, not only in the United States but also abroad, as the most important factor in the international monetary situation. There was a widespread belief that these public works would lead to a marked rise of the price level in the United States, and that consequently the whole world situation would undergo a fundamental change.

Unquestionably, commodity prices rose quite considerably during 1935, but it is impossible to ascertain to what extent this was due to public works in the United States. The fact that the rise took place in primary produce prices, while those of manufactures remained practically stationary, seemed to indicate that the extent to which public works affected the price level must have been of secondary importance. There is reason to believe that from a purely monetary point of view the result was not in proportion to the sacrifices involved.

Whether, from an economic point of view, the addition to national wealth justified the increase of the national debt on such a huge scale is also open to argument. While some of the public works undertaken are unquestionably justified, irrespective of their monetary effect or their effect upon unemployment, the same cannot be said of a very large proportion of the money spent. From this point of view it would have been wiser to go more slowly with the adoption of public works, so as to make sure that every dollar spent added as much to the nation's wealth.

(4) Inadequate Monetary Effects

From a purely monetary point of view it is an open question whether the method of financing of these gigantic public works was expedient. Given the fact that President Roosevelt aimed at raising commodity prices, and that public works were undertaken largely to that end, it was deplorable from his point of view that he had not the courage of his convictions. He allowed himself to be persuaded by his Treasury officials—who are naturally conservative and orthodox—to finance the public works by essentially non-inflationary methods. Admittedly, the Treasury had to consider the prospects of refunding maturing debts and could not afford to jeopardise its chances in that direction. Had the public works been financed by crude inflationary methods, it is conceivable that the difficulty of meeting maturities would have led to an inflation far in excess of what President Roosevelt could possibly have had in mind. Nevertheless, given the fact that he wanted to cause a rise in commodity prices by means of public works, it is impossible to escape the conclusion that, torn between the two considerations, he did not know his own mind and combined excessive radicalism with excessive timidity. A much smaller amount spent on public works but financed by inflationary means would in all probability have produced a stronger effect upon prices.

It is not as if there would have been much difference between the material effects of public works financed by means of loans and of works financed by the printing-press. The additional demand for commodities and the additional increase of purchasing power would have been the same even if the amounts required had been raised not by borrowing, but by inflationary means. In itself an increase in the monetary circulation does not necessarily lead to a rise in commodity prices. The surplus tends to find its way back to the banks and through the banks to the authorities. And yet it would have made all the difference if public works had been financed by methods of crude inflation. It would have made the producers and consumers in the United States realise that President Roosevelt meant business.

(5) American Public not Inflation-minded

The reason why President Roosevelt's various reflationary efforts produced comparatively meagre results was that the public did not believe in his determination to inflate. After every act or statement which was calculated to indicate an inflationary policy, there was an act or statement which provided a counterblast cancelling out the psychological effect of the first act. The antidote to inflation was all the more effective as the American public was not inflation-minded. It had no experience of inflation proper during and after the war, and found it unbelievable that the United States, with her huge gold stock, could possibly ever have such an experience. In countries which have suffered from advanced inflation within the memory of the present generation, the public is inflation-conscious, and is inclined to suspect and anticipate inflation at the slightest excuse, irrespective of emphatic denials by the Government. On the other hand, the American public, not being inflation-conscious, refuses to believe in the likelihood of inflation, or in the presence of inflation even if it is officially declared or admitted. For this reason, nothing short of deliberate and crude inflationary measures would have made producers and consumers in the United States realise that there was a likelihood of an inflationary rise in commodity prices. The result would have been an increase in productive activity in anticipation of profits made through higher prices and an increase in demand on the part of consumers for fear of impending rise in prices. To produce such a result it would have been worth while for President Roosevelt, in the interest of his reflationary policy, to risk the difficulties of Treasury re-financing, especially as the authorities, being in possession of a huge gold reserve, were in any case in a position to check inflation when it threatened to get beyond control.

The fact that reflation through public works failed to produce any noteworthy effect upon the American price level is in part attributable to the fact that actual total production represented only a small percentage of the productive capacity of American industries. Increase in demand would have had to go a long way before it would have resulted in an increase of prices instead of causing an increase of the output. This does not, however, mean that in times of depression, when actual production is always inevitably below capacity, a spending policy is necessarily ineffective. But if it is carried out in such a way as to minimise its inflationary effect, then the result is bound to be inferior to the effort. The American experience proves that the psychological effect of a spending policy is at least as important as its material effect. This is also evident from the experience of Gold Bloc countries, where a public works policy entirely failed even to prevent a fall in prices, much less to cause a rise.

(6) Public Works Policy in Great Britain

It was not until the beginning of 1935 that the British Government began to make half-hearted attempts to embark upon a policy of spending. Even then it was not monetary but political and general economic considerations that induced the Government to change its hitherto rigidly orthodox attitude. The approach of the general election and the appearance of Mr. Lloyd George's ambitious public works scheme induced the Government to adopt a few schemes of capital expenditure. At the same time, the international political outlook induced the Government to increase expenditure on national defence. Up to the time of writing, all this has been financed out of budgetary resources, which means that it has not in any way produced an addition to the purchasing power of the country. The Government has consistently refused to adopt a really ambitious policy of slum clearance and to finance it by means of borrowing. The much-advocated large housing loan never materialised. At the same time, there is ample evidence that the Government's attitude towards public works is no longer nearly as orthodox as it was even at the beginning of 1935. For some time past, Mr. Neville Chamberlain has in fact been moving towards expansionism, a tendency which has continued since the general election. His expansionism largely assumed the form of insistence upon the maintenance of cheap money in face of reviving trade, which in the ordinary course would cause a rise in interest rates. Simultaneously, however, he adopted a more liberal attitude towards constructive public works schemes. This is all the more remarkable in that it coincides with a rearmament programme which involves a powerful drain of the national resources.

It remains to be seen whether the necessity for rapid rearmament, coupled with this new expansionism in the sphere of public works, will induce the Government to revise its attitude towards spending and lead it to increase exceptional expenditure on such a scale as would necessitate the unbalancing of the budget. Even so, it is certain that the deficit will be covered by strictly orthodox methods of borrowing, so that there can be no inflationary effects in the narrow sense of the term.

(7) Spending Policy on the Continent

Public works expenditure in Germany, Italy and to a less extent in the countries of the Gold Bloc had no direct bearing on monetary policy. The object in these countries has not been to cause a rise in prices, or even to prevent a fall, though in practice the policy must tend to produce that effect. In adopting extraordinary programmes of public expenditure, the Governments of countries with overvalued currencies were actuated by a desire partially to counteract the adverse effect of their monetary policy, and thereby to disarm opposition against it. Even in these cases, therefore, expenditure on public works is indirectly a means of monetary policy. In countries where expenditure on public works and rearmament assumed considerable dimensions, as it did in Italy and Germany, it resulted in a marked rise in commodity prices. This, however, was not in pursuance of, but against, the monetary policy of those countries.

In every case, a spending policy has been adopted as a temporary emergency measure. In no case has there been any evidence of a desire to elaborate a permanent policy of varying public expenditure with the purpose of regulating either the price level or the volume of employment. Conceivably, in practice, with the improvement of economic conditions, most Governments engaged in the execution of exceptional public works will discontinue these works and forget about them until the next spell of depression. Thus, there would not be any scientific regulation of the volume of public works in accordance with the gradual character of the upward or downward trend of trade.

It is even conceivable that some of the Governments will continue such public works as are considered useful even after the end of the depression, in which case their policy will tend to accentuate the upward swing of the trade cycle, accelerating its development into a boom. Evidently, the policy of spending has been adopted under the influence of the crisis in a haphazard way, and it will be a long time before it becomes part of a scientifically planned monetary and economic policy.

CHAPTER XVI

MANAGED CURRENCY

(I) Expansionism *v.* Monetary Management

It cannot be emphasised sufficiently that the various schools of monetary reform to a very large extent overlap one another. As we have already pointed out, the expansionists of various classes are usually in favour of a cheap money policy and are usually opposed to the stabilisation of currencies in relation to gold. Many of them, though by no means all, also favour monetary management. Indeed, scientific expansionism necessarily implies monetary management. It is only pseudo-scientific and frankly unscientific reformers who consider expansion as a perpetual tendency which should never be checked, let alone reversed. To their mind, expansionism is essentially a one-way street, and they seriously believe in the possibility of never-ending non-stop expansion. The only kind of management they may conceivably have in mind is some regulation of the degree of expansion, so as to prevent it from getting out of control.

To imagine that it would always be possible to administer the right degree of expansion requires, however, an abnormal degree of optimism. Human calculation is always liable to err, and there are, besides, important factors which defy human reckoning altogether. A shortage of crops, for instance, is sufficient to upset calculations, while the caprices of consumers provide a highly important potential source of unexpected results. The object of monetary management is to adjust monetary policy to any such changes in the relation between supply and demand. It sometimes necessitates suspending expansion or even reversing it. The apparatus should be able to work efficiently both ways. Circumstances may arise in which management implies an increase of interest rates; a contraction of credit; a reduction of consumer's purchasing power; and a suspension of public works expenditure. This is a consideration which is often overlooked both by advocates and opponents of a managed monetary system. According to popular belief, the sole object and means of monetary management is to expand incessantly. If that were all, monetary management would be an easy task indeed.

(2) Managed *v.* Inconvertible Currency

Another popular belief is that managed currency necessarily means inconvertible paper currency. What is worse, it is widely believed that every inconvertible paper currency is a managed currency; and that the moment a country suspends the gold standard its currency automatically becomes "managed". In reality, a currency can be managed even if it is based on gold, and on the other hand, the mere fact that a currency is inconvertible does not in itself mean that it is managed. Indeed, some of the most prominent adherents of the managed currency school do not consider that monetary management and some form of limited gold standard are incompatible. They are not against retaining gold as the basis of the monetary system. What they object to is that the automatic changes in the amount of the gold reserve brought out by the caprices of gold production or by international influences outside the control of the Government of the country concerned should govern the volume of currency and credit and the level of interest rates. They are in favour of retaining gold for the purpose of settling international balances, or for the purpose of inspiring confidence in the currency system.

It is true that the moment a country suspends the gold standard, its currency ceases to regulate itself automatically. Notwithstanding this, to state that a currency becomes a managed currency simply because it is no longer automatically regulated would tend to discredit the meaning of the term "management". This indeed is the reason why the orthodox school frequently refers to every kind of inconvertible currency as being a managed currency, and whenever an inconvertible currency fluctuates orthodox economists triumphantly point out the failure of the managed system. In reality, in many cases inconvertible currencies simply become not managed but unmanageable. They have to be allowed to find their own level internationally and internally. In other cases, Government intervention is confined to a very restricted field, while, for the rest, the currency is not managed. For instance, the British Exchange Equalisation Account merely aims at reducing the fluctuations in the international value of sterling. This in itself can hardly be called monetary management. The internal value of the pound is allowed to take care of itself and the authorities do not make any extraordinary effort to regulate the volume of credit.

(3) What is Monetary Management ?

Monetary management implies a deliberate policy which aims at the systematic regulation of the volume of currency and credit with a definite object in view. This object may be either the maintenance of a stable exchange rate, or the maintenance of a stable or moderately changing price level, or the maintenance of a stable or steadily increasing volume of employment and trade. The advocates of the managed monetary system may be divided into schools according to whether they aim at the stability of prices or stability of employment. Those who aim at stable exchange rates by means of monetary management are not as a rule classed among the advocates of managed currency. Advocates of the maintenance of the stability of the international value of a currency cannot be included under the managed currency school, even if they are in favour of maintaining the international stability of the currency by means of a policy of intervention instead of relying upon the automatic working of the monetary system. Most supporters of monetary management are in favour of attaining more than one end, but some of them lay the emphasis on the exchange stabilising aspects of management, or on the price stabilising aspect, while others attach more importance to the employment stabilising aspect. Most advocates of a managed currency attach more importance to the stabilisation of the price level ; but the number of the adherents of the school advocating the stabilisation of employment as the main goal of monetary management is increasing.

The question whether or not a stable price level is desirable has been subject to much discussion. Owing to the grave disadvantages of violent price movements since 1914, the number of those who consider it of supreme importance that price levels should remain stable has increased considerably. The disturbing effects of rising or falling prices are doubtless obvious. And yet the assumption that it is to the interest of mankind that prices should be prevented from moving is not accepted unanimously. Indeed, it is opposed both by the extreme orthodox school and by a considerable section of the radical school. The former argues that since the movement of prices constitutes a valuable indicator of underlying tendencies, the artificial stabilisation of the price level would merely destroy the barometer without solving the more fundamental problems. The answer to this argument is that an improvement of statistics of production and sales would dispense with the necessity of relying upon such a doubtful barometer as the movement of prices, for this indicator can be influenced by an immense number of factors. In the absence of adequate statistics, we have to rely upon price movements as the only indicator available. If, however, we succeeded in obtaining a more scientific indicator we could well afford to dispense with the old-fashioned method of judging trends by price levels. In any case, price movements are not always the effect of underlying tendencies; almost as often as not they are the cause and not the effect. Price movements provoked by superficial influences are capable of causing a lasting disturbance in the fundamental equilibrium. This in itself is a strong argument against the theory that price fluctuations perform a valuable social function by acting as the barometer to indicate underlying tendencies. No barometer has ever yet been known to have influenced the weather: but price movements are capable of influencing underlying tendencies.

(4) Stable or Falling Prices?

Some of the economists who are in favour of monetary management do not believe in a stationary price level. In their view, the object of management should be not to maintain a stable price level but to bring about a gradual and very moderate, well-regulated decline in prices. According to them, it is only by such means that the benefits of technical progress and increased output can be passed on to the consumers. Many orthodox economists are also in favour of a declining price level on the ground that it would tend to discourage credit expansion and boom. Some radical economists believe, however, that for that very reason, a moderately rising price level is the smaller of the two evils. Those in favour of a stationary price level believe that it would be possible to pass on to the consumers the benefit of cheaper and more plentiful production by raising their purchasing power rather than by lowering the price level.

But a large number of the advocates of monetary management do not consider the non-monetary aspects of the problem at all. They simply hold the view that any price fluctuation is an unmitigated evil and should, therefore, be avoided at all costs. They are inclined to be just as dogmatic about this as orthodox supporters of the gold standard are dogmatic about the absolute necessity of maintaining at all cost the stability of currencies in relation to gold. Indeed, there is a danger that while monetary reformers are making desperate efforts to demolish some old-fashioned fetishes, they themselves set up fetishes to take the place of those destroyed. When Mr. Benjamin Anderson, one of the most extreme orthodox economists, coined the term "heterodox orthodoxy", he certainly hit the nail on the head even though he applied the term indiscriminately to any doctrine that was not strictly orthodox.

(5) A New Doctrinairism

Advocates of internal monetary stability are at pains to convince the world that international monetary stability is merely a means to an end and not the end itself. They themselves, however, are in bad need of a lesson to make them realise that the same holds good also about internal monetary stability, which they are inclined to present as the ultimate goal instead of regarding it as a means of improving the standard of living. So long as monetary stability, whether internal or international, serves that supreme object, it is worth having. The moment, however, that the efforts to maintain stability, whether internal or international, require sacrifices which are out of proportion to the results, they should be abandoned. This is what is not realised by advocates of monetary stability, whether they favour stable exchanges or stable prices. Both are inclined to attach exaggerated importance to stability and to advocate a policy which involves excessive sacrifices. The new doctrinairism favouring the defence of internal monetary stability at all costs is in no way better than the old doctrinairism which claimed that it was our supreme duty to defend our currencies at their existing parities with the last drop of our blood.

Rigid insistence upon a stationary price level can become as serious an obstacle to the improvement of the standard of living as can the stubborn defence of the international value of the currency. This is particularly the case where the monetary management is confined to the regulation of the volume of credit for production. In that case, monetary management does not cure the evil of deficient or excessive purchasing power. Even if monetary management is extended to the regulation of purchasing power, situations may arise in which a change in the price level is a more expedient solution than the adjustment of either the volume of credit or the volume of purchasing power. The contraction of purchasing power, even if scientifically managed, is bound to be unpopular, and if the same result can be achieved by raising the price level, in certain circumstances this would evidently be the better solution. For the same reason, expansion of purchasing power should not be proceeded with unless there is good reason to believe that the increase in production which appears to make it desirable is of a lasting character. Rather than run the risk of having to curtail purchasing power once more it is better if evidently temporary goods surpluses are disposed of by lowering the price level.

(6) Monetary Management and Economic Planning

All these problems are on the border-line between monetary management and general economic planning. Indeed, the two of them cannot or should not be considered separately. The great failing of the majority of those in favour of the monetary management is that they think that strictly monetary measures are in themselves sufficient to regulate the economic system in accordance with requirements. This one-sidedness characterises not only those advocates of monetary management whose aim is the stabilisation of the price level but also those whose object is the stabilisation of the volume of employment. They believe that by increasing the volume of credit and by checking or reversing the increase when necessary, it would be possible to keep the whole able-bodied population fully employed. According to this conception the volume of trade can be regulated with the aid of changes in the volume of credit in the same way as the temperature of a bath can be regulated by turning on and off the hot tap or the cold tap to suit requirements.

Here again we are confronted with an example of the fallacy of over-simplifying a situation which in reality is extremely complicated. Monetary management in the narrower sense, however skilfully administered, cannot in itself prevent disequilibrium from developing in individual branches of production, and such disequilibrium may eventually affect the general trend. The great failing of the majority of monetary reformers is that they underestimate the importance of such disequilibria. They are concerned only with the average prices, or with the total volume of production and consumption, and do not pay due regard to dislocations between individual items. Admittedly, the management which aims at regulating the volume of employment instead of merely regulating the price level is more in touch with realities, but even this type of management is bound to produce inadequate results unless it is combined with a general scheme of economic planning. Just as economic planning is unthinkable without monetary management, so monetary management is doomed to failure without economic planning. It is to be deplored that this elementary truth is not realised by the majority of monetary reformers. They have the failing of specialists who are inclined to exaggerate the importance of the narrow subject to which they have decided to devote their life. The value of their work could be increased considerably if only they were able to see the monetary sphere in its true perspective, and if they could fit their monetary reform scheme into the broader scheme of economic reform.

CHAPTER XVII

MANAGED GOLD STANDARD

(1) Compromise between Orthodoxy and Radicalism

We pointed out in Chapter IV that to a large extent the post-war gold standard was a managed monetary system. While before the war the gold standard was based almost entirely upon the automatic working of the economic tendencies, after the war Central Banks adopted the practice of interfering with these tendencies to a large extent. This fact, in itself, proves that the gold standard and monetary management are by no means incompatible. The question is whether it would be possible to reconcile the existence of the gold standard with a really advanced degree of monetary management. If so, a managed currency backed by gold might appear to be the ideal solution since it gets the best of both worlds. It would constitute a fair compromise between monetary orthodoxy and radicalism.

According to both orthodox economists and advocates of advanced monetary management, there can be no compromise between the two systems. Even those of the more progressive wing of the orthodox school who are prepared to admit the necessity of a certain degree of management, such as existed after the war, maintain that the object of such interference as they consider admissible should be to prevent only temporary fluctuations; they consider that there must be no interference with fundamental trends which, in the long run, will be dealt with by the automatic working of the gold standard. Radical supporters of monetary management also hold the view that under the gold standard the scope of management must be very narrow. They reject the idea of combining monetary management with the maintenance of the gold standard because they think that the existence of a gold standard, however limited it may be, would severely handicap monetary management.

Our task is to examine what degree of management is compatible with the existence of the gold standard. Let us begin by considering the most moderate forms of intervention and proceed towards the more advanced ones.

(2) Moderate Degrees of Management

In the broadest sense of the term even a change in the bank rate may constitute an act of monetary management. The gold standard could be considered truly automatic only if the monetary authorities were to maintain an entirely passive attitude and did not seek, by changing the bank rate, to influence the tendencies brought about by a gold influx or efflux. This, of course, is practicable only in countries which have no Central Banks, for if there is a Central Bank it must have an official rediscount rate, and if there is such a rate it has to be changed from time to time. According to the classical rules of the gold standard, it is not, however, considered incompatible with the automatic character of the system if the bank rate is changed, provided that its alteration is the result of a corresponding change in the market rates of discount, and merely confirms a *fait accompli* instead of trying to influence the tendencies. Thus, if the bank rate is put up in order to check an outflow of gold before the contraction of currency and credit brought about by that outflow has caused a corresponding rise in market rates, then it constitutes an act of monetary management in the broadest sense of the term. Similarly, if the bank rate is lowered after the drain has come to an end but before an influx of gold has resulted in a corresponding decline in the market rates, then it constitutes an act of intervention on the part of the authorities. This is what has actually happened time after time in France and other countries of the Gold Bloc since 1931. The classical automatic character of the gold standard has not altogether been upheld; a moderate degree of management has been adopted even in these countries.

Various measures applied by Central Banks before the war to check the drain on their gold reserves or to replenish their gold supplies constituted a somewhat more advanced degree of monetary management. Such measures were the paying out of silver coins instead of gold on the part of the Bank of France, the payment of an open or disguised premium on gold and various technical devices or moral pressure by which an outflow of gold can for a while be discouraged. Even the Bank of England resorted occasionally to artificial devices to encourage the influx of gold. As Mr. W. T. C. King, in his *History of the London Discount Market*, reminds us, early in this century the Bank occasionally granted loans free of interest to finance gold imports. After the war almost every country which returned to the gold standard resorted occasionally or systematically to such measures of intervention.

(3) Open Market Operations

The next degree in monetary management, which was also practised in some countries before the war and which has become the general rule after the war, was open market operations in foreign exchanges. By accumulating unofficial foreign exchange reserves apart altogether from the note cover, and by using them during times of adverse pressure, various Central Banks prevented gold movements which would otherwise have secured automatic readjustment through the normal functioning of the gold standard.

Another method of monetary management is the practice of open market operations aiming at influencing the resources of the money market. This practice assumes the form of buying or selling securities, through which means the supplies of credit can be made more abundant or more stringent. Although by no means unknown before the war, this method of management assumed great importance after the war as it provided the means of offsetting the effects of unwanted gold movements. If applied for that purpose, open market operations constitute a high degree of monetary management. By means of such operations the monetary authorities can immediately neutralise an inflow or outflow of gold by preventing it from causing an unwanted change in the volume of credit.

Since the automatic gold standard works largely through the effect of gold movements upon the volume of credit, this intervention constitutes a very advanced degree of monetary management. It has been criticised by orthodox economists, especially when it is used to prevent an outflow of gold from causing a contraction of credit. The purists are not nearly as critical of those transgressors of the laws of the automatic gold standard who neutralise an excessive inflow of gold by preventing it from serving as a basis for an expansion of credit. And yet, management in the form of neutralisation of surplus gold has a much wider scope than management in the form of offsetting the effect of an outflow of gold upon the volume of credit. After all, Central Banks are in a position to neutralise incoming gold to an almost unlimited degree, as the experience of France and the United States after the war conclusively proves. On the other hand, neutralisation of an outflow of gold cannot go very far without weakening the technical position of the Central Bank.

(4) Managed Currency with Gold Backing

While all but the extreme orthodox school are prepared to admit that a certain degree of offsetting operations is not incompatible with the gold standard, opinions differ about the degree which is admissible before such management reduces the gold standard to a mere matter of form. The most advanced degree of management of the gold standard would imply the regulation of the volume of credit entirely independently of the changes in the amount of the gold reserve. An expansion that is considered desirable in order to prevent a fall in prices or a fall in employment would be brought about even if it meant a fall in the gold reserve, which would not affect the supply of currency and credit. Similarly, an influx of gold would not in itself be allowed to produce its corrective by bringing about cheap money through a credit expansion. In other words, the monetary authorities would behave exactly as if the gold standard did not exist. They would regulate the volume of credit in accordance with the requirements of the price level or of employment, requirements which inevitably conflict at times with the rules of the automatic gold standard. Under such a system the gold reserve and the reserve ratio would be allowed to fluctuate, while the volume of currency and credit would be kept stable or would be adjusted independently of the changes in the gold reserve. Indeed, the gold reserve would be there merely as a security for the note issue or as a reserve for settling international accounts, but would have no connection whatever with the credit structure. Monetary management under that system would be guided by the credit requirements of trade, independently of the caprices of international gold movements whose internal monetary effect would become reduced to that of commodity imports and exports. Such a currency would be a managed currency with a gold backing. It would be nevertheless a form of the gold standard, since gold would be available at the Central Bank for international purposes, and the exchange would be kept stable by means of the normal working of the gold points.

An even more advanced form of managed currency is the inconvertible paper currency with a gold backing whose stability is maintained not by means of gold movements through arbitrage but by means of gold transactions undertaken by the monetary authorities themselves. There is, however, relatively little difference between this system and the one described above, for whenever a currency is subject to a strong buying or selling pressure the authorities have to buy or sell gold if they want to maintain exchange stability, whether or not they admit arbitrage.

(5) Is Gold Backing an Advantage?

What is the advantage of this system over an inconvertible managed paper currency without gold backing? If gold is not allowed to play its part as the automatic regulator of the volume of credit, what is the object of retaining it at all? This question is often asked by radical monetary reformers who would prefer the complete elimination of gold from the monetary system for fear that if it were retained, even in a subordinate and limited rôle, the monetary authorities could not escape the mentality which induces them to operate the modified gold standard on orthodox principles. The answer is that even if we prevent gold from fulfilling its part as regulator of credit supplies, there is no reason why we should prevent it from playing a useful part as a means of settling international balances and as a backing to the note issue and to the credit structure, for the existence of such a backing is calculated to inspire confidence.

The experience of the last few years has amply confirmed—if indeed there was need for confirmation—that the public all over the world has more confidence in gold than in any other security and that gold is the only commodity which is accepted in unlimited amounts in payment for goods by all countries. While since 1931 the system of the gold standard has become increasingly unpopular both in countries which have suspended it and in countries which have retained it, simultaneously with this tendency gold itself as a means of preserving values has become increasingly popular. This is indicated by the unprecedented degree of hoarding by private individuals, and by the endeavours of all Governments, whether or not they are on a gold standard, to maintain and increase their gold reserves.

The habit of mankind to prefer gold to anything else as a conserver of values is some thousands of years older than the system of the gold standard. It would in all probability survive the abolition of that system. The degree to which the public in most countries has reverted to gold hoarding during the crisis gives an idea how deeply rooted the instinct is in human nature. By far the greater number of those who hastened to acquire gold when conditions became uncertain did not argue the case for and against gold as an investment; they simply followed an instinct which is stronger than any influence of economic teaching.

(6) The Case for Gold

It is customary among radical economists to denounce this primitive instinct as the major obstacle to a rational solution of the monetary problem by the adoption of a scientific currency. In reality, the public's instinctive preference for gold is extremely useful for mankind. It is a great blessing that there is one commodity which is universally accepted without limitation in return for goods and services. If there were no such commodity it would be the duty of economists and statesmen to do their utmost to invent one, as, in its absence, it would be extremely difficult for the nations to accumulate reserves against a rainy day. There would be no shock-absorber to assist Governments in the task of tiding their countries over spells of adverse conditions.

Fortunately, we are in a position to support the case for gold with a concrete example. The experience of Germany during the second half of 1934 provides an example of the conditions that would exist in a world without a gold standard. If gold were to be universally demonetised, every country would be in exactly the same position as Germany was as a result of the depletion of her gold stock. In the absence of a gold reserve no country would be able to import unless it happened to be able to export at the same time. Were any country owing to bad harvest, or for any other reason, unable, however temporarily, to export, it would immediately have to cut down its imports to a corresponding degree, since it would not possess that universally acceptable commodity—gold—which it could use as a substitute for its commodity exports and thereby survive one or two bad seasons.

It may be objected that the international credit apparatus would tide countries over their temporary difficulties and that international lending would enable them to cover their trade deficits. It may well be asked, however, whether the absence of gold reserves would in any way facilitate international borrowing. The answer is most emphatically in the negative. Would any conscientious broker advise his client to subscribe to a loan for a country which had no gold reserves, and which would, in consequence, have to default during the first bad year? Admittedly, it is possible for the debtor to borrow an amount sufficient to maintain the interest service. That has actually been done in the past by many countries, though the result has not been exactly encouraging for investors. In the absence of gold reserve, however, investors would be asked to lend on the tacit understanding that in the first bad year the debtor would inevitably have to resort to such additional borrowing. Having no gold reserve to fall back upon, the debtor would have to choose between defaulting or borrowing on highly onerous terms the amount required for the loan service, and such borrowing again would depreciate the capital value of the earlier issue.

Nor would bankers be keen on granting short-term credits to countries without gold reserves, since such credits would become frozen as soon as conditions in the debtor country changed even slightly for the worse. It may be objected that even under the gold standard a major crisis leads to an embargo on gold exports and places creditors in exactly the same unenviable position as if there were no such thing as a gold standard. The difference is, however, that under the gold standard only an exceptionally severe crisis, or a series of bad years, could produce the effect which would be produced, in the absence of the gold standard, by quite a moderate deterioration of conditions in a single bad year.

(7) To make Credit Expansion Safer

Advanced currency reformers may well denounce the public for its foolish preference for gold. Even if we were to admit that this preference is unscientific, unjustified and unreasonable, we ought to be thankful for the "foolishness" of the public. It is of immense advantage to a country to possess a commodity which it can export to any other country at any time without difficulties. In given circumstances it is the possession of that "scrap iron" of no social utility that staves off starvation.

Another consideration in favour of retaining gold in its limited rôle is that it would make credit expansion safer. It cannot be emphasised sufficiently that credit is in practice synonymous with confidence. If the possession of a large gold stock inspires confidence owing to the "foolish" preference of the public for the metal, there is every reason to take advantage of this "foolish" preference to strengthen the basis of credit. It would be a mistake to try to prevent gold from fulfilling such a useful task, merely because its rôle as regulator of the credit supplies may in given circumstances be harmful. The extent of credit expansion that can be safely undertaken depends mainly upon the degree of confidence of the public in the soundness of the credit structure. So long as the public trusts the credit of its Government, of its Central Bank and its banks, a well-planned expansion tends to increase the nation's welfare. If, however, the expansion undermines confidence, it produces a destructive effect and leads to a decline of the standard of living. For this reason, every care has to be taken to strengthen confidence in the credit structure, or at any rate to prevent it from weakening, when embarking upon credit expansion. It is anything but wise, therefore, to advocate the abolition of gold simultaneously with the adoption of an expansionist policy.

(8) The "Gold Mentality"

If in spite of these arguments the advanced supporters of inconvertible managed currency are in favour of the complete demonetisation of gold, it is because they are afraid that in practice if not in law the monetary authorities would manage the monetary system with the object of preventing an outflow of gold and, if possible, accumulating a large surplus. It is feared that, with that object in mind, the monetary authorities might pursue a deflationary policy. Whether or not this would be the case depends in the first place upon the mentality of the monetary authorities. From this point of view, however, there is but little difference between the gold standard and an inconvertible monetary system. If the monetary authorities are inspired by orthodox principles they can run an inconvertible system on orthodox lines just as they would if they were working on the gold standard. If, on the other hand, those in charge of monetary management are inspired by radical principles, then they can manage a gold currency on unorthodox lines provided that there are ample gold resources at their disposal.

This latter consideration is of primary importance. It is utterly useless to make up our minds that when we return to the gold standard it will be managed on unorthodox lines, unless there is an ample safety margin to make it possible for the monetary authorities to disregard orthodox considerations. This is not adequately appreciated even in the camp of radical economists. Several of them—among others, Sir Arthur Salter, Mr. J. M. Keynes, and Mr. H. G. Henderson—declare themselves prepared to stabilise forthwith on the understanding that the new gold standard would be run on unorthodox lines. There is, however, no guarantee whatsoever that once the gold standard were readopted it would not be managed in accordance with time-honoured conventions. Since it is impossible to prescribe by law when the Bank rate should be raised or when credit should be restricted, the execution of monetary policy would have to be left to the Central Banks. The latter are certain to revert to orthodox methods the moment the gold reserve is threatened with depletion. The only safeguard against such a deflationary mentality would be to abstain from returning to the gold standard unless and until it can be done in circumstances which secure an adequate safety margin of gold reserve. If the reserve ratio amounts to several hundreds per cent, then money can be managed under the gold standard in the same way as if it were an inconvertible currency.

CHAPTER XVIII

MANAGED PAPER CURRENCY

(1) Meaning of Monetary Management

The ideal of the majority of radical monetary reformers is a scientifically managed inconvertible paper currency. Such reformers denounce the gold standard on the ground that it makes the volume of currency and credit largely dependent upon the caprices of nature and upon disturbing international influences. In their view, the volume of currency and credit should be determined by scientific considerations in accordance with sound and genuine requirements. To that end, they advocate the complete dissociation of the currency from gold.

As we pointed out in Chapter XVI, it is a popular belief that, once a currency ceases to be attached to gold, it necessarily becomes a managed currency. This belief contains a grain of truth, for the moment the volume of currency and credit ceases to be regulated by the automatic working of the gold standard, it has to be regulated by the decision of the monetary authorities. In that sense, the currency is "managed", but in the real sense of the term management implies scientific control and in many cases the monetary authorities are unable to control, scientifically or otherwise, the value or volume of the currency. In particular, during and after the war inconvertible paper currencies were essentially unmanageable. Indeed, it would be absurd to suggest that the German mark and the Austrian krone after the Armistice were managed currencies. Such suggestions are at times put forward by adherents of the orthodox school in order to discredit the idea of monetary management.

Nor can efforts to maintain the international stability of an inconvertible currency be regarded as monetary management, except in the broadest sense of the term. The suggestion that since the establishment of the Exchange Equalisation

Account sterling has become a managed currency in the sense in which the term is generally used, is absurd. In themselves, endeavours to limit the fluctuations of a currency by means of intervention of the authorities in the foreign exchange market are not as a rule regarded as monetary management. It is true that they constitute acts of Government intervention for the purpose of influencing the international value of the currency. Monetary management, however, should imply something more than purely negative efforts to counteract international fluctuations. It should imply a positive endeavour to regulate the volume and value of a currency in a way that is considered to be in accordance with the interests of the increase of the welfare of the community, independently of the technical international considerations which have in the past been regarded as being of paramount importance.

(2) International and National Management

The supreme ideal of radical advocates of managed currency is international management by some organisation set up for that purpose. Mr. Keynes, in his *Treatise on Money*, advocates the establishment of a super-national bank which would be in charge of monetary management. To some extent, the Bank for International Settlements was meant to fulfil that task, though the idea that national Central Banks should relinquish part of their power in favour of the Basle institution has never been considered seriously by those who control it. Conceivably if the world crisis of 1931 had not intervened, the B.I.S. would have developed into a most influential body, capable of influencing the international monetary situation to no slight degree. So long, however, as political frontiers exist, Governments will not relinquish their right to determine the volume of national currency. For this reason, the scheme of an internationally managed currency is under existing conditions impracticable.

Most advocates of a managed currency are aware that there is no likelihood that their dream will ever become reality. They therefore advocate national managed currencies as an alternative, and maintain that, in the absence of a uniform monetary policy regulated by common consent, these managed currencies must be kept independent of one another and of gold. It is argued that those who seek international stability of currencies which are managed on lines different from one another are guilty of grave inconsistency. While under the gold standard there is a tendency towards automatic readjustment, under a system of independent managed currencies there is no such tendency, and any attempt to maintain them stable in relation to one another would inevitably come into conflict with the fundamental principles pursued by monetary management. Thus, if one country is inflating while the other is deflating, adverse pressure on the former's currency is bound to develop, and if an attempt is made to maintain its international stability, it inevitably entails contraction of credit, as under the gold standard.

(3) Purchasing Power Parities

For this reason, the view is held that the choice lies between internal and international stability, and that the former can be attained only at the expense of the latter. The solution suggested is that the currencies should be managed nationally, independently of one another in accordance with national requirements, and that if the different degree of expansion or contraction leads to pressure upon any one of them, the exchange rate concerned should be allowed to adjust itself accordingly, or it should be adjusted by deliberate action.

The proposals for the international application of this system of managed inconvertible paper currency have been largely influenced by Professor Gustav Cassel's " Purchasing Power Parity " theory of exchanges. According to that theory, in the long run exchanges always adjust themselves to the ratio between the price levels of the two countries. Applied to managed currencies, this would mean that if only exchanges were allowed to take care of themselves, any discrepancy between price levels caused by the different degree of expansion or contraction of currency would be automatically readjusted through a corresponding change in exchange rates.

Experience during the last fifteen years has amply proved that things do not work out in this fashion in real life. Owing to the existence of speculative influences, the movement of exchanges is usually greater than is justified by the movement of the ratio between the price levels. Nor are these " temporary " deviations from purchasing power parities as temporary as Professor Cassel would like us to believe. As often as not—in fact more often than not—such exaggerated movements provide in part their own subsequent justification by causing an adjustment in the purchasing power parities themselves. If an exchange depreciates, it is bound immediately to affect the prices of commodities imported from abroad, and less directly also the prices of commodities exported. Thus it inevitably affects the price level. This is true not only if the depreciation of the exchange is exaggerated but also if it corresponds exactly to the change in the purchasing power parity. If the purchasing power parity between countries A and B declines by, say, 10 per cent, and the exchange rate is allowed to adjust itself accordingly, before long it will be found that the purchasing power parity will decline by a further 2 or 4 per cent, in consequence of the effect of the exchange depreciation upon the price of imported and exported commodities.

(4) The Disturbing International Factor

It is, therefore, a mistake to imagine that the exchange rate is a purely passive factor. Under the system proposed the rate would very often react upon the internal price level and would upset the calculations of the authorities in charge of monetary management. A fluctuating exchange rate would provide an unsettling influence and sooner or later the authorities would be induced to take steps to maintain the stability of the exchange. In doing so, they would have to depart to a large extent from a policy of management dictated solely by consideration of the interests of internal expansion and the improvement of the standard of living.

Let us suppose that, instead of allowing the exchanges to take care of themselves in the hope that they will adjust themselves to their purchasing power parities, the authorities aimed at achieving a deliberate adjustment of the exchanges to those parities whenever deviations from them caused an inconvenient buying or selling pressure. Such a system would unquestionably be an improvement upon the combination of internal management with external *laissez-faire* policy. The principle of intervention would be applied more consistently, operating externally as well as internally. From a practical point of view, such a policy would safeguard internal trade from some of the disturbing influences of an irregularly fluctuating exchange. Nevertheless, the inconvenience of frequent changes in international exchange rates would remain. And it is well to realise that in the absence of a limited use of gold the changes of parities through devaluation would have to be very frequent.

The possibility of settling international balances by means of gold transfers would go a long way towards obviating the necessity for frequent changes in international parities between independently managed currencies. While the pressure is relatively moderate and not too persistent, it can always be counteracted by means of gold exports or imports. This would not merely postpone the change in the parities until the gold stocks of the weak countries were exhausted; in many cases the tide would turn before the weak countries had come to the end of their resistance, and the change of the parities on account of temporary influences could thus be avoided. In the absence of the shock-absorber of gold movements, however, even slight and temporary pressure would lead to changes of the parities. Internal trade would be exposed to more frequent shocks through international influences. Indeed, the frequency and large extent of disturbing changes of parities might jeopardise the success of internal monetary management.

(5) Managed Inconvertible Currency and Isolation

In the long run an inconvertible paper currency without gold backing can be managed successfully only if the country concerned isolates itself to the highest possible degree from all other countries. If foreign trade and international financial intercourse is reduced to a minimum and is placed under water-tight control, then and only then can the country in question afford to pursue an independent policy of monetary management with the exclusion of gold as a shock-absorber. Since no country is completely self-sufficient, this is impracticable. Every country has to import, and the higher its standard of living, the more it will have to import in the way of food and raw material. In order to be able to do so it must export, and to that end costs have to be kept at a competitive level.

There is, of course, one alternative solution—that the community should export at a loss in order to pay for the goods imported. If, thanks to independent monetary management, it is possible to exploit to the utmost the country's natural resources with the aid of all technical devices and efficient methods, then the community might be able to afford to lose on its export trade. This, however, is conceivable only under a high degree of economic planning whereby losses of exporters are borne by the community as a whole. It has been done in Russia and also to a less degree in Germany and Italy. Even under this system the ability to sell gold instead of having to sell goods at a loss would be helpful to no slight degree.

The establishment of exchange clearing on an international scale would go a long way towards facilitating monetary management without compelling a reduction of international commercial and financial intercourse to a minimum. The question will be dealt with in detail in Chapters XXVI and XXVII. Even under exchange clearing it would be easier to manage successfully a currency with gold backing than one without gold backing.

Beyond doubt, in the absence of a gold reserve which could act as a shock-absorber, a managed monetary system is exposed to shocks which could easily be mitigated by the adoption of a limited gold standard. Radical reformers would doubtless realise this if they were not guilty of the same dogmatism which they are the first to denounce when it is encountered in the orthodox camp. They would also then be aware of the fact, raised in the last chapter, that if a managed currency is backed by gold it is likely to inspire more confidence than an inconvertible paper currency. A Government whose currency has a strong gold backing can afford to indulge in expansion to a much larger degree than a Government with an inconvertible paper currency which has no gold backing. Even if the currency is not freely convertible, the mere existence of a strong gold reserve is regarded as a sufficient safeguard against the spectre of uncontrolled depreciation.

This leads us to a solution which is a compromise between a managed gold currency and a managed paper currency. A country need not necessarily restore the gold standard in the generally accepted sense of the term, but could accumulate a large gold reserve which would be available for international purposes and which, psychologically if not legally, would constitute the basis of its currency and credit system. The difference between such a system and the gold standard is merely one of degree. After all, most gold currencies after the war were in fact or in law inconvertible for internal purposes. As in many cases the authorities themselves undertook gold shipments, instead of leaving them to private arbitrage, there is no essential difference between such a system and an inconvertible currency which has a gold backing and which is maintained reasonably stable in relation to gold. And since, according to the new conception of the gold standard, the parities should be liable to alteration in face of major pressure, once this principle is admitted it would disarm much of the criticism of the inconvertible managed currency backed by gold.

The advantages of a gold backing to an inconvertible paper currency are too obvious to be overlooked. The system should be acceptable even to some of those radical reformers who object to the managed gold standard on the ground that the authorities would be inspired by orthodox principles. It would also disarm opposition on the part of those who maintain that international stability of a currency is detrimental to management which aims at internal expansion. An inconvertible paper currency with gold backing can be adjusted as and when required without any necessity for the process of suspending the gold standard or devaluing the currency. At the same time, while an inconvertible currency without gold backing is at the mercy of speculative influences, an inconvertible currency with strong gold backing can be managed independently of that factor. It is thus evident that even from the point of view of radical monetary reformers, it is a mistake to advocate the complete demonetisation of gold. In the absence of universal and international exchange clearing scientific management is inconceivable without a strong gold backing. Even under the system of exchange clearing the possession of gold backing is a great advantage and assists the authorities to no slight extent in the task of monetary management. None but extreme fanatics can disregard these considerations and demand the reduction of the value of gold to that of scrap iron.

CHAPTER XIX

MONETARY MANAGEMENT DURING THE DEPRESSION

(1) Management before 1931

There is nothing new under the sun, and students of economic history find it relatively easy to prove that the idea of monetary management is about as old as that of the monetary system itself. Examples are quoted of certain States of Ancient Greece which practised monetary management, and with a little effort it is even possible to prove that Ancient Egypt had a managed currency. Monetary management in the modern sense, however, is essentially a post-war development. The monetary systems that existed throughout the nineteenth century and until 1914 were substantially automatic. As we saw in Chapters IV and XVII, however, the automatic character of the monetary system was considerably curtailed after the war. Indeed, the gold standard that existed in most countries after 1925 was to a large degree a managed system. At the same time, a strong movement was afoot demanding the application of a higher degree of management.

There was after the war much more reason for a movement in favour of a managed currency than there had been before the war. Prior to 1914, the main argument against the automatic gold standard was that the monetary resources of mankind were dependent upon the caprices of nature by reason of their effect on the fluctuation of gold production. After the war, the " caprices of nature " argument was reinforced by the " disturbing effect of the international monetary factor upon home trade " argument, and by the " handicap to the utilisation of technical progress for the welfare of mankind " argument.

(2) Attitude of British Authorities

Post-war Britain provided a particularly fertile soil for the managed currency movement. Owing to the relative technical weakness of the pound, and to the desire to safeguard trade as far as possible from international monetary influences, the British authorities had resorted to a high degree of monetary management. Gold movements which under the automatic system would have led to a contraction of credit were neutralised. To do the British authorities justice, it is necessary to point out that for them monetary management during 1925–31 was by no means a one-way street. It did not mean only the offsetting of the effect of a gold efflux, but at times also the neutralising of a gold influx. When it was assumed that an influx—such as the somewhat artificial import of gold arranged by the Midland Bank in 1928—was purely temporary, steps were taken to sterilise it rather than allow it to lead to an expansion of credit which would subsequently have had to be followed by a contraction.

The tendency towards monetary management received a strong stimulus through the crisis of 1931 and the following years of depression. This does not mean that in suspending the gold standard Great Britain and a number of other countries have adopted managed currencies. Indeed, it may well be asked whether the degree of management in Great Britain, for instance, was really as much greater after 1931 as is generally assumed. Admittedly, after the suspension of the gold standard the authorities intervened to regulate to some degree the international value of the currency, but then this was done also to some extent before 1931. In particular, during the last months that preceded the suspension of the gold standard, official intervention constituted the major factor in the foreign exchange market. On previous occasions, the authorities had also played an active part, though to a relatively less degree. As for the management of the internal volume of credit, unquestionably there was a deliberately engineered expansion during the first half of 1932. After that, however, there was no indication that the Bank of England intervened by open market operations to prevent an unwanted expansion or contraction. Indeed, the Bank of England's rôle in the discount market and money market since 1932 has become almost entirely passive. Simultaneously with the suspension of the gold standard, it created stringency by the time-honoured method of raising the Bank rate to the panic level of 6 per cent. During the first half of 1932, however, the Bank rate was gradually reduced to 2 per cent and there it has remained ever since. For the first time in the history of the Bank the Bank rate was left unchanged for over three years. This fact speaks for itself as to the degree of official intervention with market tendencies since the middle of 1932. Nor was any other method employed deliberately to control the money market. Indeed, in that market things were allowed to take care of themselves to a much larger degree than under the gold standard.

(3) The Exchange Equalisation Account

It is true that at the same time the newly established Exchange Equalisation Account became an important factor not only in the foreign exchange market but also in the money market. Indeed, it is argued sometimes that it is because of the operations of the Exchange Equalisation Account that the price level in Great Britain has been relatively stable while prices have fluctuated in the countries of the Gold Bloc. In some quarters this fact is presented as a triumph of monetary management. The truth of the matter is that the circumstances to which Great Britain owes the relative stability of her price level during the last four years have been largely accidental. The result has not been in any way due to any conscious efforts of the Exchange Equalisation Account to maintain such stability. Indeed, the Exchange Equalisation Account does not concern itself in any way with the price level. Its operations are not guided by any endeavour to cause or prevent a rise or a fall in commodity prices. The sole consideration which induces the authorities in charge of the Exchange Equalisation Account to intervene or abstain from intervening in the foreign exchange market is their desire to moderate the fluctuations of sterling.

Admittedly, the operations of the Exchange Equalisation Account have influenced the money market to no slight degree. Whenever the Exchange Equalisation Account has to buy gold or exchange in order to prevent an unwanted rise of sterling it has to raise funds by selling Treasury bills. Whenever it has to sell gold in order to prevent an unwanted fall of sterling it makes use of the funds thus released for a reduction of the volume of publicly held Treasury bills. It is inevitable that from time to time these operations should affect the money market. They inevitably affect the volume of funds and that of credit available for trade. It would be impossible to argue, however, that the authorities in increasing and reducing the volume of Treasury bills pursue the same object as they did through their open market operations before 1931, namely, that of expanding or contracting the volume of credit. They have nothing of that kind in mind this time. The changes in the volume of credit resources are the inevitable and accessory consequences of operations undertaken purely for the purpose of reducing the fluctuations of sterling.

The Exchange Equalisation Account has no desire to expand or contract the volume of credit. It does not know and probably does not care what effect these expansions and contractions have upon the internal credit situation. Its sole concern is the international situation. Considering the existence of a large volume of credit, the fluctuations caused by the operations of the Exchange Equalisation Account are in any case of no consequence from the point of view of trade and prices. Possibly if business activity were in full swing and the credit resources available fully employed, the operations of the Exchange Equalisation Account would produce noteworthy repercussions on the volume of credit used by trade. In that case, the authorities could not afford to disregard the internal aspects of the operations of the Exchange Equalisation Account.

The operations of the Exchange Equalisation Account, then, do not seek to maintain the stability of the price level or to regulate the volume of employment through the volume of credit. If prices are relatively stable in Great Britain it is because every depreciation of sterling tends to cause a fall in world prices and every appreciation tends to cause a rise in world prices. Since world prices tend to adjust themselves to sterling, there is no need for prices in Great Britain to adjust themselves to world prices.

(4) Cheap Money and Management

The cheap money policy of the Government is sometimes represented as a policy of monetary management. The authorities claimed to have made money cheap and plentiful in order to increase the volume of employment. Doubtless this comes within the definition of monetary management. It has to be borne in mind, however, that even under the gold standard a prolonged period of depression inevitably leads to a period of cheap money. In the 'nineties, when the automatic gold standard was in operation, money rates declined through the automatic working of normal factors to nearly as low a level as during the period of 1932–6. After the middle of 1932, the Government's policy did little more than merely confirm the natural tendency prevailing in the market. Indeed, the authorities would have had to go out of their way to prevent money from becoming cheap. There was no need for them to go out of their way to cause money to become cheap.

While monetary management cannot be regarded as being responsible for cheap money, it can be regarded as the cause of the prolongation of the spell of cheap money. Under the automatic gold standard, even a limited degree of trade recovery such as was experienced in Great Britain, especially in 1935, would have been followed by a stiffening of money rates. In pursuance of the Government's policy of cheap money, the Bank of England had to abstain from making money tighter, although there were obvious signs of expansion. Rather than check the upward trend of employment and commodity prices, the authorities preferred to allow money to remain cheap and plentiful and allowed a substantial increase in the note circulation to take place. At this stage, the cheap money policy was distinctly in accordance with the principles of monetary management. The pound during this period provided a good example of a managed inconvertible paper currency with gold backing.

For the same reason, the countries of the Sterling Bloc also benefited by a relatively stable price level. Only one of them, Sweden, adopted a deliberate policy of monetary management. In her case a relative stability of price level coupled with a satisfactory degree of internal expansion was to a large degree due to a deliberate policy of monetary management.

(5) Management and the United States

In the United States, the suspension of the gold standard in 1933 was not followed by the adoption of a managed currency in the real sense of the term. President Roosevelt's aim was to raise commodity prices on a large scale and as quickly as possible, and to that end the subtle devices of scientific monetary management would not have sufficed. There was a policy of crude and deliberate depreciation of the currency coupled with public works on a gigantic scale and the increase of purchasing power by various devices. Such measures are outside the scope of monetary management proper. In a sense, the gold policy adopted towards the end of 1933 aimed at monetary management since it aimed at the regulation of the internal price level by monetary means. It was based on the assumption, supported by Professors Irving Fisher, Warren and Pearson, that changes in the gold value of a currency would be accompanied by corresponding changes in its commodity value. The theoretical aspects and the results of this policy will be discussed in detail in the following two chapters.

In the United States, as in Great Britain, there was little scope for monetary management during the period of reflation, for the simple reason that owing to the existence of a huge volume of idle funds, changes in the volume of credit were unable to affect trade or prices. A further artificial increase in the already excessive volume of credit resources would not have created any additional employment, while a contraction of credit would have had to go a very long way before it could have materially checked trade activity. It is only when the volume of credit available roughly corresponds to, or is inferior to, the normal requirements of trade that changes in either direction would immediately affect the volume of employment and the level of prices.

(6) Management and the Gold Bloc

Monetary management played a certain part in the monetary policies of the Gold Bloc countries. It cannot be said that the gold standard in France was managed to a higher degree after 1931 than before. The difference was mainly one of the method of management. Prior to 1931, the main object of monetary management in France was to prevent the natural working of the gold standard from bringing about a credit expansion which would raise commodity prices in France to the world level. Since 1931, the more especially during 1934 and 1935, the main object has been to prevent an outflow of gold from causing a corresponding contraction in the volume of credit. This policy was particularly noticeable during the months that followed the crisis of May 1935. In order to defend the franc against a violent speculative attack, coupled with a wholesale outflow of French capital, the Bank of France raised the Bank rate to 6 per cent. At the same time, however, it took good care that there should be no contraction of credit, and thus sought to avoid grave repercussions upon trade. When the crisis was over, the official monetary policy aimed at the reduction of the Bank rate before this became justified by any fall in open market rates brought about by dishoarding and repatriation. Instead of following the tendency of the open market, the Bank of France departed from its traditions by influencing it in a downward direction. The declared object of French monetary policy both under M. Flandin and M. Laval was to bring about a trade revival by means of a policy of easy money. In practice, the results of that policy were negligible, but the good intention was there.

It is safe to say that during the depression the idea of monetary management made considerable progress. Even though the degree of its application in practice remained limited, the experience of Sweden and to a less extent of Great Britain and other countries prepared the way for future progress. The chances are that, even in countries on a gold basis, a higher degree of management than that existing in the past will be considered admissible. As for the countries which are at present off gold, they are not likely to return to the gold standard except in circumstances in which they can enjoy the advantages of a managed monetary system. Even formerly highly orthodox and conservative statesmen such as Mr. Neville Chamberlain have become converted to the idea of monetary management. It is reasonable to assume, therefore, that even though *laissez-faire* may return to a high degree in many spheres of economic life, it will never return in the monetary sphere.

CHAPTER XX

ELASTIC GOLD STANDARD

(1) Internal *v.* International Stability

One of the results of the world's experience during the last twenty years has been an increase in the attention paid to the question of internal monetary stability. Before 1914, the movements of commodity prices were not sufficiently pronounced over short periods to make public opinion realise the disadvantages of the fluctuating purchasing power of money. From 1914 onwards, however, there was ample opportunity for the world to become aware of the consequences of rising and falling prices. It is no wonder that the movement in favour of internal monetary stability, even at the expense of international monetary stability, has gained ground among theoretical economists, practical statesmen and the general public.

As we have seen in earlier chapters, one of the objects of scientific monetary management is to regulate the volume of credit in order to prevent any unwanted changes in the price level. According to one school of thought, this end can be attained without, necessarily, the sacrifice of international currency stability. There is, however, another school of thought which claims to achieve the same end by means of manipulating the international value of the currencies. Instead of advocating control of the volume of credit, this school maintains that it is possible to regulate the price level by changing the gold value of the monetary unit.

The originator of this scheme was Professor Irving Fisher, who in his book *Stabilising the Dollar*, published in 1920, elaborated a most ingenious system based on the principle of maintaining the stability of the monetary units in terms of commodities by changing their gold contents in accordance with requirements. Although the idea was subsequently taken up by various writers in Europe, it remained essentially American, and more recently has received strong support from Professors Warren and Pearson.

(2) Professor Fisher's System

Professor Fisher suggests that the gold weight of the dollar should be varied so as to keep its purchasing power invariable. " We now have a gold dollar of constant weight and varying purchasing power," he said, but " we need a dollar of constant purchasing power and, therefore, of varying weight." In this way he claims to be able to control the price level. The more gold in the dollar the greater its buying power and the lower the price level. If prices tend to rise or fall, he claims to be able to correct the tendency by loading or unloading the gold in the dollar, employing an index number of prices as the guide for such adjustments. If we believe Professor Fisher, the process is as simple as clock-shifting for daylight saving, and would produce its effects as unobtrusively. It is necessary to emphasise that in his view the effect on prices produced by the change in the gold weight of the currency would be automatic, instantaneous, and complete. We all know that a devaluation tends to raise prices, partly because it directly affects the price of imported commodities, partly because it opens the way to internal credit expansion, partly because of its psychological influences. It is not, however, such factors as these, through which devaluation works, that Professor Fisher has in mind. He believes that the mere fact that the gold content of the dollar is changed would in itself be sufficient to produce an exactly corresponding effect upon the price level.

Professor Fisher's system is based on the strictly mechanical conception of the monetary and economic system. As in his quantity theory of money, so in his compensated dollar scheme, he claims to have reduced highly involved tendencies to simple mathematical formulæ and claims to be able to express them in terms of simple arithmetic. The very fact that, throughout his writings, Professor Fisher compares the standard of value with other standards and sees no difference between the rôle of a yardstick and that of the dollar, discloses the fundamental fallacy of the system. The yardstick is applied to measure something very definite and concrete. The monetary unit is applied to measure something essentially vague and abstract.

We are not concerned, however, with the metaphysical aspects of the compensated dollar scheme. The questions that matter are whether in practice it would be possible to manage a currency by systematic adjustment of its gold content; whether such a policy would obviate the necessity for managing the currency by credit control; and whether such a system would have disadvantages which would more than offset the beneficial effect it is claimed to have.

(3) The "Compensated" Currency

It is beyond doubt that the rigidity of the gold parities has been responsible for many of our troubles since 1925. The conception that it is our sacred duty to defend the existing gold parities at all costs has demanded heavy sacrifices at one time or another from practically every country. It is, therefore, not surprising that there is a tendency in world opinion to favour the elastic gold standard. By this system, the currency would remain backed by gold. What is more, it would be even convertible into gold, though not at a fixed figure. The amount of gold obtainable from the monetary authorities for the monetary unit would vary in inverse ratio to the purchasing power of the monetary unit in terms of commodities. If there were a rise in commodity prices and therefore a fall in the purchasing power of the monetary unit, the gold content of the monetary unit would be increased, while if there were a fall in prices and therefore an increase in the purchasing power of the monetary unit, its gold content would be reduced. This system is usually referred to as a "compensated" currency.

According to Professor Fisher and the supporters of his theory, by raising the gold content of the dollar it would be possible to check the rise in prices, while by reducing its gold content the falling tendency of the price level could be brought to a halt. Broadly speaking, there is some truth in this theory. After all, every devaluation (a reduction of the gold content of the monetary unit) is followed by a rise in commodity prices; and although there has been no example to show the effect of a revaluation of the monetary unit in an upward direction (the increase of the gold content of the monetary unit), there can be no doubt that such an act would be followed by a fall in commodity prices.

(4) Simultaneous Devaluation and Prices

The question is, would the same phenomenon occur if the gold content of all monetary units, or at any rate of all important monetary units, were changed simultaneously and to the same extent? And is there any arithmetical ratio between the change in the gold content of the monetary units and its effect upon the price level? It is as difficult to answer the first question as it is easy to answer the second. So far we have had no experience of simultaneous devaluation of all currencies and it is not easy to arrive at definite conclusions as to what would happen. As a matter of common sense, however, it seems probable that simultaneous devaluation of all currencies would not in itself automatically cause a rise in commodity prices. If devaluation in any individual country produces an instantaneous effect upon the price level, it is for two reasons. First of all, it leads to a depreciation of the exchange rate, as a result of which the price of imported commodities rises automatically in proportion. The effect upon commodities produced within the country is less direct, but, given a certain degree of freedom in international trade, the chances are that the internal price level as a whole will tend in the long run to adjust itself to the world level.

This process of readjustment is hastened by the monetary expansion that usually follows devaluation. If the authorities of a country prevent the volume of currency and credit from adjusting itself to the new level of the monetary unit, then the process of internal readjustment can be delayed and held up altogether. This was in fact the case of France after the devaluation of the franc. Evidently, it is not the mere fact of the change of the gold content of the monetary unit that brings about the change in the price level. The change is due to two tendencies of readjustment, namely, the readjustment of inland prices to the world level and the readjustment of the volume of currency and credit to the new level of the monetary unit.

If all currencies are devalued simultaneously and to the same extent, there is no need for prices in any country to adjust themselves to the world level, since the latter will remain unchanged in terms of both national and foreign currencies. There would of course be a tendency towards credit expansion, and to that extent there would be a tendency towards a rise in prices. What matters is that in itself a change in the gold content of the monetary unit does not affect the price level.

(5) Price Adjustment never Complete

Even if the devaluation were carried out by one isolated country only, the effect upon prices would never be in exact proportion to the extent of the change in the gold content of the monetary unit. It would be possible to quote innumerable examples to show the wide discrepancy between the extent of the devaluation of currencies and its immediate effect upon prices. It is true that in the long run prices to a large extent become adjusted to the new value of the currency, though the adjustment is never complete. Even in 1931, several years after the devaluation of their currencies, France and Belgium were cheaper countries to live in than Great Britain or Italy. It was not until the world price level began to decline towards the price level of the countries with undervalued currencies, that the readjustment began; it was, however, soon unsettled once more by a depreciation of a number of currencies.

In any case, from the point of view of the efficiency of Professor Fisher's scheme, it is the immediate effect on prices, and not the effect in the long run, that matters. His aim is to readjust a movement of commodity prices immediately it is noticed, not in twelve months' time or three years' time. From this point of view, the proposed method of adjusting the gold content of the unit in exact proportion to the change of the ideal index number which represents the true purchasing power of the currency cannot possibly be satisfactory. If, according to his suggestion, a rise in the index number by 1 per cent is followed by an increase of the gold content of the dollar by 1 per cent, the result will not be a fall in the index number by 1 per cent as Professor Fisher anticipates. Conceivably, there may be an immediate fall by, say, ¼ per cent, and a fall in six months' time by ½ per cent. In order to provoke an immediate fall of prices by a full 1 per cent it would be necessary to increase the gold content of the dollar not by 1 per cent but probably by 4 or 5 per cent. In the long run, such an increase would, needless to say, lead to an unnecessary and uncalled-for fall of prices of rather more than

1 per cent, so that the disturbing effect of the remedy would be much stronger than that of the disease which it claims to cure.

According to a modified version of Professor Fisher's scheme, the index number which would serve as the basis for the adjustment of the gold content of the currency should not be that of the general level of wholesale prices but that of a selected group of basic products. As far as these products are concerned, the existence of a good market in them in most of the important countries, and the possibility of regular arbitrage between these markets, secures a high degree of uniformity in their prices in various countries. Thus, if one of the countries changes its parity through changing the gold content of its currency, the effect upon the selected group of prices of basic products is instantaneous. To that limited extent the effect of a change in the gold contents of the currency would thus be fully effective. It would not, however, achieve the desired end, which is to prevent the wide fluctuation of the general price level in the broadest sense of the term. Indeed, if excessive internal expansion should lead to a rising tendency in the price level, the reduction of the price of basic products might in given circumstances accentuate the rise of other groups of prices.

(6) Frequent Changes of Parities Undesirable

The readjustment of the monetary unit at frequent intervals—possibly every day, for the daily index number of commodity prices seldom remains the same for two days running—would be anything but desirable. It would produce an unsettling effect which would deprive the gold standard of one of its main advantages. Since the index numbers of various countries fluctuate in different proportions and often in different directions, the proposed system would perpetuate the fluctuation of exchanges. This in itself would have an unsettling effect upon internal price levels, and would necessitate more frequent and larger scale changes of the monetary unit.

It is very easy to reduce Professor Fisher's proposals to absurdity. Many opponents of monetary reform have done so repeatedly, thinking that by exposing the weakness of one particular reform scheme they can prove the superiority of the orthodox system. Professor Fisher's scheme, like every other reform scheme, whether put forward by economists of international reputation or by obscure currency cranks, should be approached in a constructive spirit. Untenable though it may appear in the form in which it is proposed, it may contain some useful element which can and should be retained. While the literal application of Professor Fisher's scheme for the adjustment of small percentages in the change of the price level would be utterly futile, the underlying principle that strong and lasting tendencies in the price level of a country can be readjusted by the change of its parities should be remembered.

Professor Fisher is hopelessly wrong in trying to establish arithmetical relation between cause and effect where there is none. He is right in claiming that an increase in the gold content of a currency tends to cause a fall in prices and that a reduction tends to cause a rise in prices. If it were proposed that the monetary unit should be adjusted, not every day in a futile attempt to readjust price fluctuations of 1 per cent and less, but only once in ten years or twenty years to correct changes amounting to 10 or 20 per cent, then the idea would be both feasible and useful. In Chapter XXII, which deals with proposals concerning alterable gold parities, we shall try to explain how the principle in this modified form would work. Even though elastic parities are impracticable, the system of alterable parities represents a happy medium between this extreme and that other extreme which demands the defence of existing parities with the last drop of our blood. Professors Fisher, Warren and Pearson have certainly done a valuable service in stimulating the development of a sceptical attitude towards the belief that parities are absolutely unalterable and sacrosanct. Even though they are guilty of going to the other extreme, they have nevertheless achieved a useful result by attacking the orthodox conception from their professorial chairs. Their academic position and their world-wide reputation secured them a hearing where less fortunately placed reformers would have been merely sneered at. The fact that scientifically trained first-rate minds consider an alternative to perpetually rigid parities possible and desirable must have set many people thinking. Even those who refused to accept the gospel of the elastic gold standard may have become more receptive to the moderate conception of alterable parities.

CHAPTER XXI

THE "RUBBER DOLLAR" IN PRACTICE

(1) President Roosevelt's Experiment

Professor Irving Fisher is among the few academic economists who have had the satisfaction of witnessing—even if for a short time—the adoption of their reform proposals by their countries. Thanks mainly to the influence of Professor Warren, towards the middle of 1933 President Roosevelt became converted to a policy aiming at the maintenance of the stability of the dollar in terms of commodities. This idea was expressed in the President's famous message of July 3, 1933, addressed to the World Economic Conference, in which he said: "Old fetishes of so-called international bankers are being replaced by efforts to plan national currencies with the objective of giving to those currencies a continuous purchasing power which does not greatly vary in terms of commodities. . . . The United States seeks the kind of dollar which a generation hence will have the same purchasing and debt paying power as the dollar value we hope to attain in the near future. That objective means more to the good of other nations than a fixed ratio for a month or two in terms of the pound or franc."

President Roosevelt went even further in identifying himself with the idea of an elastic gold dollar in his broadcast message of October 22, 1933, when he announced the inauguration of the famous gold buying policy. In authorising the Reconstruction Finance Corporation to buy gold newly mined in the United States at prices to be determined from time to time, President Roosevelt declared that his aim in taking this step was "to establish and maintain continuous control". He went out of his way to emphasise that the arrangement thus established was a policy and not an expedient. "It is not to be used merely to offset a temporary fall in prices." He added, " We are thus continuing to move towards a managed currency."

Although the terms in which the President declared his new policy were rather vague, in substance the gold buying arrangement amounted to the restoration of a limited gold standard with elastic parities. It is true that the object of this policy was not to maintain the stability of the price level but to raise it. Nevertheless, the fact remains that, acting upon Professor Warren's advice, President Roosevelt attempted to achieve monetary management by means of changing the gold parities of the dollar. Indeed, the opponents of the system indulged in cheap sarcasm by coining the phrase " the rubber dollar ", to describe President Roosevelt's system, alluding to the elasticity of the monetary unit.

(2) Prices Unaffected

President Roosevelt's system was, however, even more inadequate than the scheme put forward by Professor Irving Fisher. The latter's scheme at any rate would have had the merit of bringing about an instantaneous adjustment of the dollar exchange rate in the desired direction. If the gold contents of a gold currency are changed there is naturally an immediate adjustment of the exchange rates to the new parities. The changes in the gold buying price brought about by President Roosevelt's policy did not produce a similar effect, for the simple reason that the price concerned only newly mined American gold. The discrepancy between this price and the world market price for gold was not allowed to be adjusted by means of arbitrage shipments in either direction. For this reason, discrepancies were inclined to be rather wide. At first the dollar-franc exchange lagged far behind the changes in the gold parity caused by the increases in the gold buying price. Subsequently, towards the middle of November 1933, the continuous advance of the gold buying price resulted in speculative selling of dollars which caused the exchange to depreciate far beyond the new provisional parity.

Owing to the excessive depreciation of the dollar, there was every reason for the changes in the gold parities to produce a strong effect upon commodity prices. In reality, between October and December 1933, the wholesale index in the United

States fell from 102 to 101·4, notwithstanding the reduction of the gold value of the dollar during that period. The index number of cost of living also declined from 78 to 77·3. This experience is a glaring illustration of the failure of Professor Fisher's theory, which is based entirely upon the assumption that the effect of a change in the gold value of a currency upon its commodity value is automatic and instantaneous. It was only subsequently that the depreciation of the dollar caused by the reduction of its gold content began gradually to produce its effect. Twelve months after the inauguration of the gold policy the rise of wholesale prices was only 7·6 per cent, while the rise in the cost of living was barely 3 per cent. Not until eighteen months after the dollar was devalued did the policy produce its effect, and even then the effect was far from proportionate to the extent of the change in the gold content of the dollar.

The experience of the United States goes a long way towards proving that in the form Professor Fisher proposed it, the system of the elastic gold standard is impracticable. At the same time, it also proves that, taking a long view, it is possible to provoke a trend in commodity prices or check an unwanted trend by altering the gold value of a currency.

(3) Elastic Gold Standard in Britain

The United States was not the only country in which a kind of elastic gold standard has been in operation. It is not generally realised that, ever since September 1931, Great Britain has also adopted a peculiar form of elastic gold standard. Although Great Britain suspended the gold standard on September 21, 1931, the pound sterling has never for a moment ceased to be convertible into gold. In other countries which suspended the gold standard, holders of notes ceased to be in a position to acquire gold in a legitimate way, and their facilities for acquiring gold illegitimately were limited. In Great Britain, thanks to the existence of an open and unrestricted market in gold, everybody remained at liberty to exchange his notes for gold. All that happened was that the notes ceased to be convertible into gold at a fixed parity. They could be converted, however, to an unlimited extent at the current market price. Indeed, it may be said that Great Britain adopted a new monetary system, a kind of elastic gold standard in which notes remained convertible into gold and the export of gold remained free, and which differed from the orthodox system mainly in that the gold parity was elastic instead of being rigid.

The mere fact that there was an open market for gold in London, which was allowed to exercise its function without the legal restrictions customary in countries which had suspended the gold standard, would not in itself justify this interpretation of the new monetary situation in Great Britain. Had the facilities of the London gold market remained approximately the same as before the suspension of the gold standard, the market would not have assumed this significance from a monetary point of view. For before 1931 the facilities provided by the London gold market were by no means unlimited. As often as not, buyers were able to satisfy their requirements only on one day during the week, and even a most persistent demand would not have resulted in an increase in the supply. Sellers were in a better position to dispose of their stocks than buyers to cover their requirements, but this was only because between 1925 and 1931 there happened to be a persistent monetary demand for gold.

(4) The London Gold Market

At present, however, the London gold market is in a position to satisfy any requirements and to absorb any supply. Although there is no official seller bound by statutes to sell on demand an unlimited amount of gold, the supply in the open market is practically unlimited. Although there is no official buyer bound by law to take over at a fixed price any supplies which no one else wants, the open market is in a position to absorb a practically unlimited quantity of gold.

Apart from the increase in the turnover and the greater elasticity of supply and demand in the London gold market, its rise to prominence has also been due to the freedom from legal interference or moral pressure to which would-be purchasers of gold are exposed in other countries. After the suspension of the gold standard, the legal status of the gold market remained unchanged. As before, everybody was at liberty to buy or sell gold in unlimited amounts at any price, to hold it in this country, or to have it shipped abroad. Other countries suspending the gold standard imposed restrictions on the acquisition and holding of gold by private interests. Some countries went so far as to compel holders to surrender their gold stock against the payment of the statutory buying price of the monetary authorities. In Great Britain the only limitation of this kind is the right of the Bank of England under the Currency and Bank Notes Act of 1928 to compel holders resident in this country to surrender their holding in excess of £10,000 against the payment of the statutory selling price. Even this power has not been utilised except in the case of gold held by British banks. In any case, the power existed before the suspension of the gold standard. As for foreign holders, their freedom is as complete as in any country on an effective gold standard. British subjects are of course also entitled to buy gold in unlimited amounts for the purpose of exporting it; and to import gold for sale to foreigners without running the risk of being compelled to surrender it at a lower price. In this respect, the situation in Great Britain resembles much more closely that of a country on a gold basis than that of a country with an inconvertible currency.

(5) Exchange Equalisation Account's Rôle

The elastic parities of sterling are to a large extent controlled by the Exchange Equalisation Account. It is true that other influences are at times predominant, but it is safe to state that, taking a long view, sterling has moved in accordance with the official policy. In this sense, the British Government has thus pursued a somewhat similar policy to that of President Roosevelt between October 1933 and January 1934. In Great Britain the aim of the official policy was merely to prevent excessive fluctuations of sterling, at the same time allowing it to find its natural level. There was no deliberate attempt to cause a rise in commodity prices through the operations of the Exchange Equalisation Account, or even to prevent any fall in commodity prices that might otherwise have taken place. In practice, however, a fall of prices was actually avoided as the result of the official policy. The difference between the British and American attitude towards a policy of elastic parities is that, during the short period of its application in the United States, President Roosevelt regarded it as a permanent policy that had inaugurated a new era, while the British Government has always regarded the elasticity of sterling as a necessary evil which must be avoided as soon as conditions have improved sufficiently for the restoration of the gold standard. Nevertheless, the system has been in operation in Britain for four years. The saying that "ce n'est que le temporaire qui dure" is sometimes true outside France.

In a sense, any policy which aims at a depreciation or appreciation of the national currency, even if the policy has no bearing upon gold parities, is similar to the system of the elastic gold standard. Every country which either devalues or depreciates its currency in order to bring about a rise in its price level is thus, consciously or otherwise, a follower of Professor Irving Fisher. After all, even if a currency is not convertible into gold either *de jure* or *de facto*, its depreciation involves a reduction of its gold value, so that if the depreciation is engineered for the purpose of raising the internal price level or avoiding a fall, then it amounts to the application of Professor Fisher's principle. Indeed, we may even go so far as to say that the changes in the international value of a currency produce just as instantaneous and direct an effect upon the price level as could possibly be expected of the Fisher scheme of elastic parities. Apart from this effect, the effect of the change in the gold content of a currency can manifest itself only through a credit expansion or contraction following upon the increase or reduction of the gold basis of credit through the change of the gold content of the monetary unit. As the American experiment of 1933–4 showed, in itself the increase of the internal price of gold in terms of the monetary unit does not produce the magic effect Professor Fisher expects it to produce.

The prospects for the adoption of the elastic gold standard in the narrower sense of the term are anything but bright. Since the end of January 1934, when the dollar was pegged to gold at a definite parity, nothing further has been said in America about the adoption of the scheme as a definite system. Professor Warren faded into the background and those who at present constitute the so-called "brain trust" of President Roosevelt are definitely opposed to a further reduction of the gold weight of the dollar. In Great Britain, too, the fluctuations of sterling in terms of gold became quite narrow during the second half of 1935. Even though developments such as the devaluation of the gold currencies may lead to fresh fluctuations, the declared aim is the eventual definite stabilisation of sterling in terms of gold. In any case, the idea of the elastic gold standard as a permanent system never had any following in Great Britain or in any other country outside the United States. The broader application and interpretation of the scheme in the form of alterable gold parities will be dealt with in the following chapter.

CHAPTER XXII

ALTERABLE GOLD PARITIES

(1) Parities no longer Sacrosanct

Throughout the nineteenth century it was taken for granted that the interests of mankind could best be served by a monetary system in which the currency was maintained at a fixed parity in relation to gold. This conception had taken such deep roots in the minds of statesmen, economists and the general public that even after the war, in spite of the fundamental changes of conditions, most countries considered it their supreme duty to restore their currencies to their pre-war parities and maintain these parities at all costs. Even countries such as France and Italy, where post-war conditions resulted in a substantial depreciation of the exchange, were reluctant to give up hope of the eventual return to the pre-war parity. Great Britain and the Scandinavian countries restored their currencies to their pre-war gold value at the cost of heavy sacrifices, and maintained them there until the crisis, in spite of the obvious disadvantages of this policy. Once the gold standard was restored at the old parities, it would have been regarded as sacrilege to suggest that these currencies should be devalued. Similarly, when countries where post-war inflation assumed high dimensions reluctantly consented to devalue their currencies, public opinion became determined that these new parities should be maintained, and regarded them as just as sacrosanct as they did the old parities before the war.

The experience of 1931–6 has gone a long way towards undermining this well-established conception. The world has witnessed the suspension of the gold standard in countries which have always been regarded as the outstanding examples of commercial and financial integrity. Even though Great Britain was driven off the gold standard when her means of defending the pound were completely exhausted, several countries of high standing followed her example while still in possession of substantial gold reserves. The Scandinavian countries, which had always been considered first-class, were the first to forsake their parities without being actually driven off them. It is true that, had they attempted to defend their parities, they would have had to yield in the course of a few months or a few years, but the fact remains that, at the time when they suspended the gold standard, they were still technically in a position to defend it. The same holds good for Japan and to a much larger degree for the United States. President Roosevelt's action in 1933 has created a precedent for the suspension of the gold standard by a country with a very strong gold reserve, for the purpose of relieving pressure caused by a heavy fall of prices. It is a precedent which will be of importance in future financial history. It has prepared the ground for the monetary reform scheme of alterable gold parities.

(2) A Matter of Expediency

While the suspension of the gold standard by a number of countries which were not forced off gold draws attention to the possibility of abandoning old parities as a matter of expediency, the examples of the devaluation of currencies under adverse pressure indicate the line which is suggested by the advocates of the policy of alterable parities as a basis for future monetary policy. Czechoslovakia, Belgium, Luxemburg and the Free City of Danzig, instead of suspending the gold standard, changed their parities overnight, reducing the exchange value of their currencies to a level at which they hoped that the adverse pressure would cease. To suggest that they were prompted by a recognition of the fact that the defence of parities is only a means to an end and not the end itself, and that such a defence should be abandoned if and when it is realised that the sacrifices involved would outweigh the results obtained, would be reading too much into the decision of the Governments concerned. In each case, the devaluation was decided upon as an emergency measure, and little attention was paid to its theoretical background. Nevertheless, these acts of devaluation constitute important precedents which have assisted in the development of the monetary scheme of alterable gold parities.

The system of alterable parities is not identical with Professor Fisher's system of elastic parities. According to the latter even a moderate price movement should be met by an adjustment of the gold parity. According to the system of alterable parities, the adjustment should be reserved for major emergencies, when the pressure against the existing parities threatens to be intolerable. While under the Fisher scheme the changes would be small and frequent, under the system of alterable parities they would be substantial and infrequent. A compensated currency with elastic parities might necessitate weekly or monthly changes in its parity, to the extent of one per cent or even less at a time. Under the system of alterable parities, conceivably there would be no change for years or even decades; but when the change became inevitable it would have to be at the rate of 10 per cent or more in order to remedy the accumulated disequilibrium. In fact, unless there were a disequilibrium of considerable magnitude, the necessity for altering the parity would not arise. When it did arise it would be considered as the smaller of two evils; but according to the philosophy of the compensated currency the adjustment of parities to price tendencies would be a normal procedure.

(3) Experimental *v.* Alterable Parities

The system of alterable parities is something totally different also from that of experimental parities. The latter are the result of pre-stabilisation or *de facto* stabilisation or possibly of some form of experimental stabilisation. The idea of the system of alterable parities, however, is that they should be regarded as subject to alteration not only during the first few months or years following upon stabilisation, but at any time in the future. While experimental parities, as the name implies, constitute a temporary expedient, alterable parities constitute a definite system, a modified form of the gold standard.

In his book on *The Future of Gold* published in 1934, the author was among the first to put forward a suggestion for alterable parities. On page 68, he pointed out that it was possible that the general conception of the sacrosanct character of mint parities might change, and that many people would be willing to support the idea of a stabilisation, provided that the parities chosen were not regarded as something absolutely unalterable, and provided that their defence was not considered the supreme duty of the nation in any circumstances and at all costs. He repeated and elaborated this suggestion in his book *World Finance since 1914*, published in May 1935. Since then several economists of international reputation have pronounced themselves in favour of such a solution. In an article in *The Economist*, Sir Arthur Salter put forward an identical suggestion, while an international conference of economists held at Antwerp arrived at a similar conclusion, among others. The report of this conference, advocating alterable parities, was signed by three leading English economists, Mr. J. M. Keynes, Mr. H. D. Henderson and Mr. R. F. Harrod.

The difference between the views held by these economists and those put forward by the author is that the former would like to stabilise immediately on the understanding that the parities could always be modified if necessary, while the author is opposed to stabilisation unless and until conditions are such as to remove the likelihood of an alteration of the parities. In his view, once the currency is stabilised, there will be a tendency to defend it at the price of sacrifices out of proportion to the advantages of its stability. Public opinion is not yet ripe for the system of alterable parities, even though, as we have already pointed out, the experience of the last few years has gone a long way towards undermining the belief in the sacrosanct character of parities. The longer we keep off gold, the more the idea of alterable parities will establish itself.

In any case, a change of parities is not something essentially desirable which should be resorted to light-heartedly at the slightest pressure. To avoid the necessity for too frequent changes it is advisable to stabilise currencies in circumstances which secure an ample safety margin of reserves. This question will be dealt with in detail in Chapter XXV.

(4) Defence of Alterable Parities

Those opposed to the system of alterable parities argue that, if it is understood that a Government is entitled to change the parities of its currency, the task of defending that currency against an adverse pressure will become very difficult. It is argued that the reason why it is easier to defend a gold currency than an inconvertible currency is that, at any rate, some of the speculators rely upon the defence of the gold parities at all costs. When an exchange depreciates to gold export point there are always speculators who are willing to buy that exchange on the assumption that it will not be allowed to depreciate any further. This support by speculators does not exist to the same extent as far as inconvertible paper currencies are concerned. Although there may be speculators who consider a currency undervalued at the prevailing market price, there is not the same inducement for them to buy that currency as there is in the case of a gold currency which depreciates to gold export point. For, in the case of inconvertible currency, one rate is more or less as good as another, and there is no special figure, such as the gold export point of a gold currency, at which the authorities are likely to defend it even at the cost of great sacrifice.

It is also argued that, if the parities are not unalterable, every time there is an adverse pressure there is bound to be a feeling of uncertainty as to whether the Government is likely to resist or to yield. Such an uncertainty is bound to be detrimental to trade and is bound to accentuate the flight of capital. Admittedly there is also a high degree of uncertainty when a gold currency is subject to adverse pressure, as we have witnessed time after time during the last few years. This uncertainty will be quite considerable now that we have had the experience of a number of gold standard suspensions and devaluations by countries whose gold reserves were not actually exhausted.

(5) "Unalterable" Parity not Adequate Safeguard

Until 1931, it was generally assumed that in time of peace a country could, or would, suspend the gold standard only after it had spent practically the last penny of its gold reserve in defence of the parity. This principle was confirmed by the British experience. On the other hand, it was disregarded by every other country which went off gold or devalued its currency after September 21, 1931. Thus, the fact that the gold reserve of a country whose currency is subject to adverse pressure is not exhausted can no longer be regarded as a guarantee that its Government will not decide to abandon the defence of its parity. From this point of view, the difference between a gold currency and an inconvertible paper currency is merely one of degree. Similarly, the difference between a gold currency whose parity is declared unalterable and another whose parity is admittedly alterable is also merely one of degree.

The only safeguard against uncertainty caused by the possibility of a change in the parities is, as we have already pointed out, stabilisation in circumstances which secure such an ample safety margin as to place the currency in question above suspicion. Needless to say, this is not the only circumstance required to safeguard the currency. A much more important condition is that, before the currencies are stabilised, all major disequilibria, internal or international, should be removed, or at any rate reduced to tolerable proportions.

The system of alterable parities has found practical application in the United States since January 30, 1934. It was adopted to take the place of the system of elastic parities which was in operation between October 22, 1933, and January 30, 1934: from the latter date, the parity of the dollar was fixed at 41 per cent under its old parity and the President was authorised to change it to any figure between 40 and 50 per cent below the old parity. It is true that this arrangement was adopted only temporarily, although the system of alterable parities implies a more or less permanent arrangement. As, however, at the time of writing, the American system has been in operation for over two years (and the discretionary powers have lately been extended for a further year), it may be regarded as an example of the system of alterable parities. There has so far been no need for President Roosevelt to avail himself of his right to change the parity because it was fixed in circumstances which provided an ample safety margin, and which secured a steady buying pressure on the dollar instead of a selling pressure. The authorities of a country can always defend their currency almost indefinitely against a buying pressure; it is only in face of a selling pressure that their power is limited.

(6) Widening the Range between Gold Points

The system of alterable parities should not be confused with a reform measure proposed by Mr. Keynes, according to which under the new gold standard there should be a wider margin of fluctuation for exchanges than was possible under the old system, and that to that end Central Banks should be at liberty to alter their gold price within a certain range. The difference between this proposal and the system of alterable parities is that under the former the range within which parities could be altered would be very narrow, while under the system of alterable parities there would be a fairly wide range, if indeed the extent of possible alteration were fixed at all. Moreover, the two systems differ in their objects: Mr. Keynes's proposal merely aims at counteracting temporary disturbing influences, while the system of alterable parities is intended to become operative only in face of sweeping fundamental tendencies. As, however, both reforms would in practice work in the same way, and the difference between them is largely one of degree, we propose to examine Mr. Keynes's proposal in the course of this chapter.

There is indeed a good deal to be said in favour of widening the margin between gold points. In an article in the *Economic Journal* of March 1927 and in his book on *International Gold Movements*, the author pointed out the tendency towards a contraction of this margin and emphasised the inconvenience of frequent gold movements caused by the narrowness of the range between the gold points. He cannot but approve, therefore, Mr. Keynes's concrete proposal by which the widening of the margin could be effectively achieved. Since 1927, when the author's article appeared, the contraction of gold points has continued, mainly as a result of the fall in interest rates which, to some extent at any rate, will be of a lasting nature. Moreover, the contraction of gold points between sterling and the dollar through the establishment of Transatlantic air services foreseen by the author in 1927 is likely to become a reality in the not-too-distant future. There is, therefore, more reason than ever to be concerned about the unduly narrow range between gold points after the restoration of the gold standard. It is anything but desirable that, owing to the low cost of gold arbitrage, there should be frequent gold movements in both directions as a result of relatively insignificant passing tendencies. There is, therefore, everything to be said in favour of a proposal which would maintain the range between gold points at a reasonable level. In Volume II of his *Treatise on Money*, Mr. Keynes suggests that the difference between a Central Bank's statutory buying and selling price for gold, which at present is in most countries a mere fraction of one per cent, should be widened to, say, 2 per cent. As a result, the range between gold points would widen to somewhere between 2½ and 3 per cent. To the author's mind, this would be about the ideal range. Fluctuations up to 3 per cent certainly would not unsettle international trade. As the Central Banks would be at liberty to alter their gold buying and selling price within the suggested range of 2 per cent, they would be in a position to influence the gold points in a desired direction whenever necessary.

(7) Normal *v.* Abnormal Pressure

With the aid of this technical device, it would be possible to reduce considerably the disturbing effect of gold movements originating in normal circumstances as a result of a discrepancy between interest rates in two centres, or of some passing adverse pressure on one of the currencies. In a way, a reduction of the gold parity by, say, 2 per cent would tend to produce the same effect upon the international movement of funds as an increase of the bank rate. With the exchange at about 1½ per cent under par and 3 per cent under gold import point, there is to speculators of a conservative type a strong inducement to acquire funds, for such speculators are satisfied with a relatively moderate profit provided that their risk is limited. Banking houses which would not think of keeping overnight open positions in an inconvertible currency, would yield to the temptation of a possible profit of 1½ to 3 per cent from "going long" in a currency which was at gold export point. That is, they would be prepared to take a position so long as they saw no reason to distrust the currency concerned.

It cannot be sufficiently emphasised that the proposed device can be applied successfully only if the pressure is not due to a flight from the currency. But if the selling pressure is due to distrust—whether or not distrust is justified by the existence of fundamental disequilibrium—then all technical devices, including the increase of the bank rate, are useless. Unquestionably, if there were a flight from the currency, the fact that the Central Bank reduced its parity to the lower limit would be likely to encourage the flight rather than discourage it. This would be especially so if the gold standard were restored on the understanding that in face of fundamental pressure the Government reserved the right to make substantial alterations in the parity. It is sometimes difficult even for the monetary authorities to ascertain whether or not a selling pressure is due to fundamental causes. As for the market, it is always inclined to exaggerate the significance of any movement that happens to occur, whether in an upward or in a downward direction. Thus, if the public is nervous about the safety of the currency, then the lowering of the gold price by the Central Bank would in all probability increase the prevalent pessimism.

(8) The Example of 1930

Mr. Keynes in his various writings made it quite clear that he did not mean to suggest an alteration of the parity in face of a sweeping attack on a currency. Such a change could be effective only when the temporary and technical nature of the weakness is evident. Had such a device been applied by Great Britain at any time between 1925 and the middle of 1929, it would in all probability have been effective. Had it been applied, however, at a time when foreign holders of sterling were beginning to feel uneasy, it would have been useless. This is duly illustrated by the experience at the end of 1930 and the beginning of 1931, when the unwillingness of the Bank of France to accept gold of standard fineness and the inability of the Bank of England to pay out fine gold resulted in a considerable widening of the gold points of sterling. Once there is uneasiness about the safety of a currency the exchange will inevitably depreciate to gold export point wherever that gold export point happens to be. If gold export point is lowered, by no matter what measures, the exchange is bound to decline to the lower level instantaneously.

This is what actually happened in 1930, when sterling depreciated well below its former gold export point. Admittedly, the example is not perfect, because amidst the circumstances prevailing at the time the new gold export point of sterling was very vague and arbitrageurs were not in a position to ascertain exactly the limit beyond which its depreciation could not continue. It stands to reason, however, that even if there had been a definite lower gold export point the distrust of sterling would have induced speculators to sell rather than to buy.

(9) Complementary Technical Devices

While it is evident that the proposed broadening of the margin between gold points would be useless against a flight from the currency, its advantages as a means of counteracting normal seasonal influences or international transfers of funds through arbitrage are incontestable. It is solely for such purposes that Mr. Keynes has put forward his proposal. For the same purpose he also advocates the control of forward exchange rates by Central Banks. This second proposal will be examined in detail in Chapter XXIII. Here we will confine ourselves to pointing out that the two proposals are to a large degree complementary. They both serve the purpose of counteracting temporary selling pressure on the currency, as an alternative to the orthodox method of allowing gold to leave the country or of raising the bank rate to check the efflux. Suppose, for example, that there is a selling pressure on sterling owing to a higher level of interest rates prevailing in the United States, coupled with a moderate degree of distrust in sterling, and the Government is anxious to abstain from interfering with home trade by raising the bank rate or by allowing the outflow of gold to cause a contraction of credit. In such a case, Mr. Keynes's proposals would provide the ideal means for their purpose. The Central Bank would lower the price of gold to its legal limit, thereby making sterling attractive to speculators. At the same time, it would keep the discount on forward sterling reasonably narrow or would even put it at a premium, in spite of the distrust in sterling, so as to make it worth while for foreign holders of sterling balances to retain or even increase their holdings notwithstanding the higher rate offered in New York. The lowering of the gold price would tend to facilitate the task of keeping the forward rate at an overvalued level, for there would be a natural demand for forward sterling on speculative account. Conversely, the control of the forward rate by the Central Bank would assist the lowering of the gold price in producing the desired effect, for it would prevent withdrawals of funds by arbitrage and thus would enable speculative buying to cause an appreciation. All this assumes, of course, that there is no *fundamental* cause for distrust in the stability of the currency.

The technical devices proposed by Mr. Keynes would be able to do all the work done in the technical sphere by the bank rate under the orthodox system. Admittedly, they would not produce the whole effect of the bank rate, for, as is well known, in addition to influencing the international movement of funds, the bank rate tends to affect the exchanges also by forcing down commodity prices at the cost of destroying trade. It is only this destructive function of the bank rate that cannot be replaced by the devices proposed by Mr. Keynes. His proposals have the merit of exposing the destructive character of the orthodox bank rate policy. Anything that the raising of the bank rate could achieve by constructive means could be achieved just as well by the control of the forward exchange and the reduction of the gold price by the Central Bank. If in spite of this the orthodox bank rate policy is resorted to, it is evidently with the object of counteracting international influences by deliberately destroying home trade. It is well that this fact should be duly realised.

CHAPTER XXIII

FORWARD EXCHANGE OPERATIONS BY CENTRAL BANKS

(1) Mr. Keynes's Proposal

Among the proposed technical devices which, it is claimed, would be reforms of fundamental importance, the suggestion that Central Banks should operate systematically in forward exchanges occupies a prominent place. The proposal was made originally at the Genoa Conference, but the resolution passed to that effect was never applied by the majority of Central Banks; to a large extent, it remained a dead letter. Its chief supporter is Mr. J. M. Keynes, who, in his books *A Tract on Monetary Reform* and *A Treatise on Money*, and more recently in an article in *Lloyds Bank Monthly Review*, strongly emphasises the advantages of the operation of Central Banks in the forward exchange market. He considers that the adoption of this device is a means by which short-term pressure upon the exchanges could be overcome without disturbance of the internal credit structure.

Mr. Keynes's argument runs on the following lines: Occasions arise on which it is desirable from the point of view of internal trade to maintain a low rate of interest while at the same time it is also desirable to attract or retain foreign balances. In order to be able to attain the latter end without having to raise the bank rate, Mr. Keynes suggests that the Central Banks should fix forward exchange rates at a level at which it is profitable for foreign holders to maintain or increase their balances in the national currency notwithstanding the relatively low interest rates they obtain.

(2) The "Interest Parity"

To understand this highly involved argument—which the Macmillan Committee refused to consider on account of its highly technical character—it is necessary to cast a glance at the relation between interest rates and forward exchange rates. Under normal conditions the forward exchange rate between two stable currencies tends to represent the difference between interest rates on short-term loans in the two markets. We may conveniently call the figure the "interest parity". If there were a perpetual state of equilibrium between the interest parity and the forward exchange rate, there would never be any particular advantage from the point of view of the yield in shifting funds from one centre to the other. In practice, however, discrepancies arise frequently and, pending their readjustment, it becomes profitable to transfer balances between the two centres. Discrepancies which give rise to such shifting of funds may arise either through a change in the ratio between interest rates in the two centres or through a change in the forward exchange rate.

In theory, the change in the interest parity should always automatically cause a corresponding adjustment of the forward rate, so that, apart from a very brief transition period, the state of equilibrium is not supposed to be disturbed. In practice, however, things do not always work out in this way. Forward exchange rates are subject to influences other than those of relative interest rates, and it may take some time before the readjustment is complete. Meanwhile, one of the centres is bound to lose foreign balances and gold unless it raises its interest rates so as to accelerate the restoration of equilibrium between the interest parity and the forward exchange rate. This latter measure was in the past considered as the classical remedy to be employed on occasions when a rise of the bank rate in a foreign centre was followed by a selling pressure on the national currency.

(3) An Alternative to Bank Rate

The increase of the bank rate for such purposes involves, however, unjustified hardships for internal trade. Mr. Keynes suggests, therefore, that instead of allowing foreign funds to leave the country as a result of the increase of the forward discount—under the gold standard such an efflux tends to cause a contraction of credit, and therefore unduly penalises internal trade—the monetary authorities should take steps to readjust the discrepancy by influencing the forward exchange rate in the direction required. They can do so by undertaking to deal in the national currency for forward delivery at a rate corresponding to the interest parity between the two centres.

Conversely, if a centre suffers from *embarras de richesse* as a result of an unwanted influx of foreign funds, attracted by relatively high interest rates, it is in a position to discourage the movement without having to stimulate excessive speculation by unduly lowering the bank rate. In accordance with Mr. Keynes's proposal, it would have to quote favourable rates for forward foreign currencies, thereby causing a depreciation of the forward national currency. As a result, the transfer of funds to the centre concerned would cease to become profitable and the influx of funds would, therefore, cease. As Mr. Keynes rightly points out, the fixing of forward rates provides good scope for quiet collaboration between the Central Banks. They may jointly arrive at an understanding to fix the forward exchange rate between two currencies at a figure at which the unwanted movement of funds ceases.

To illustrate the case, let us quote the example given by Mr. Keynes in his *Treatise on Money* (p. 326).

> In the autumn of 1928, local conditions in the United States convinced the Federal Reserve Board that the short-period interest rate should be raised in the interest of business stability. But local conditions in Great Britain were of a precisely opposite character and the Bank of England was anxious to keep money as cheap as possible. The Federal Reserve Board did not desire that its high rates should attract gold from Great Britain, for this had it occurred would have tended to defeat its efforts. Nor did the Bank of England desire to impose high rates in Great Britain (to which it might be driven) in order to prevent its gold from flowing out.

Here was a case in which the desired end could well have been achieved by means of fixing the forward sterling-dollar rate at a figure at which the higher rates prevailing in New York ceased to attract funds from London. In the absence of such arrangements, the Bank of England was forced by the outflow of gold to raise its bank rate in 1929, however inconvenient this was from the point of view of the internal situation.

(4) Limitations of the Reform

It is necessary, however, to bear in mind that the adjustment of forward exchange rates in itself would not influence the whole of the international transfer of short-term funds, for many holders of such funds do not always consider it essential to cover the forward exchange. Therein lies one of the limitations of the proposed device. It would have been able to check only part of the movement of funds from London to New York in 1928 and 1929—that part which was transferred solely for the purpose of taking advantage of higher interest rates, and which was, therefore, covered against exchange risk. At the same time, possibly the attraction provided to interest arbitrage funds by an artificially favourable forward rate might have partly counteracted the withdrawal of funds from London to New York for the purpose of investment or speculation. It is impossible to deny that during 1928–9 the manipulation of forward rates by Central Banks would have mitigated the evil even if it had not been able to eliminate it altogether.

Hitherto we have been dealing with discrepancies created by changes in the interest parity. Discrepancies can, however, arise also from deviations of the forward exchange rate from its interest parity. If through seasonal influences or speculative operations the forward rate departs from its interest parity, it becomes profitable to transfer funds to the centre in whose favour the forward rate has moved, since the profit on the swap would be added to the interest rate obtained. Could the device suggested by Mr. Keynes be applied in such cases with the same advantage as in cases of discrepancies caused by a change in the interest parity? The answer depends on the nature of the selling pressure on the forward exchange. If it is due to seasonal operations or bear speculative anticipation of the seasonal or other normal factors the extent and duration of which can be foreseen, there is no reason why the device should not be applied with advantage. If, however, the Central Bank is confronted with a sweeping speculative pressure due to distrust in the stability of the currency, then the matter requires careful reconsideration. Indeed, Mr. Keynes himself never intended his proposed device to be applied against a flight from a currency. We propose to return to this point later in the chapter. Meanwhile, let us examine how the policy would operate technically.

(5) Central Banks' Rôle

Needless to say, for the policy to become effective it would be necessary for the Central Banks to operate in forward exchanges to an unlimited degree whenever intervention became necessary. It is also essential that the Central Banks should be prepared to become the final buyers or sellers. If all that Central Banks were prepared to do was to buy or sell forward currencies and then to seek to find a counterpart for the transactions so as to cover their exchange risk, then their activity would be of relatively little significance and it would be unable to control forward rates. After all, if there are counterparts to be found at the desired rates, there is no need for the Central Banks to assume the rôle of intermediary between the ultimate buyer and the ultimate seller. It is precisely because sellers or buyers of forward exchange are unable to find a counterpart at rates which are considered desirable by the Central Banks that it is proposed that the latter should intervene.

Nor is it sufficient for Central Banks to confine their activities in the foreign exchange market to quoting swap rates, i.e. being prepared to sell spot exchange and buy forward or vice versa. When there is a pressure on a currency it usually affects both spot and forward exchange. It would be useless to try to stem the tide by supporting the forward exchange through buying spot and selling forward currencies, for the operation would then only swell the tide of pressure on the spot exchange. In order to be able to control forward rates without influencing spot rates in an undesirable direction, Central Banks would have to be willing to buy or sell forward exchanges outright.

(6) Gold Market *v.* Foreign Exchange Market

As to the method by which the proposed system should operate, Mr. Keynes suggested in his *Tract on Monetary Reform* that the Central Banks should quote a buying and selling price for gold for forward delivery, and that they should change this price whenever necessary. The object of this proposal, which was made soon after the Genoa Conference, was not so much to enable the monetary authorities to acquire the control of the forward market as to stimulate the development of that market. At that time the forward market was still highly inadequate and it appeared as though its development would be slow without official intervention. Since then, however, a highly efficient forward exchange market has developed. It is doubtful whether in the existing conditions the quotation of a forward gold price would in itself be sufficient to control the forward exchange market. Intercourse between the gold market and the foreign exchange market is by no means flawless, and experience during recent years, when there has been a fairly active dealing in forward gold, has shown that there is frequently a disparity between forward gold rates and forward exchange rates. The forward gold rates barely fluctuated while the forward quotation of the French franc—a currency easily convertible into gold—moved within a very wide range. Apart altogether from this, unless there is a large volume of speculative activity in forward gold, the volume of transactions in that market would not be sufficiently large adequately to influence forward exchange rates.

Mr. Keynes, being aware that in itself the fixing of a forward price for gold would not be sufficient, in his more recent references to the subject suggests that Central Banks should operate actively in the forward exchange market itself. He does not want Central Banks to operate regularly in the forward market, still less to quote rates at which they are prepared at any time to buy or sell unlimited amounts. What he wants is that the monetary authorities should intervene with discrimination when the situation is such as to make their intervention desirable. He emphasises that the device should never be used for trying to counteract a deep-seated disequilibrium. This attitude disposes of one of the main criticisms against operations by Central Banks in forward exchanges. There remains, of course, the difficulty of ascertaining when the pressure is due to temporary causes and when it is due to fundamental disequilibrium. As, however, this same difficulty is encountered in many spheres of activity of the monetary authorities, it can hardly be used as an argument specifically against Central Bank operations in forward exchanges.

(7) Should Central Banks take Risks?

Admittedly, it is perhaps too much to expect that Central Banks should have open commitments in a currency which is liable to wide fluctuations in terms of the national currency. From this point of view, however, the acquisition of a holding of foreign currency is just as undesirable as the creation of an open position through a forward exchange operation. If one or both currencies are off gold, then the Central Banks concerned are well advised to abstain from such operations, so as to avoid the risk of heavy loss. It is true that the holding of gold by a Central Bank with a fluctuating currency also involves a certain risk, but in this case the remedy lies in the hands of the authorities themselves. If they do not want to make a loss on their newly acquired gold, then they must stabilise eventually the price of gold in terms of national currency at a rate at which it involves no loss. They have no such safeguards if they acquire a currency—spot or forward—on a gold basis, since that currency may depreciate considerably in terms of gold. To be on the safe side, the monetary authorities engaged in exchange control operations must acquire spot currencies which are freely convertible into gold and must convert them as soon as possible. The risk involved in forward operations under existing conditions is too great to make them worth while. Indeed, what Mr. Keynes has in mind is forward exchange operations by Central Banks after the stabilisation of currencies, but not in existing conditions.

Assuming that the device is applied only after the return to some form of gold standard, the risk involved will in normal conditions be relatively limited, especially if the monetary authorities exercise wise discrimination between temporary and lasting influences. The Central Bank either trusts the stability of its own currency or it does not. If it does, it should have the courage of its conviction so long as the selling pressure does not assume menacing proportions. If it does not trust its own currency, then it is just as unreasonable on its part to sell gold as to sell foreign currencies for forward delivery. Buying of foreign currencies for forward delivery is, of course, a different matter. It involves confidence in another currency and it also involves, after a point, the bolstering up of that currency.

(8) Defence against Flight from Currency

It is also essential that, in addition to discriminating between temporary and fundamental pressure, the monetary authorities should discriminate between pressure due to technical discrepancies between forward rates and their interest parities, and pressure due to distrust in the stability of the currency. We have seen earlier in this chapter that, in the circumstances, intervention in the forward market can fulfil a useful task. The question now is whether forward exchange operations by Central Banks would facilitate the task of defending the currency against adverse pressure due to distrust. As is well known, such adverse pressure can assume four different forms. There is, in the first place, a flight of capital which involves withdrawals of deposits—national or foreign—from the banks, and withdrawals of gold from the Central Bank. There is, apart from this, the flight which takes the form of borrowing from the banks and the transfer of the proceeds into gold or foreign currency. This involves a credit expansion by the Central Bank and loss of gold. The third method is the contraction of a short position in the national currency by means of forward exchange operations. This in itself involves neither a loss of deposits, nor a credit expansion, nor a loss of gold. On the other hand, it leads to the fourth form of adverse pressure, through stimulating swap operations which involve all these evil consequences.

Although the psychological effect of the widening of the discount on the forward currency may be unfavourable, it is not nearly so strongly adverse as that of the outflow of gold or even of the withdrawals of deposits. If the discount on the forward exchange is kept within normal limits through intervention by Central Banks, then this adverse psychological effect can be reduced, if not altogether eliminated. At the same time, the high yield on swap transactions would also be reduced. Needless to say, the publication of the amount of forward commitments of the monetary authorities would produce an adverse psychological effect, but it would not be nearly so strong as the publication of a corresponding loss of gold. In any case, as most countries have established Exchange Equalisation Accounts, and as the figures of these accounts are not disclosed, there is no need to give any publicity to the extent of forward operations.

(9) Diverting Pressure from Spot Market

If the adverse pressure could be diverted from the spot to the forward exchange by means of reducing the discount on the forward exchange through official intervention, then the monetary authorities would stand to gain. One of the reasons why an adverse pressure on the exchange is in these days accompanied by such an unusually heavy efflux of gold and such a decline of bank deposits is because of the difficulties of hedging against currency depreciation by operating in the forward market at a reasonable cost. Holders of francs would in many cases rather hedge against devaluation by forward selling than by transferring their capital abroad or by acquiring gold. Those who seek to hedge against, or to speculate on, a depreciation of the franc would also prefer to create short positions by means of forward selling if that could be done more cheaply than borrowing francs for the purpose of transfer abroad. As, however, every time adverse pressure develops, the discount on the forward currency is allowed to widen to a fantastic figure—in fact, in some instances the increase is deliberately engineered—there remains nothing but to undertake operations which lead to wholesale loss of gold.

On the surface it appears that it would be short-sighted on the part of monetary authorities not to adopt a policy aiming at reducing the discount on forward currencies. There is, however, another side to the picture. If a policy aiming at the contraction of the discount on the forward currency were to do nothing more than divert selling pressure into the forward exchange market, then there would be everything to be said in favour of such tactics and nothing against them. In reality, however, the maintenance of the discount on the forward exchange at an artificially low level would stimulate speculative selling on a very large scale, over and above the extent to which it diverts selling pressure from the spot market into the channels of the forward market. It ought to be borne in mind that, in the absence of cheap forward exchange facilities, the extent of the selling pressure has its natural limits. Only those who have the capital or who are in a position to borrow it can export it. The amount of liquid resources which can be withdrawn from the economic system of a country is limited. On the other hand, there is practically no limit to the extent to which foreign currencies could be purchased for forward delivery. It is reasonable to assume, therefore, that should forward selling be made easier its volume would exceed that of the capital outflow several times over.

It may be objected that the monetary authorities of a country can view such a wave of forward selling with equanimity provided that they have faith in the stability of their own currency. But would they have the courage of such a conviction? If a Central Bank has sold the equivalent of its gold stock in the form of forward exchange, it may well hesitate to go on selling. Indeed, it would be reckless gambling on the part of the Central Bank to sell foreign currencies beyond the amount which it was in a position to deliver at any moment by disposing of its gold stock. Presumably, Central Banks would stop selling forward exchange long before the limit of their gold stock had been reached.

(10) Widening the Margin between Gold Points

The encouragement given to speculation by reducing the discount on the forward exchange unduly can, of course, be counteracted by lowering the spot rate accordingly. Under the gold standard, the limits to which this can be done are rather narrow, owing to the close range between the gold points. Mr. Keynes suggests, however, that the range between gold import point and export point should be widened by authorising the Central Banks to lower their gold price. If this is done, then the advantage to speculators of a narrow discount on the forward exchange can be counteracted by increasing the risk of loss through an appreciation of the spot exchange. Such a move would, moreover, provide an opportunity for the Central Banks to squeeze the bears, which cannot be done effectively under the orthodox gold standard.

Even with this corrective the useful scope for intervention by Central Banks in the forward exchange market is necessarily limited. When there is a widespread speculative attack on a currency—especially if it is justified by the existence of basic disequilibrium—the lowering of the gold price makes resistance to the attack, if anything, more difficult, especially if the parities are established on the understanding that in case of strong pressure the Government will be at liberty to alter them materially. This question was dealt with more in detail in the last chapter.

The utility of the intervention by Central Banks in the forward exchange market is confined to international transfers arising through interest arbitrage. Notwithstanding the limitations of its scope, the proposal is well worth considering as one of the conditions on which the gold standard should be restored. It would undoubtedly help under normal conditions to safeguard internal trade from international influences. But in order to deal with this proposal according to its merits, it would be necessary to examine the whole problem of forward exchanges, with its profound theoretical background and with all its intricate technical details. To do so would be, however, outside the scope of this book. The author must refer those of his readers who are interested in the subject, and who are not afraid of its technicalities, to his forthcoming book *The Theory of Forward Exchanges*. Meanwhile, the attitude of Central Banks in practice towards forward exchanges is examined in the next chapter.

CHAPTER XXIV

OFFICIAL FORWARD EXCHANGE OPERATIONS IN PRACTICE

(I) Three Alternative Courses

We examined in the previous chapter the suggestion made by Mr. Keynes for the control of the forward exchange market by the monetary authorities. The question whether Central Banks should take an interest in forward exchanges, and, if so, in what manner, has been the subject of controversy for some years past. There are three main schools of thought among theoretical and practical experts. According to one, the monetary authorities should assume an attitude of complete neutrality towards forward exchange operations. They should confine their controlling activities to the market for spot exchanges and should allow forward rates to take care of themselves.

Those who are opposed to neutrality in regard to forward exchanges are again divided into two schools. According to those who agree with the views of Mr. Keynes, intervention of the monetary authorities in the forward exchange market should aim at keeping forward rates at or above their interest parities (the ratio between interest rates in two financial centres). For a currency with a weakening tendency, this would involve the maintenance of the forward exchange at an artificially high level. According to the other school, the object of official intervention in the forward exchange market should be to discourage speculation by making its cost prohibitive. This can be achieved by artificially depreciating the forward exchange. Indeed, some go so far as to favour the complete prohibition of speculative operations in forward exchange.

(2) Exchange Equalisation Account's Practice

The series of financial crises experienced since 1931 provided examples of the practical application of each one of these three policies. The Exchange Equalisation Account—to mention only one outstanding example—has ever since its establishment in 1932 preserved an attitude of strict neutrality towards the forward exchange market. It has confined its operations entirely to spot exchanges, allowing forward rates to find their own level. It has refrained from taking any steps to influence forward rates in either direction. It has not taken advantage of the immense possibilities of squeezing bears which were exploited with such beneficial results by the French exchange control in 1924 and 1926. The reason why, during periods of selling pressure, the Exchange Equalisation Account authorities do not support sterling by forward selling of foreign currencies is probably that they consider such operations as equivalent to support by means of borrowing abroad. Since this expedient produced disastrous results in 1931, the British monetary authorities prefer to abstain from repeating it even in changed circumstances.

The reason why sterling is not defended against an unwanted rise by means of purchases of foreign currencies for forward delivery lies in the desire of the British authorities to convert their holdings of foreign exchange into gold at the earliest opportunity. It would indeed be risky to have a long position in French francs. There is reason to believe that such practical considerations as these rather than any fundamental objection on principle, are primarily responsible for the Exchange Account authorities' adoption of a neutral attitude towards forward exchanges. With other Central Banks, however, the neutral attitude is the result of an objection, on principle, to what are regarded as speculative operations by Central Banks. It is for such considerations that the Bank of France, for instance, has refrained, since 1929, from dealing in forward exchange.

(3) Bank of France's Neutral Attitude

The attitude of the Bank of France towards the forward exchange market is not, however, one of absolute neutrality. While it abstains from direct intervention, it pursues by indirect methods the policy of discouraging forward selling of francs. Every time there is a speculative attack on the franc the Bank of France raises its bank rate, thereby increasing the difficulty of creating a short position by borrowing francs and selling them outright. As a result, speculative operations are diverted from the spot to the forward market and the discount on the forward franc widens to a figure at which the cost of short selling becomes almost prohibitive. Intervention in forward exchanges on the part of the Bank of France proceeds, however, on strictly orthodox lines, by the employment of that classical remedy-for-all-ailments, the bank rate. Possibly its effect upon the forward rate is not deliberate but merely incidental.

Other Central Banks go much further in their policy of causing artificial depreciation of the forward exchange. The Netherlands Bank, for instance, whenever there is a speculative attack on the guilder, usually brings pressure to bear upon Dutch banks to induce them not to buy forward guilders from foreign sellers except in connection with genuine commercial transactions. The idea is that, in the absence of adequate Dutch demand for forward guilders, the discount is bound to widen and the cost of bear operations thus becomes prohibitive. The policy of deliberate depreciation of the forward exchange is based on the assumption that the selling pressure on the currency is solely or mainly due to speculative operations in the forward market. Those who accept this assumption believe that, should the cost of speculative selling of the national currency be made prohibitive, the selling pressure would come to an end. We propose to show later that this is by no means necessarily the case. It is true that in the case of Holland, for instance, the speculative attack has come to an end every time the authorities have resorted to the device of widening the discount on forward guilders. Those who conclude, however, that this proves the effectiveness of the device are guilty of the fallacy of *post hoc ergo propter hoc.* The attacks on the guilder came to an end because their cause—usually a political crisis—came to an end, and because while the political crisis lasted the Netherlands Bank was technically strong enough to withstand the drain on its gold reserve. In all probability the attack would have come to an end even though the forward exchange had been allowed to take care of itself.

(4) Bolstering up Forward Exchanges

The policy of bolstering up the forward exchange by Government intervention was adopted by the British authorities during the sterling crisis of 1931. Simultaneously with the heavy selling of spot francs and dollars out of the proceeds of the Franco-American credits, the British authorities supported forward sterling and maintained its discount at an abnormally narrow margin despite heavy speculative selling. Their tactics were influenced partly by considerations of prestige; they were anxious to prevent forward sterling from depreciating below the gold export point for spot sterling. The main reason, however, was a desire to divert pressure from the spot to the forward market. Had they allowed forward sterling to depreciate below its interest parity, considerable foreign balances would have been withdrawn with the forward exchange covered.

The alternative would have been to raise the bank rate further, but in doing so the authorities would have only aggravated the panic. The attempt was foredoomed to failure, for even in the absence of large withdrawals of foreign balances with their exchange risk covered, there was sufficient selling pressure on sterling to exhaust the resources available for its defence. Moreover, the cheap facilities for forward sale of sterling provided additional encouragement to bear speculation. The authorities were wise in discontinuing the defence of sterling when the amount of spot and forward sales of francs and dollars exhausted the Franco-American credits. The experience of 1931 shows the futility of supporting the forward exchange at times of fundamental pressure. Since 1931 the British monetary authorities have refrained from intervening in the forward exchange market.

Indeed, in the existing conditions of instability little useful purpose can be served by systematically supporting the forward exchange. At present by far the larger part of international short-term balances is not covered against exchange risk by forward operations. Indeed, for most holders the very object of keeping balances abroad is to enable them to benefit by the depreciation of their national currencies and to that end the forward exchange is left uncovered. Bank balances abroad with the forward exchange covered are reduced to a minimum and do not constitute a major factor. In any case, the relative influence of interest rates in various centres is at present not nearly as strong as in normal times.

(5) Depreciating the Forward Exchange

If it is a mistaken policy in the existing conditions to support the forward exchange, it is an even greater mistake to pursue a policy aiming at depreciating the forward exchange. The widening of the discount usually produces an unfavourable psychological effect and tends to encourage the flight of capital. In addition, selling pressure is diverted from the forward exchange to the spot exchange. Those who are unable to cover their risk by operating in the forward at a reasonable cost will leave no stone unturned to cover their risk in the spot market. They will borrow or sell securities in order to be able to transfer their capital abroad. Foreign bankers holding balances with the exchange covered will repatriate their funds owing to the excessive cost of covering the exchange risk. This consideration plays an important part in the case of financial centres with substantial foreign balances. In other centres foreign banks usually keep only relatively small balances in the national currency for their current business requirements, and these balances would remain in any case. It is the nationals of the country concerned who would increase the selling pressure on the spot exchange, by selling the spot currency instead of selling forward. Moreover, unduly weak forward exchanges lead to an increased pressure on spot exchanges, as a result of the high yield on the swage, i.e., selling spot and buying forward, the part of those who possess spot currency.

It appears that the most satisfactory policy for the monetary authorities in the existing conditions of monetary instability is to adopt an attitude of neutrality towards forward exchanges, without being unduly dogmatic about it. While occasionally it may appear expedient to depart from this self-imposed restriction, the general rule for Central Banks pending international stabilisation of currencies should be to confine their activities to the spot market.

(6) A Policy of Discrimination

A method of intervention which has been subject to criticism is the efforts by the monetary authorities to discourage forward dealings of a speculative nature. There is, however, much to be said both for and against such efforts. As we pointed out above, the difficulty of covering the exchange risk in the forward market tends to increase the pressure on the spot market. Moreover, the policy of discouraging speculative forward business is liable to do harm by narrowing down activity in the forward exchange market. Speculation is indispensable even in the spot market, for the purpose of making good short-term discrepancies between supply and demand. It is much more indispensable in the forward market where, in addition to the difference between amounts of buying and selling orders, there is also the difference between the maturity dates. The forward exchange market cannot possibly be efficient unless there is a good deal of speculative activity, or unless the Central Banks are prepared to take the place of speculators in providing the counterpart to commercial requirements.

The view that it is to the interest of the monetary authorities to discourage forward operations, or at best to adopt an attitude of neutrality towards them, reduces the likelihood of the adoption of the proposals made by Mr. Keynes for a constructive forward exchange policy. Indeed, unless the mentality of those responsible for the monetary policy of the leading countries changes considerably between now and the stabilisation of the currencies, there seems to be but little chance of the adoption of the reform—even though within its limited sphere it would go a long way towards creating greater stability of interest rates and towards safeguarding internal trade from the disturbing influences of developments abroad. In any case, however, the question cannot arise until the general stabilisation of currencies has become a matter of practical politics.

CHAPTER XXV

DRASTIC DEVALUATION

(1) Creating a Safety Margin

Devaluation in itself does not constitute a reform of the monetary system. The gold value of the monetary unit may be changed without thereby causing any change in the system itself. It is only if devaluation results in a fundamental change in the working of the monetary system that it can be considered as a monetary reform. Devaluation cannot bring about a fundamental change in the system unless it is a drastic devaluation. A devaluation that merely adjusts a currency to its changed economic parities does not in itself alter the system in any way, even though it facilitates the working of the old system. But a devaluation which is sufficiently drastic creates a large real surplus in the gold reserve, and thus may be considered to have brought about a reform of the monetary system.

In the preceding chapters we have several times referred to the desirability of stabilising the currencies in such a fashion as will produce a safe surplus of the gold reserve above normal requirements. Those who believe in the theories of Professors Fisher and Warren must consider it impossible to increase the safety margin by means of devaluation. In their view, a devaluation of a currency by, say, 50 per cent is bound to be followed by a rise in commodity prices by 100 per cent, so that the goods value of the gold reserve—which is the only value that matters in the long run—remains unchanged in spite of the fact that its book-keeping value has doubled. In Chapter XX we pointed out the fallacy of this conception. In practice, commodity prices never move in proportion to the devaluation. Their rise is bound to lag far behind that of the book value of the gold reserve, and in normal conditions it will be many years before the two curves meet, if indeed they meet at all. In the meantime, the community will enjoy the benefit of a real surplus gold reserve. Strange as it may sound, the community will thus get something for nothing. The surplus thus obtained constitutes a windfall for the nation and an unearned increase in its resources.

If this increase should be large enough to enable the monetary authorities to manage the gold standard in an unorthodox spirit and if the drastic devaluation has been carried out for that specific purpose, then it may be said to constitute a monetary reform measure. In what circumstances, then, can the net surplus be substantial enough to make a lasting difference to the monetary policy of the country concerned? A relatively moderate surplus would make no substantial difference, and in any case the chances are that it would gradually disappear.

In order that the devaluation should produce a lasting effect upon the monetary system, it is necessary that it should result in an increase of the reserve ratio to an exceptionally high figure. While it would be impossible to name an actual figure as the desirable reserve ratio from this point of view, past experience suggests that it is necessary that the reserve ratio should be considerably higher than any of the reserve ratios registered after the war. We have seen that, with a reserve ratio of 80 per cent, France none the less pursued an orthodox monetary policy. Even Switzerland, whose gold reserve was at one time 125 per cent of the note circulation, showed no inclination to abandon the self-imposed handicap of monetary orthodoxy. It appears, therefore, that the reserve ratio must be something like 200 to 300 per cent or more to enable the monetary authorities to view an outflow of gold with equanimity. It is also necessary that the devaluation should take place in circumstances which would minimise the rise in commodity prices which it produces. Otherwise the rise in commodity prices would sooner or later necessitate a corresponding increase in the monetary circulation and the volume of credit, and the reserve ratio would gradually decline to a normal figure.

In order to create a sufficiently large initial surplus, it is necessary to devalue a currency to something like 25 per cent of its original value. The pound sterling, for instance, would have to be devalued to about 5*s*. This idea was put forward by the author in his books *The Future of Gold* and *World Finance since 1914*. His critics may be divided into two groups. Some of them criticised his proposal on the ground that it would lead to a spectacular rise in commodity prices and would, therefore, result in a social upheaval. Others, on the other hand, criticised the proposal on the ground that it would lead to no increase of commodity prices and that it would therefore be ineffective.

(2) How Prices adjust themselves to Devaluation

The truth lies somewhere between the two extreme suggestions, though only experience could show to what degree either of them is correct. Much depends on the circumstances in which stabilisation takes place and upon the monetary policy pursued after stabilisation. If the devaluation is carried out during a period of rising prices, then the chances are that prices will adjust themselves to a relatively large extent to the new monetary parity. If, on the other hand, devaluation is carried out during a period of stagnant or falling prices, then the chances are that the immediate effect upon the price level will be negligible. In any case, it is safe to conclude that, during the first few months at any rate, the rise would proceed rather less than half-way towards complete adjustment to the new level. Thus, even a drastic devaluation would not be followed by a rise in prices comparable with the rise witnessed after the war—it would not be comparable even with the rise which occurred in countries like the United States or Great Britain, where inflation remained relatively moderate.

The opponents of drastic devaluation argue that, to the extent that prices follow the change in the monetary unit, the community would not benefit by an increase in the commodity value of the gold reserve, and to the extent that prices do not follow the change in the unit, the community would not benefit by the rise in prices. This argument, however, could easily be reversed, for it is evident that in so far as prices rise the community would benefit by that rise, and in so far as the rise lagged behind the increase of the book value of the gold reserve the community would benefit by the net surplus thus obtained, which would constitute a welcome windfall.

(3) Rise of Prices Relatively Moderate

If it were possible to arrange a drastic (and equal) devaluation of all currencies simultaneously, then there would be no reason why it should cause any immediate rise in the price level of any country. In that case, the increase in the book value of the gold reserve would represent also the increase in its commodity value. If the devaluation did not take place simultaneously in the leading countries, then it would be likely to lead to a relatively moderate rise in the price levels of countries which had devalued. Even then, however, the rise would probably not be marked to begin with, unless the devaluation took place during a period of rising prices.

In theory, commodity prices in a country which devalues drastically should rise immediately to a large extent, so that if all countries devalued each in turn would experience a marked rise in its price level. In practice, however, what happens when a country devalues is that its price level rises to a relatively moderate extent while the price level of other countries tends to fall, for the simple reason that these other countries have to compete with the undervalued currency of the country which carried out the devaluation. If country A, for instance, devalues to the extent of 50 per cent, the short-period rise in its commodity prices will be not the 100 per cent which would correspond to the change of the monetary unit, but only, say, 20 or 30 per cent. At the same time, commodity prices in countries B and C would fall by, say, 10 to 15 per cent. When it is the turn of country B to devalue to the extent of 50 per cent, there will be similar effects on the price levels of countries A and C. When the turn of country C comes, its devaluation will cause a fall in the price levels of countries A and B. As a result, when all countries had devalued the net change in the price levels would be found to be relatively small.

(4) Moderate Rise Desirable

Thus, a devaluation of currencies to one quarter of their original mint parities would not in itself cause a rise in the price level by 300 per cent, as Professor Fisher's school assumes, but would probably cause a rise of well under 100 per cent and conceivably under 50 per cent. In itself such a rise would certainly not cause a social upheaval. After all, France, Belgium, Italy, etc., experienced a much more substantial rise in commodity prices after the war without suffering in consequence any vital disorganisation of their social system. On the contrary, such a relatively moderate rise would go a long way towards solving the problem of excessive indebtedness, public and private. As the author explained in detail in his book *World Finance since 1914*, the increase in the burden of fictitious wealth since the war has been at the root of most of our difficulties. Unless and until the normal relationship between fictitious wealth and real wealth is restored, there can be no hope of genuine and lasting equilibrium. Drastic devaluation is practically the only way in which the burden of fictitious wealth can be materially reduced. Moreover, a rise in commodity prices without an all-round devaluation of currencies would simply restore the shortage of gold which was among the immediate causes of the crisis of 1931.

It would have been the best possible solution if in 1920 commodity prices had been allowed to rise by several hundreds per cent, and the currencies had then been devalued to a corresponding extent. By such means the excessive increase of fictitious wealth during the war would have been liquidated to a large extent. Instead, the leading countries restored their currencies to their pre-war parities and allowed commodity prices to decline to their pre-war level. It would be difficult to repair the damage done by this mistaken policy. No Government is likely deliberately to bring about a rise in commodity prices amounting to several hundreds per cent. In the circumstances, the best solution would be a sufficiently drastic devaluation to cause a rise of wholesale prices by something like 50 to 100 per cent, and consequently a rise in the cost of living to the extent of something like 20 to 40 per cent. Such a rise would go a long way towards relieving the burden of the public debt without at the same time inflicting unbearable losses upon the classes with fixed incomes.

(5) Safety Margin and Expansion

In itself, the reduction of fictitious wealth through such a rise in prices would not be sufficient to restore a reasonable equilibrium between fictitious and real wealth. On the other hand, the increase in the commodity value of gold reserves, through the failure of commodity prices to rise to an extent corresponding to the devaluation, would open up immense possibilities for safe expansion.

It is from this latter point of view that drastic devaluation may be considered as a method of monetary reform. By no other methods would it be possible to pave the way for credit expansion on a large scale without abandoning the gold standard. It is only when a Central Bank possesses a safety margin amounting to 200 per cent or more that it can afford to allow credit expansion to take place on a really extensive scale. Provided that the expansion is well planned and provided that it leads to an increased production coupled with an increased purchasing power, there is no need whatsoever for it to lead to any further material rise in prices. After the initial rise caused by drastic devaluation is completed, the authorities will be in a position to maintain the price level reasonably stable. There would be a further adjustment of the ratio between fictitious wealth and real wealth through the increase of the latter.

Evidently, the execution of every kind of monetary reform would be greatly facilitated by a drastic devaluation of currencies. By creating a comfortable safety margin, it would give the reforms a fair chance to establish themselves through trial and error. If the safety margin is narrow, there is but an inadequate chance for the reformers to carry out their experiments.

In the circumstances, it is astonishing how little attention most reformers pay to this aspect of the problem. Some of them believe that devaluation to the existing level of exchange depreciation would give them all the safety margin they require. Others even believe that the surplus gold reserves that would arise if the currencies were devalued on their existing levels would lead to dangerous inflation. In reality, there is nothing easier than to sterilise the surplus that is not wanted and to keep it sterilised as an emergency reserve. The examples of various countries in recent years have proved that it is possible for a Central Bank to maintain a reserve ratio of 80 per cent and over without having to allow credit to expand to a corresponding degree. There is no reason to suppose that it would be any more difficult to sterilise a surplus of hundreds per cent, especially if the surplus is created mainly by the book-keeping revaluation of the gold reserve and not by new acquisitions. The purchase of huge amounts of gold by the monetary authorities would inevitably lead to a certain expansion of credit, even though it would be possible up to a point to neutralise the expansion by open market operations. The creation of a surplus by a mere book-keeping entry does not, however, involve any credit expansion. It only creates a possibility of expansion should the authorities decide to increase the volume of credit.

(6) Excessive Timidity

The devaluations which were carried out after the war were in every instance on a drastic scale, but they failed to produce a surplus because they followed a period of inflation which had already caused a substantial rise in commodity prices. Even so, it was found that countries, such as France, which devalued their currencies to a larger degree than was absolutely necessary, benefited by an increase of their margin of gold reserve. The devaluations which have been carried out since the beginning of the crisis have on the whole been characterised by an excessive timidity. Czechoslovakia was the first country to devalue and she devalued to an extent of $16\frac{2}{3}$ per cent only. This was evidently barely sufficient for the requirements of the country. Even the Belgian devaluation of 28 per cent was anything but excessive. The only country which has so far obtained a large book-keeping surplus of gold reserve through the devaluation of its currency is the United States. In none of these cases was the monetary aspect of drastic devaluation duly considered among the motives that influenced the decision as to the extent of the devaluation.

There is no reason to suppose that a drastic devaluation on the lines proposed by the author would be carried out by deliberate action. It is, however, conceivable that the trend of evolution will in the long run move in that direction even in the absence of any deliberate policy to that end, and even in defiance of efforts to check the trend. Conceivably, the Gold Bloc may resist a moderate devaluation until its technical position has become so weak as to make further resistance impossible. In that case, the Gold Bloc currencies may have to be allowed to depreciate and find their level, or they may have to undergo a drastic devaluation. The United States would then go further in devaluing the dollar and sterling would also have to find its new level. Thus, conceivably, the right solution might be reached by the wrong means, through a currency depreciation race. On the other hand, it is possible that the adjustment of the gold currencies to the level of sterling and the dollar will take place in an orderly manner and that it will not lead to any further depreciation either of sterling or of the dollar. In that case, the excess of fictitious wealth will remain, and will lead sooner or later to another crisis which will necessitate fresh devaluations. In the long run a definite solution can be found only by stabilising currencies at a level at which it becomes possible to liquidate the excessive fictitious wealth, and at which the revaluation of the gold reserves creates a sufficient safety margin to enable the monetary authorities to embark upon a policy of reasonable expansion.

CHAPTER XXVI

A COMMODITY STANDARD

(1) Commodities as Substitutes for Gold

We tried to prove in Chapter XVII that it is essential to maintain some form of limited gold standard in order that there shall remain one commodity which is accepted in payment to an unlimited extent by every country. We argued that in the absence of a gold reserve which could be used to tide a country over a difficult period, even a passing crisis might be sufficient to reduce a country to starvation. This all-important aspect of the problem of the gold standard has not received adequate attention from any of the opponents of the system, for these opponents merely urge that the gold reserves should be sunk at the bottom of the sea and do not propose any alternative international medium of exchange. Little constructive had ever been written on this aspect of the controversy until the publication of Major L. L. B. Angas's book *The Problem of Foreign Exchanges.* Major Angas refused to accept the suggestion that gold is the only commodity which can be used for the purpose of accumulating reserves for "rainy days". He maintained that certain non-perishable staple products could be used for the same purpose. According to him, instead of accumulating gold stocks which have little or no social utility, the monetary authorities should accumulate stocks of useful metals such as copper, tin, lead, etc., and other commodity stocks. He believes that these commodities could well take the place of a gold reserve, not only by enabling the countries concerned to import less during times of pressure, but even by enabling them to increase their exports by liquidating these stocks.

The suggestion made by Major Angas certainly has the merit of being constructive, which is rather more than most suggestions aiming at the scrapping of gold reserves could claim to be. It therefore deserves close examination. Would it be possible and desirable to replace gold reserves by reserves of other commodities? The first part of the question can be answered in the affirmative. There is no technical reason which would prevent Governments from acquiring and maintaining large commodity stocks. Indeed, they would find it incomparably easier to do so than to acquire large gold stocks. During the last few years the world has been suffering from an excessive supply of raw materials. Even though as a result of rearmament during 1935 much of this surplus has been liquidated in the case of some commodities, generally speaking, the supplies, actual or potential, are still far in excess of demand.

(2) Glut of Raw Materials

The Governments of several raw-material-producing countries have had to undertake directly or indirectly to assist in the financing of the surplus which has accumulated and which constitutes a constant threat to the market. Any solution which would enable them to liquidate these embarrassing stocks, and which in addition would enable them to remove restrictions upon raw material production, would unquestionably be welcomed. In some instances attempts have been made to liquidate the surplus by dumping it on the world market at a price that did not cover the cost of production. These liquidations, of course, made it more difficult to dispose of the current output. The establishment of commodity reserves by various Governments, on the other hand, would create an exceptional demand, thanks to which all surpluses could be liquidated without interference with the marketing of the normal current output. From the point of view of raw material producers this would be an ideal solution.

The fact that raw-material-producing countries are anxious to get rid of their accumulated surplus shows that it would not be advisable to attempt to establish commodity reserves consisting exclusively or even mainly of commodities produced in the countries concerned. It would be essential that as far as possible Governments should accumulate commodities which are not produced on a sufficient scale in their own countries and which in the ordinary course they have to import. The accumulation of such stocks is of great importance from the point of view of national defence, as well as from the monetary point of view.

While most countries are doing their utmost to keep the gold they possess, they are only too keen to get rid of any surplus stocks of home-produced raw materials. They would even be prepared to import more manufactures in order to be able to liquidate their raw material stocks. Indeed, they would even be willing to reduce their foreign indebtedness by exporting their raw material surplus in payment for frozen debts. While they are unable to pay cash, they are both able and willing to pay in kind. It is for this reason that it would be technically possible for the creditor countries, at any rate, to accumulate large commodity reserves.

The fact that the commodity stocks acquired for monetary purposes would not come to the market but would remain stored up for years would make all the difference from the point of view of producing countries. In existing circumstances, they are not prepared to exchange their raw material stocks for additional imports of manufactures, or to sell them in payment for their frozen debts, for fear that in doing so they would spoil the market for their own current output. Once this fear is removed it will be much easier to come to agreements for the purchase of raw material stocks against the supply of capital goods or against the liquidation of frozen debts.

(3) Unfreezing Frozen Debts

As far as Great Britain is concerned, the scheme of acquiring a commodity reserve would work in the following way: The amounts that have accumulated in the various blocked accounts in raw-material-producing debtor countries would be used to purchase raw materials which would be taken over by the British Government. In order to satisfy the Governments of the debtor countries that the transaction would not reduce their chances of exporting their products against cash, the British Government would give the assurance that the commodities in question would be blocked for a period of at least, say, two years. The equivalent of the purchase price of the commodities would be paid over to the British creditors by the British Government. Where the defaulting debtor was a foreign Government itself, it would have to issue internal bonds to the equivalent of the amount defaulted upon and spend the proceeds on the purchase of staple commodities which would be taken over by the British Government; the latter would then pay the amount due to the British bondholders. The producers in the debtor countries would derive a substantial direct benefit from the scheme, but the rise in the world prices of commodities would be beneficial to producers and holders of stocks all over the world. Thus, producers in the British Dominions would not be victimised by the transaction, even though the purchases were made from foreign countries. The contraction of the surplus supplies would be beneficial to all.

The reduction of the amount of foreign indebtedness which is at present in default owing to transfer difficulties would make an appreciable difference to the position of debtor countries and creditor countries in general. The direct beneficiaries would be those debtors who would thus recover their solvency, and those creditors who would obtain reimbursement. Indirectly, however, all debtors and creditors would benefit, for the reduction of the amount of frozen debts would improve the quality of the outstanding balance. The significance of this consideration cannot be sufficiently estimated. It is a commonplace of newspaper articles that there can be no substantial revival in foreign trade without the resumption of foreign lending. The reduction of the total in default, and the improvement of the chances for the repayment or unfreezing of the rest, would go a very long way to prepare the ground for the resumption of well-regulated lending abroad.

This unfreezing of frozen credits would be the more valuable in that the alternative in many cases would be the loss of the whole, or at least a great part, of the amounts involved. Barring a very sharp rise in commodity prices, there is not the least chance that the debt services of most defaulting raw-material-producing countries will ever be resumed in full. The creditors will have to consent to debt settlements by which they will forgo a large percentage of their claims. Anything obtained through the suggested scheme could thus be regarded as a sheer windfall for the creditor.

Great Britain is not the only country which would be in a position to acquire substantial commodity reserves. Indeed, most countries would find no difficulty in acquiring substantial commodity stocks either by means of collecting debts or through exchange clearing and compensation transactions. Even raw-material-producing countries like the United States could use up their frozen credits in Latin America and elsewhere by acquiring materials which they do not themselves produce. There is a distinct world-wide tendency towards the acquisition of stocks of all materials and manufactures required for the national defence. This tendency has become accentuated by the adoption of economic sanctions against Italy, for this step made the nations aware of the importance of such commodity reserves. This tendency would go a long way to help the realisation of a commodity reserve scheme.

(4) Need for Gold Reserve

It is thus possible to visualise a situation in which practically every country possesses substantial commodity stocks as currency reserves. So far, Major Angas is on sound ground. Where he becomes unconvincing is when he suggests that these commodity reserves should be used as an alternative to gold reserves and that the latter should be sunk in the ocean or disposed of by some similar means. In the author's view, commodity reserves would be very useful as additions to the gold reserves, but would be no substitute for them.

Admittedly, it would be possible to defend a currency against adverse pressure by liquidating part of the commodity reserve. This, however, could not be done on too large a scale without provoking a disastrous slump in the commodity market. Nor would it be possible to depend upon being able to sell the commodity stocks abroad exactly at the moment when a sale was most necessary from a monetary point of view. We have seen during the last few years how difficult it is to dispose of commodities in times of depression. It is much more convenient to possess gold which can be disposed of without the least difficulty and without unsettling commodity markets at home and abroad. So long as they possessed a gold reserve, the authorities could choose their own moment for unloading their commodity stock for the support of the exchange. In the absence of a gold reserve, they might be forced to sell their commodities at the worst possible moment and in the worst possible circumstances. Indeed, it stands to reason that, whenever the exchange weakened and whenever, in consequence, official sales of commodities might be anticipated, the market would put the prices against the Government and the latter would stand to suffer losses. Moreover, it would be unwise to use commodity reserves by means of arbitrage for the purpose of meeting day-to-day fluctuations. For such purposes, and even for the purpose of meeting seasonal and other normal fluctuations, the use of gold would be much more convenient—assuming, of course, that under a managed gold standard such fluctuations of the gold reserve would not be allowed to react upon the volume of credit. The costs of transport, etc., for a million pounds worth of commodities are many times larger than those of a million pounds worth of gold. For this reason alone they are less suitable than gold for settling international balances when the settlement can be achieved most conveniently through arbitrage shipments.

Even if the principle of a commodity reserve is admitted, the commodity stocks should always be regarded as a " second line of defence ", to be resorted to in face of a persistent pressure. The more mobile gold reserve should be allowed to play the part of offsetting normal fluctuations.

If only from the point of view of national defence, it is necessary and desirable that Governments should accumulate commodity reserves. It would be a mistake, however, to expect these commodity reserves to fulfil the same functions as the gold reserves and to fulfil them as smoothly. Commodity stocks would be very useful as supplementary reserves, but there would be no need to include them in the metallic reserve on the same footing with gold or even with silver. There could, of course, be no question of free arbitrage in commodities. The commodity stocks need not be included in the metallic reserve at all, but should merely form part of the note cover. Or, to meet the objection of purists, the commodity reserves might be excluded altogether from the Central Banks' assets. They might be owned by Exchange Equalisation Accounts. But, whatever the precise arrangement, the knowledge that there is a strong second line of defence in the form of a commodity reserve might in itself go a long way towards inspiring confidence. For this reason the adoption of the principle is desirable. It would further extend the limit to which well-planned credit expansion may safely be undertaken.

(5) Strengthening the Pound's Backing

As a result of the adoption of commodity reserves as a "second line of defence", the task of re-establishing the gold standard would become much easier. So long as the British authorities do not possess a gold stock comparable with that of the United States or France, it is not safe to return to the gold standard. The experience of 1925–31 has shown the disadvantages of attempting to make the gold standard work while Great Britain is in a state of inferiority compared with countries which do not possess a banking centre with the organisation and traditions of London. Unless sterling were technically as strong as the dollar and the franc, the gold standard would be exposed once more to adverse pressure or to shocks through the inexperience and gambling spirit of the United States or through the hoarding habits and political-mindedness of France.

In order to eliminate or at least to reduce the discrepancy between the British gold reserve on the one hand and the French and American gold reserves on the other, it would be necessary for Great Britain to double, or even to treble, her gold stock. Given the fact that the British balance of payments is barely at equilibrium, it is not easy to visualise such a multiplication for a few years. The creation of a large British export surplus is naturally impossible amidst the rising tide of economic nationalism all over the world, while if the amount of the gold reserve were increased simply by a corresponding increase in foreign balances, the technical position of sterling would not be improved. Again, it is unthinkable that this country will in the ordinary course obtain the repayment of its foreign investments on a sufficiently large scale to produce so large an influx of gold, and it is equally unlikely that the British Government would ever consent to issue external loans running into hundreds of millions of pounds for the sole purpose of stimulating such an influx. While the skilful handling of the Exchange Equalisation Account may result in some further increase in the gold stock, it would take many years before the amount would be large enough to permit a restoration of the gold standard.

It is thus conceivable that a moment might arrive when all circumstances, save only the technical position of sterling, favoured stabilisation. In such circumstances, the possibility of adding commodities to the gold reserve would be extremely useful. The possession of, say, a hundred million pounds worth of commodities would, from the point of view of the technical position of sterling, be equivalent to the possession of a similar amount of gold.

(6) Objections to Commodity Reserve

Let us now deal with the objections that may possibly be raised against the commodity reserve scheme. The question may be asked whether foreign debtor countries would be both able and willing to pay their debts by selling raw materials to the British Government. As far as Germany and one or two other industrial debtor countries are concerned, the scheme would obviously be impracticable. Countries of Latin America and continental debtor countries such as Hungary, Rumania, Jugoslavia, etc., are, however, well in a position to produce a surplus of the kind of commodities that would be acceptable in payment of debts. As for their willingness, there can be no doubt that most of them would be only too pleased to take the opportunity thus provided for the liquidation of part of their debts, especially as at the same time the operation would provide direct assistance to their producers. In some instances, agreements to this particular end have actually been concluded. For example, Hungary settled her accumulated frozen commercial indebtedness to Switzerland in the form of special wheat exports. As we have already pointed out, the attractions of the scheme from the point of view of the debtor countries could be increased by an undertaking that the commodities purchased would not be sold for a given period. Although the agreement on the details of such transactions would require lengthy negotiations, there is no reason to suppose that the negotiators would encounter insurmountable difficulties.

It may be objected that the scheme would favour a certain group of creditors at the expense of others. This objection might have carried considerable weight a few years ago, but in the meantime the principle that all creditors are entitled to equal treatment has been discarded on so many occasions that its application now is almost the exception rather than the rule. In any case, other creditor countries would be at liberty to follow the British example and accept payment in commodities. Moreover, the unfreezing of part of the credits without a corresponding reduction in the debtors' resources available for debt payment could only be advantageous to the remaining creditors. It would change the ratio between the debtors' assets and liabilities in favour of the creditors.

(7) Effect on Production and Stocks

Another possible objection is that the British purchases might unduly encourage an expansion of the production of staple commodities. There is undoubtedly something in this point, but the same may be said about any influence which leads to an increase in demand and in commodity prices. The Governments of the raw-material-producing countries would fully understand that the transactions in question were essentially non-recurring. It would be for them to prevent their producers from being misled, and thus from stimulating an undue increase in production. In any case, an amount of £100 million or even twice that figure, spread over a large number of countries, would hardly do more than liquidate a relatively small part of the surplus stocks. It is not as if it would be necessary to increase actual production in order to satisfy the additional demand.

Another possible objection would be that, though it would be all very well while the Government bought commodities, the good effect of its operations would be reversed the moment it began to sell. The importance of this argument should not be exaggerated. If, as there is every reason to hope, the application of the scheme were followed by a revival of trade, the movement, once it had been set in motion, would not be halted, even by the complete liquidation of the stocks originally acquired.

(8) Intervention *v.* *Laissez-Faire*

There remain the conventional objections against Government intervention in economic life, and the usual arguments against the inefficiency of Governments in business. We do not propose to examine here the whole controversy of *laissez-faire v.* intervention. It is sufficient to point out that the trend of evolution is decidedly in favour of increased Government intervention, and the adoption of the scheme would be in keeping with this trend. Finally, it may be argued that the possession of commodities by the Government might entail financial losses. Even if there were that danger, the advantages of the scheme would make it worth while to put up with losses, especially as the amount employed in connection with the scheme would represent an unearned profit on the revaluation of the gold reserve. There is, however, no reason to suppose that there would be any material losses; in fact the probability is that on balance the Government would make a profit, since it would be initiating an upward movement in commodity prices. This is, however, a purely secondary consideration, just as the profit or loss on the operations of the Exchange Equalisation Account is a matter of secondary importance.

In the author's view, the admission of the principle that non-perishable staple commodities can be included in currency reserves to a limited extent would go a long way towards solving the world's monetary problems and also the present problem of surplus stocks. The acquisition of commodity reserves and the desire for their increase by various countries would create a permanent demand for such commodities. This demand and the stocks themselves could be regulated in accordance with broader considerations of economic policy and could be made to become a most important stabilising factor in the world's economic system. This aspect of the problem, however, goes far beyond the scope of this book.

CHAPTER XXVII

BIMETALLISM

(1) What is Bimetallism?

When it is recalled that a large part of the civilised world was for many centuries *de jure* or *de facto* on a bimetallic basis, it may be open to question whether proposals for the restoration of bimetallism can be termed reform proposals. As, however, bimetallism would involve a fundamental change in the monetary system, to the author's mind it can justly be regarded as a reform measure, even though the result would be the restoration of a state of affairs similar to that which existed in the past. After all, if bimetallism cannot be called a reform measure on the ground that it restores conditions which once existed, on the same ground exchange clearing can also be denied the term reform since it is to some extent similar to the mercantilist system that was in force some centuries ago. And yet nobody would hesitate to regard exchange clearing as a reform; nor should there be any doubt about whether bimetallism can be viewed as such.

The bimetallist controversy has such a vast literature that it is difficult to examine it from a new point of view. The substance of bimetallist proposals is that silver should serve jointly with gold as the basis for the currency system. It is usually taken for granted that bimetallism implies a fixed ratio between gold and silver; and the ratio at which bimetallists would like to see silver fixed is usually very much in favour of silver compared with existing relative market prices of the two metals. Perhaps it is desirable to emphasise at the outset that the remonetisation of silver, like the remonetisation of gold, has no hard and fast rules fixed once for all. Most ardent bimetallists would like us to believe that bimetallism necessarily means the restoration of the old fixed ratio of 1 to 16 between gold and silver, just as the extreme wing of the ardent supporters of the gold standard like to take it for granted that the gold standard can mean only the orthodox automatic system with gold coins in circulation. By adopting such an uncompromising attitude these extremists do immense harm to the system they defend. In reality, the remonetisation of silver is quite conceivable without a return to the old fixed ratio of 1 to 16, indeed without a return to any fixed ratio at all. If silver were admitted as part of the metallic reserve, this in itself would amount to a high degree of remonetisation.

(2) Arguments in Favour of Bimetallism

The main arguments in favour of the remonetisation of silver are as follows:

1. It would increase the purchasing power of the silver-using countries by increasing the value of silver in terms of commodities.
2. It would make for greater stability if the currency and credit structure were to be based on two metals instead of one.
3. It would prevent the recurrence of conditions caused by the gold shortage during the post-war stabilisation period.
4. By broadening the basis of currency and credit it would facilitate a reasonable expansion well secured by an adequate metallic reserve.
5. It would enable silver producers and holders of silver stocks to obtain reasonable prices for the metal.

The first argument is the one which has been heard the most in recent years. It was argued that one of the reasons for the world depression was the absence of adequate purchases on the part of the Chinese and other silver-using nations, whose purchasing power had suffered as a result of the decline in silver. This is the reason why some, but by no means all, large business firms engaged in trade with the Far East have played such a prominent part in advocating the remonetisation of silver. Impassioned appeals were addressed to the world demanding in the name of justice and equity that silver should be remonetised and revalued for the sake of raising the purchasing power of the poor destitute Chinese people. Few of the advocates of bimetallism troubled to enquire into the question whether the increase in the gold and commodity value of silver though its remonetisation would benefit the Chinese people as a whole, or merely certain classes to the detriment of the majority. Nor did the supporters of bimetallism specify whether, in demanding the remonetisation of silver in order to raise the purchasing power of the Chinese people, they had in mind their total purchasing power or merely their ability to buy foreign goods. The appreciation of the exchange value of a currency does not in itself raise the total purchasing power of the country concerned. It is true that, since it leads eventually to a fall of internal commodity prices, it increases the purchasing power of the monetary unit. Since, however, the national income also falls—partly through the fall of nominal earnings and partly through the increase of unemployment and of bankruptcies—it usually falls to a larger degree than that of the fall of prices, the net result is a diminution of the total purchasing power of the nation concerned. At the same time, however, its willingness to buy foreign goods will increase, owing to the relative cheapness of those goods in consequence of the appreciation of the national currency. It is this increased willingness to buy foreign goods that is mistaken by foreign observers for an increase of purchasing power. In reality, should the contraction of the total purchasing power through the deflationary effect of the appreciation of the currency go too far, it leads to an actual decline in the volume of imports, even though their proportion to home trade may increase. These remarks hold good for the appreciation of a silver currency in terms of gold as well for the appreciation of a gold currency in terms of other gold currencies. The ardent bimetallists were not concerned with the total purchasing power of the Chinese population but solely with its willingness to buy foreign goods. They were too short-sighted to realise that in spite of the stimulus given to Chinese imports by the appreciation of silver, its internal deflationary effects might assume such proportions as to reduce the nation's capacity to pay even the lower price for imported goods.

(3) "Honest" Inflation

The argument that it would secure greater stability if the monetary system were to be based on two metals instead of one has lost much of its force as a result of the adoption of a managed gold standard after the war. Under the automatic gold standard, even temporary fluctuations in the world gold output tended to result in corresponding fluctuations in the credit structure, trade and price level. Once, however, the practice had been adopted of neutralising gold movements, the world's dependence upon the caprices of nature was considerably reduced. The ratio between the volume of credit and that of the metallic reserve is now much more elastic than it was in days gone by. For this reason the argument that the total output of gold and silver is likely to be subject to less fluctuation than the output of gold alone has lost much of its force.

On the other hand, the argument in favour of bimetallism on the ground that it would obviate a lasting shortage in the monetary metal has gained in strength under the influence of the experience of 1925–31. A permanent shortage of gold, as distinct from the temporary fluctuations in its output, could evidently be cured by the remonetisation of silver. Bimetallists have made full use of this argument, and have convinced many people who were hitherto opposed to bimetallism. During the nineteenth century this aspect of the monetary problem was not nearly so prominent as it was during the period of post-war stability.

Many supporters of bimetallism advocate the system as a means of "honest inflation." Being in favour of currency and credit expansion, they argue that it is better if the surplus credit to be created is based upon a metallic reserve. And since they do not consider the possibility of expanding the gold reserve to an adequate degree by means of drastic devaluation, they see in the remonetisation of silver the only possible means to the desired end.

(4) Bimetallist Self-Interest?

The argument that the remonetisation of silver would be beneficial to silver producers was hardly mentioned by bimetallists. Those are the things one does not talk about. It was nevertheless one of the chief motives of the whole movement as far as the United States was concerned. The influence—conscious or subconscious—of one's material interest upon one's views has never been so clearly illustrated as in the case of bimetallism in the United States. Notwithstanding this, it is a mistake to dismiss the American bimetallist movement—as many of its opponents do—as being solely inspired by the greed and selfishness of a numerically insignificant clique which would like to interfere with the world's monetary system for the sake of increasing its profits on silver production. The number of those directly concerned in the prosperity of silver-mining in the United States is negligible. They would not be able, in themselves, to command such powerful support in Congress and in public opinion were it not for the idealism of a large number of disinterested believers in bimetallism. The opponents of the movement do more harm to themselves than to the bimetallists in indulging in cheap accusations of political corruption, accusations which in the case of the predominant majority of bimetallists are not justified.

(5) Three Aspects of Bimetallism

In dealing with the bimetallistic monetary reform proposals it is necessary to distinguish between three aspects of the problem. There is, in the first place, the question whether or not silver should be remonetised. In the second place, there is the question whether, if silver should be remonetised, a fixed ratio should be maintained between silver and gold. In the third place, the question arises whether, if it is admitted that a fixed ratio should be maintained, that ratio should be as high as is advocated by bimetallists. It is important that there should be no confusion between these three distinct aspects of the controversy.

The idea of remonetising silver appears in itself desirable. The author is in favour of every device by which the security behind the currency and credit structure can be strengthened in order to prepare the ground for the highest possible degree of credit expansion that can be undertaken without undermining confidence. To that end, in Chapter XXV he declared himself in favour of a drastic devaluation by which the book value and the commodity value of gold reserves could be increased considerably. What is more, as was seen in Chapter XXVI, he is in favour even of acquiring non-perishable raw materials as an additional security to the note issue. It would be inconsistent on his part if he were to disapprove of the idea of including silver among the security for the monetary circulation. If, in his view, tin, copper, lead, etc., are good enough to serve as subsidiary reserves to the currency, there is no reason why he should not consider silver suitable. It should be eligible to serve as note cover up to a limited percentage of the total.

It would be a mistake, however, to admit silver on an equal footing with gold, and to enable producers and holders of stocks of silver to dump unlimited supplies upon Central Banks. The reason why gold is so eminently suitable to serve as a monetary metal lies in its relative scarcity. Even if the price of gold were to be raised through drastic devaluation, the extent to which this would lead to an increase of the annual output would be relatively moderate. This fact has been confirmed by the experience of recent years. This quality of relative scarcity does not exist for silver to anything like the same degree as for gold. It would, therefore, be undesirable to multiply silver production by admitting silver as note cover to an unlimited degree. Such a system might easily lead to the watering down of the metallic reserve to an extent which might undermine confidence and defeat its own object. From this point of view, the limit of 25 per cent fixed by the United States errs if anything on the generous side.

(6) Fixed Ratio between Gold and Silver

Once it is admitted that silver should be remonetised to a limited degree, the question arises whether it should bear a fixed relation to gold. The main argument in favour of a fixed ratio is that in its absence fluctuations in the price of silver might inflict losses upon Central Banks. This is doubtless true. At the same time, if the percentage of silver in the note cover is not too large, the possible losses are also moderate. They can well be borne out of the profit arising from the note-issuing activities of Central Banks. In any case, the remonetisation of silver should be made conditional upon control over the new silver production, control which would reduce the degree of fluctuation.

A strong argument against a fixed ratio between gold and silver is that it caused much difficulty in the old days of bimetallism. From time to time, the ratio became largely artificial as a result of the appreciation or depreciation of one of the two metals. Doubtless, if all countries were to adopt bimetallism, the task of maintaining the ratio between gold and silver would be greatly facilitated. It is highly doubtful, however, whether such uniform arrangement could ever be achieved. In its absence a limited remonetisation of silver without a fixed ratio in relation to gold would be possible if a number of leading countries were to agree to it.

Thus, remonetisation without a fixed ratio appears to be more within the realm of practical politics than the establishment of a fixed ratio by international agreement. Similar arrangements existed in a number of countries before the war; among others the members of the Latin Monetary Union included silver at its metallic value in the metallic reserve. The same system still operates in Spain and in a few other countries.

(7) The Price of Silver

There remains the question whether, in connection with the remonetisation of silver, its price should be raised or should be allowed to rise. World-wide remonetisation would of course lead to a higher price without any artificial price-raising efforts. It is essential, however, that the price should not be allowed to rise to a level which, though possibly justified by temporary demand for the replenishment of silver stocks, would in the long run prove untenable. It would be possible to maintain a relative *de facto* stability of silver in terms of gold, provided that the price of silver were not too high. If, however, silver were allowed to rise to an unreasonably high level, then it would be risky for Central Banks to acquire large amounts. In the interest of bimetallism, it is important, therefore, that there should not be a spectacular rise in the price of silver in connection with its remonetisation.

The insistence of bimetallists upon such a rise is unquestionably the weakest part of their campaign. Besides being economically unsound in many instances, it has the flavour of self-interest. No effort to present the rise of silver as a means of improving the situation of silver-using countries can conceal the fact that some of those who demand a higher price for silver are prompted by the desire to be able to sell their output or their stock at a higher price, or to be able to increase their merchandise sales to the silver-using countries. It is evident that an appreciation of silver has strong deflationary effects upon silver-using countries and that while rentiers and those in receipt of fixed incomes may benefit from it, on the other hand, trade in general is bound to suffer. It is by its insistence upon a high price for silver that bimetallism has become discredited to a large extent by recent experience—notably, of course, by the experience of the effects of a rise in silver upon China.

CHAPTER XXVIII

THE AMERICAN BIMETALLIST EXPERIMENT

(1) Bimetallism before the Crisis

Unquestionably, the United States under President Roosevelt went further towards applying various monetary reform measures in practice than any other country has done at any time in history. Cheap money, an expansion of credit and of purchasing power, a public works policy, an elastic gold standard and devaluation were all tried in turn. Most of these devices, however, were applied not so much as permanent reform measures as merely for the purpose of raising the United States from the depth of depression into which she had sunk between 1929 and 1933. One of the few measures which was adopted with the declared object of providing a permanent reform was the restoration of bimetallism. As is well known, bimetallism lingered on in the United States for many years after it had been abandoned in most other parts of the world. A presidential election was fought over bimetallism in the 'nineties. Throughout the first three decades of the twentieth century, agitation for the restoration of bimetallism continued in the United States. While in Europe the question was regarded as of merely historical interest, it remained very much alive in the United States, where the silver-producing interests succeeded in keeping the problem before the eyes of the public. Apart from financial considerations, the question of remonetising silver commanded a certain sentimental interest in the United States.

It was not, however, until the advent of the economic depression that the bimetallists' chance arrived. There was a revival of bimetallism even in Europe, especially in Great Britain where Mr. J. M. Darling, whose idealistic and persistent campaign "kept the flag flying", succeeded in obtaining support from some leading business men concerned with trade with the Far East. In Great Britain, however, the agitation found but little response. It was unable to prevent the Government even from continuing to liquidate the Indian monetary silver stock. Nor was the Continent any more receptive to the idea of bimetallism.

(2) The U.S. "Silver Group"

In the United States, on the other hand, bimetallism was wholly successful. It was taken up by a powerful political group headed by Senator Pittman, who played his hand with remarkable skill. Although the importance of the silver-mining industry in the United States is negligible—it is often pointed out by the opponents of bimetallism that peanuts are a more important commodity in the United States than silver—Senator Pittman nevertheless succeeded in convincing a large number of Congressmen and a large section of public opinion that the remonetisation of silver was of primary importance to the United States. His "silver group" in Congress included, in addition to the representatives of silver-producing States, all those who were in favour of monetary expansion and also those who hoped that a rise in the price of silver would improve American trade with the Far East. The group has become a factor of great importance in the American political situation. President Roosevelt could not afford to ignore it. It is difficult to say whether in any other country than the United States, or in any other circumstances than those prevailing during the prolonged depression, it would have been possible to mobilise such a force behind a relatively insignificant movement. History has many examples to show that the intrinsic importance of a movement is not necessarily proportionate to the number of its supporters or the strength of their support. At the same time, the atmosphere in the United States was, for historical and political reasons, as well as for financial reasons, eminently suitable for working up a wave of enthusiasm in favour of bimetallism.

(3) The Reform of 1934

While the President was wholly in favour of monetary expansion he did his utmost to resist pressure in favour of extreme inflation. To disarm his radical opposition he had to make concessions and one of these concessions was the silver policy he adopted in 1934. Legislation was passed by which silver was admitted to form part of the metallic reserve to the extent of 25 per cent of the total metallic stock. At the same time, the privately owned silver stocks were nationalised, and the Treasury began to purchase silver on a large scale both at home and abroad, in order to bring the stock up to 25 per cent of the total reserve. The dream of bimetallists has thus become reality. The United States has definitely decided to adopt the bimetallic standard.

So far so good. The broadening of the metallic basis of the American currency and credit structure by the admission of silver to a limited degree was definitely a step in the right direction. Although to begin with the United States was isolated in her policy, had she adopted bimetallism in reasonable circumstances, it might have been possible to gain for it the support of other countries. Unfortunately, the United States Administration did not confine itself to the partial remonetisation of silver. It also embarked upon an entirely unnecessary and uncalled-for effort to revalue silver artificially. While it was natural that the remonetisation of silver by such an important country as the United States should cause a certain rise—especially as it was evident that the American authorities would have to purchase large quantities during the coming years—this in itself was not sufficient to satisfy the demands of American silver interests. These interests insisted that the price of silver must be raised artificially to a level at which it represented a multiple of its cost of production. Yielding to the pressure of the silver group, President Roosevelt had legislation passed which provided for the raising of the price of silver eventually to $1·29 per fine ounce. In addition, he began to raise the price at which the United States Treasury was prepared to buy newly mined American silver.

(4) Silver Boom and Slump

The absurdity of this policy was glaringly obvious. Given the fact that the United States Treasury had to purchase a large quantity of silver within a few years, it would have been to the interest of the American authorities to delay the rise in the price of the metal so as to be able to acquire the stock they needed at the lowest possible cost. Instead, the Treasury deliberately raised the price of silver against itself and thus gave free gifts running into millions of dollars to silver producers in the United States and abroad. On several occasions the official buying price was raised and, even though this price applied only to the American silver output, the world price of silver moved more or less in sympathy. During the first half of 1935, there developed in consequence a reckless speculation in silver. Large bull positions were accumulated in anticipation of a further rise in the American buying price and the London price rose to 36*d.*

This speculative fever was followed by a heavy slump in the summer of 1935. In order to prevent it from assuming disastrous dimensions, the United States Treasury had to step in and support the market. Ever since June 1935, the United States Treasury has been practically the only large buyer of silver, while everybody else has been selling. For months the silver market was wholly artificial and one-sided. The price was pegged by the American authorities, which at times had to buy huge amounts to neutralise the selling pressure. Eventually, in December 1935, the United States Treasury got tired of supporting the market, and allowed the price to find its level. There was a disastrous slump, from over 29*d.* to under 20*d.* The American authorities withdrew their support almost completely from the London market, though they continued to purchase substantial amounts from silver-producing countries.

(5) Unnecessary Fluctuations

The United States Government cannot be too severely criticised for having brought upon the world these entirely unnecessary fluctuations in silver. There was no need whatever to raise the buying price of silver, thereby initiating a wave of bull speculation. When subsequently the boom had to be liquidated, official American quarters complained much about the unwanted rise of silver through the activities of speculators. In reality, it would never have occurred to speculators to run up long positions had it not been for the encouragement received from Washington. While the main object of raising the buying price for American domestic silver was to satisfy the powerful "silver group", it was evident that the inevitable consequence of repeatedly raising the internal price would be a speculative rise in the world price. The Roosevelt Administration is fully responsible for that rise.

Admittedly, once the mischief had been done, it was difficult for the American authorities to solve the dilemma of whether to support silver indefinitely or allow it to collapse. The latter alternative was chosen after the decision of China formally to suspend the silver standard and to demonetise silver. This was a hard blow to the American silver policy, but again it was only a natural consequence of that policy, and the Washington Administration was the perpetrator, not the victim. This being so, the American authorities cannot very well disclaim responsibility for either the boom or the slump in silver. If they had not, for political reasons, raised the price of domestic silver in the spring of 1935, the bull position whose forced liquidation was responsible for the slump would never have been created. Nor would China have been driven to despair and compelled to suspend the silver standard.

Worst of all, since the official American policy continues to aim at eventually raising the world price of silver, there is not even the reassurance that the recent slump may create a state of lasting equilibrium in the silver market. There will be more superfluous fluctuations before the failure of the policy is realised in Washington.

(6) Effect on China

In itself, the wholesale acquisition of silver through the support of the market in 1935 would not have been contrary to the interests of the United States and of bimetallism, for in any case the American silver stock had to be increased. In a sense, the American silver purchases were useful, since they mitigated the flow of gold from Europe to the United States, which was all to the good. Unfortunately, the boom and the following slump in silver did irreparable harm to the cause of bimetallism. Not only were European countries less inclined than ever to consider the idea of remonetising such an undependable metal, but even China, the last stronghold of the silver standard, was forced to the conclusion that in the existing circumstances she could not remain on a silver basis any longer.

For the American silver policy had disastrous consequences upon China. During the years while the price of silver was falling, the silver-using countries benefited by the effect of that fall upon their price level. When, however, the trend was reversed because of the silver policy of President Roosevelt, the rise in the price of silver was accompanied by a slump in commodity prices. China had her full share of the blessings of deflation, which her population had been spared during the years of gradually declining silver prices. What is more, the tempting price offered for silver induced many Chinese holders to sell out. There was a heavy outflow of silver which to a large extent depleted the country of its monetary resources, causing an acute scarcity of currency and a series of bank failures.

It was useless to try to counteract the outflow by the imposition of large export taxes, for the authority of the Chinese Government was not sufficiently established to enable it to prevent smuggling on a large scale. Nor did China benefit by the relapse in the price in silver, for this, by its suddenness and violence, simply caused fresh disturbances. The drain on the country's silver stock went on unabated through boom and slump. In November 1935 there was a violent speculative attack on the Chinese dollar, against which the Government was powerless. In such circumstances, the Nanking Government decided to suspend the silver standard, to demonetise silver and to adopt an inconvertible paper currency stabilised in relation to sterling and the yen.

(7) Silver Policy Doomed

At the time of writing it appears that the ill-advised American silver policy is doomed to failure. Evidently, the United States, in spite of all her immense resources, is in herself unable to carry the burden of the silver stocks of the whole world. Indeed, as the extent to which the American authorities can hold silver as note cover is limited to 25 per cent, once an amount equivalent in value to one-third of the gold stock has been acquired, the American authorities will have to cease buying silver. Similarly, official purchases abroad would have to be discontinued once the American internal price has reached the statutory figure of $1·29. Nor would it be safe to go quite up to the statutory limit of the proportion of silver to gold reserve, for in doing so the American authorities would place themselves in a position in which they would have to sell silver to a reluctant market every time there was an outflow of gold. In addition, it is not to the interest of American silver producers that the American authorities should complete their purchases by acquiring silver abroad. A point would be reached when the silver group would be opposed to any further purchases abroad, on the ground that a margin must be allowed for American silver output in coming years. Given the fact that the American official purchases will thus come to an end sooner or later, it is difficult to see how the price of silver can be kept up at its present level, much less forced to, or maintained at, the figure of 1·29 dollars. At present, only American purchases in the silver-producing countries prevent a further heavy fall of silver, and the moment these purchases cease a slump will be inevitable. This is evident to all holders of silver, who are naturally anxious to take advantage of the American support while it lasts—hence the persistent selling from the East.

The example of the American bimetallistic experiment shows how easy it is to bring discredit upon a monetary reform scheme by its mistaken application. Had the United States confined herself to maintaining the price of silver at the level at which it stood when the silver policy was inaugurated, bimetallism would in all probability have been adopted to a limited degree by a number of leading countries. At that time, in fact, President Roosevelt held all the trumps, for the threat of further depreciation or devaluation of the dollar would perhaps have been sufficient to induce the British, French and other Governments to fall into line with a sensible silver policy. In the meantime, however, he discarded his trumps by virtually stabilising the dollar at its present level, and by pursuing a mistaken silver policy which has placed the United States at a great disadvantage. In all probability the result of this mistaken policy will be a fatal set-back to the movement of bimetallism.

CHAPTER XXIX

CONSISTENT DEFLATION

(1) An Orthodox Reform

It is a popular belief that all monetary reformers are necessarily radicals, and that the orthodox camp is opposed to every kind of monetary reform proposals. The main object of the orthodox school is to restore the monetary system that operated before the crisis, or preferably before the war. There is, however, one monetary reform proposal which claims a marked departure from the old system and yet has actually been elaborated in the orthodox camp. Although the object of the reform is to maintain the orthodox gold standard, the methods proposed to that end are none the less monetary reform measures. The system in question is that of " consistent deflation ", a system elaborated entirely by practical men. While theoretical experts were debating, the statesmen of the Gold Bloc evolved a new system without any theoretical background. For some time the system did not even possess a name, but in the course of the budget debate in the Dutch parliament in July 1935, it became known under the name of " consistent deflation ".

According to classical principles, deflation must be carried out in accordance with rules which are compatible with the automatic gold standard. If the price level of a country is out of equilibrium with the world level, it must be allowed to adjust itself through the normal working of gold movements. An influx or efflux of gold causes respectively an expansion or a contraction of credit, which should be followed by a reduction or an increase of the bank rate. Where there is necessity for a downward readjustment of the price level—this is the readjustment with which we are primarily concerned here—the classical rule is that the credit restrictions that precede and succeed the increase of the bank rate will tend to cause a fall of prices, and that this in turn will induce individuals, firms, and the Government to reduce their expenditure to the level of their reduced incomes. While this downward adjustment is not expected ever to be absolutely perfect, and while it is admitted that there are bound to be wide discrepancies between the extent to which various prices, cost items, incomes, etc., fall, it is contended that the law of averages works out in accordance with requirements. Until a few years ago every orthodox economist would have considered it heretical to suggest that the process of readjustment should be regulated by Government intervention so as to secure a higher degree of uniformity in the all-round fall of prices and other items. To-day, however, many members of the orthodox school—even among academic economists—recognise, or at any rate do not oppose, the admissibility of Government intervention with the object of regulating deflation in the interest of maintaining the existing gold parities.

(2) Regulating Downward Trend

The underlying idea of consistent deflation is the theory that a sharp downward movement of prices causes depression and crisis because it does not affect every kind of price and every item simultaneously, or to the same degree. It is the sluggishness of the cost of living and of fixed charges in following the decline of wholesale prices that is largely responsible for unemployment during a period of falling prices. In the main, it is the increase of the real burden of fixed charges, and especially of debt charges, that leads to wholesale insolvency during a deflationary period. Accordingly, if a solution can be found by which all items can be made to move in the same direction at the same time and to the same extent, the greater part of the disadvantages of deflation will thereby be avoided. In the past, both inflation and deflation have been essentially irregular and haphazard movements. "Consistent" deflation regulates the downward trend. Instead of allowing the various items to adjust themselves in the best way they can, under "consistent" deflation they would be adjusted by means of Government intervention.

Needless to say, this involves a high degree of interference with economic freedom. To be consistent, orthodox economists ought to oppose the idea to the utmost. They are, in fact, confronted with a conflict of loyalties. On the one hand, they are anxious to strengthen the defence of gold parities. On the other hand, they are also anxious to reduce Government interference with business to a minimum. So far, few orthodox economists have defined their attitude towards this dilemma. As, however, the maintenance of gold parities is of predominant importance to them, many of them are probably willing to sacrifice their *laissez-faire* principles to this end. Indeed, from their insistence that in a time of falling prices nothing should be done to bolster up wages it is but a short step to the demand that the fall of wages should actually be encouraged by Government intervention. A much more bitter pill is the admission of the principle that the Government has the right to control commodity prices, hotel charges and even wages of non-Government employees. Even more difficult a dose for orthodox economists to swallow is the extension of consistent deflation to embrace loan contracts through what amounts to a partial repudiation of the public debt and, what is worse, through interference with the terms of purely private loan contracts.

(3) Economists' Dilemma

It would be too much indeed to expect the academic members of the classical school to endorse such a violation of their most cherished principles. Statesmen, confronted with the practical task of defending their gold parities, are not so particular about choosing their weapons, and are prepared to overthrow some of their orthodox principles to secure the success of their efforts. They duly realise that in present-day conditions the classical remedies would be impracticable and futile. Politicians have to be opportunists. It is only academic economists that can afford to be absolutely dogmatic, not only about their aims but also about the means by which they should be sought. Once the statesmen had adopted measures to enforce consistent deflation, they received the tacit support of the orthodox economists of their countries. Nevertheless, the system of consistent deflation is lacking in adequate theoretical background. Those who are best qualified to provide it are for obvious reasons reluctant to pursue the idea to its logical conclusions. Confronted with their dilemma, they confine themselves to a grudging or tacit approval of intervention as a necessary evil in order to avert what they consider to be a still greater evil.

In substance consistent deflation—and its counterpart, consistent inflation—is the reversal of the idea of the elastic gold standard. According to the latter system the gold content of the monetary unit should be subject to frequent changes, so that prices, wages, cost of living and various fixed charges can remain constant in terms of the monetary unit. According to the consistent deflation scheme, prices, wages, the cost of living and fixed charges should be elastic in terms of monetary unit so that the gold content of the monetary unit can remain unchanged.

(4) A Constant State of Flux

Should it be possible to carry through the system completely, it would mean that all the bases of reckoning in everyday life would be in a constant state of flux. Day after day the items of our revenue and expenditure would be subject to changes in terms of monetary units. In theory, this would not cause any difficulty so long as all items were made to move together. In practice, however, the constant changes in prices, wages, etc., would cause a great deal of inconvenience to the masses, owing to the virtual impossibility of a rapid adjustment of everyday transactions to these frequent changes. Having to think in terms of different prices and incomes day after day or even week after week would mean an almost intolerable strain on the majority of people.

Moreover, it would be technically difficult to carry through consistent deflation completely. For instance, even a 10 per cent reduction in tram fares would be unthinkable, let alone reductions of 1 per cent or fractions of it. For such minor items, the adjustment could be only approximate. To those to whom such items represent a large percentage of expenditure the system would be anything but ideal. To avoid the necessity of reckoning in fractions of pence in order to carry through relatively small changes, it would be necessary to defer the adjustment until the discrepancy was, say, 5 or 10 per cent. Should that rule be adopted, temporary injustices would develop. The fact that too frequent all-round changes would, under a policy of consistent deflation, cause great inconvenience, would make it imperative that adjustments should be made at infrequent intervals only. Instead of making changes of 1 per cent every day or every week, changes of 5 to 10 per cent would be made every quarter or every year. Meanwhile, some of the prices, wages, etc., would fall automatically, while others would not, and during the transition periods the community would suffer the disadvantage of haphazard deflation. Thus, both frequent and infrequent all-round cuts would cause considerable inconvenience.

In any case, even if consistent deflation were to be carried to its logical conclusion, it would not remove the injustices caused by fluctuating prices. If a man pays his rent on June 25 and receives a half-yearly interest payment on July 1, whilst between the two dates an all-round cut has been carried through, he will evidently suffer a loss.

(5) Resistance to All-round Cuts

Hitherto we have assumed that the Government is in a position to effect changes in prices, wages, etc., without meeting any resistance. This is certainly not the case in practice. As we shall see in the next chapter, experience to date shows that the enforcement of consistent deflation meets with the utmost resistance from the various interests concerned. Would it, however, be possible to persuade the public that, since deflation is carried through consistently, they are no worse off after it than they were before? It is doubtful. It is only human nature to resist to the utmost any cuts in our money income, even though we are assured that our real income will be unchanged. It is almost unthinkable that all classes of the community would submit to money cuts without a murmur. On the contrary, in all probability the classes which have the political power would endeavour to shift the burden of the changes upon the other classes. They would try to make the all-round changes an opportunity for increasing their relative share in the national income. Such attempts are much easier to resist under conditions of stable prices than under conditions of frequent all-round changes, when wages would in any case be in the melting-pot.

It may well be asked whether it would be worth while to put up with all the disadvantages of having to change the price of every single commodity and service merely to avoid having to change the price of one single commodity, that of gold. Indeed, consistent deflation appears to be the best way of reducing to absurdity the conception that the stability of the monetary unit in terms of gold is or should be the supreme goal of nations. While it is theoretically impossible to make all-round cuts in prices, wages, various items of the cost of living and fixed charges, the regulation of profits is obviously unthinkable. That is, while it is always possible to cut down profits by means of higher taxation, it is impossible to raise them, maintain them or prevent them from falling beyond a certain point by means of Government intervention. Thus, even in theory consistent deflation could never be altogether consistent. When it comes to practice, it would inevitably be grossly inconsistent.

(6) Constructive Elements in Consistent Deflation

What is worth retaining from the idea of consistent deflation is the principle that the Government should have full power to adjust prices, wages, cost of living and fixed charges, not necessarily in the interest of the stability of the monetary unit but in the interest of regulating distribution. Such powers are essential in order to prevent or counteract maldistribution of purchasing power. Particularly useful would be retention of the principle that the debt charges must not be considered as absolutely sacrosanct. The experience of Great Britain during the last three years has proved that, notwithstanding the Government's policy of cheap money, the effective reduction of the interest burden by normal means is a long and difficult process. Indeed, after promising progress in the right direction, the decline in the yield of Government securities has come to a halt, while progress in the decline of mortgage and other interest charges has been altogether unsatisfactory. Even if conversion to a lower basis were practicable, the existence of long-term contracts would prevent many debtors from taking advantage of its possibilities. It is evident that, in order to reduce the burden of deadweight debt, Government intervention is indispensable.

Until recently, a time-honoured conception of legality prevented the Governments of the first-rate countries from reducing the burden of public and private indebtedness by cutting interest rates. The gold-clause legislation of President Roosevelt was the first step towards overcoming this legalistic conception. It was followed by forced conversion operations under the disguise of voluntary conversions in Italy, Germany and Belgium. The action of the French Government in directly reducing interest rates constituted an even more severe blow to legalism. It created a highly important precedent and indicated the way in which excessive interest burdens can be reduced. There still remains the problem of excessive capital burdens. Even if the supporters of consistent deflation do not dare to tackle this problem, the reduction of the interest burden in itself goes a long way towards reducing the disequilibrium between fictitious wealth and real wealth, a disequilibrium which has been largely responsible for all the world's troubles since the war.

(7) Consistent Inflation

Before closing this chapter, it is perhaps worth examining how the principles involved in the system of consistent deflation can be applied for inflation. Under the orthodox system an inflationary movement takes place in just as haphazard a way as a deflationary movement. Discrepancies develop between the rise in the various groups of prices, wages, etc., while fixed charges remain, of course, unchanged. The lack of uniformity in the rise inflicts hardships on various classes of the population. Among others, wage-earners are usually at a disadvantage during the interval between the rise in the cost of living and the upward adjustment of their earnings. Needless to say, the same orthodox economists who are so anxious that wages should fall during a period of falling prices are not nearly as anxious that wages should rise during a period of rising prices. And yet, humane considerations apart, such a rise is essential in order to prevent a maldistribution of purchasing power which might lead to an economic crisis, as indeed it did in 1929.

To the extent to which the principles of consistent deflation are worth retaining, they are also worth applying to consistent inflation. The evil of an upward movement, like that of a downward movement, can also be mitigated by Government intervention to hasten the process of adjustment. Applied to wages, consistent inflation amounts to a "new deal", about which more will be said in the next chapter. Applied to debt contracts, it can fulfil a useful task by mitigating outstanding cases of hardship caused to the rentier classes by rises in prices. While there can be no question of rigid enforcement of either consistent deflation or consistent inflation, there is much in both that is worth retaining as essential parts of a comprehensive scheme of economic planning. This aspect of the problem is, however, outside the scope of this book.

CHAPTER XXX

CONSISTENT DEFLATION IN PRACTICE

(1) Consistent Deflation in Italy

As we pointed out in the last chapter, the system of consistent deflation developed without any theoretical background. It was practical statesmen and not theoretical economists who hit upon this solution, not for any theoretical considerations but out of practical necessity. Their object was to reduce budgetary expenditure, and it was in order to make the cuts in civil service salaries more bearable that efforts were made to lower the cost of living. Apart from this, the desire to be able to compete with foreign rivals and to attract tourist traffic also contributed to the endeavours to lower prices and charges in general. Those who applied this new method were unaware that they were inaugurating a new system. They merely thought that they were applying a rather more drastic and less orthodox method of deflation. Having realised the difficulty and grave disadvantages of deflating by means of credit restrictions, they had to devise some alternative method, and in their search for a practical solution they hit upon consistent deflation.

The originator of the new system was Signor Mussolini. As early as 1931 he carried through an all-round cut in Civil Service salaries, and, to make the sacrifice more tolerable, he also ordered the reduction of rents, hotel charges and certain other items of the cost of living. Thanks to his dictatorial power, and to the economic discipline established in Italy, he was well in a position to carry out so drastic and unprecedented an intervention in economic life. He made a similar all-round cut in 1934. In that year, too, independently of these cuts, he reduced charges on Government municipal and mortgage loans by the encouragement of "voluntary" conversion operations which were, in fact, if not in law, forced conversions. The degree of consistent deflation applied by Signor Mussolini was not, however, sufficient to adjust the lira to its economic parities. Admittedly, it was helpful in that it obviated the necessity for deflating by means of credit restrictions.

(2) A Smaller Evil

There can be no doubt that the direct method, inasmuch as it can be employed without causing grave political or industrial unrest, is incomparably less harmful to trade than the indirect method of reducing prices by a high bank rate and by contraction of credit. Indeed, in Italy, the acceleration of the adjustment of the cost of living to the lower level of wholesale prices made cuts in wages and salaries less burdensome and reduced the extent of the contraction in purchasing power. There is reason to believe that the absence of any obvious aggravation of the economic depression in Italy during 1931–4 was largely, if not exclusively, due to the unorthodox method by which deflation was carried out. Indeed, it was thanks to his unorthodox method that Signor Mussolini was able to deflate to a high degree for years, in spite of the reflationary effect of large public expenditure on ambitious public works schemes. It was possible to avoid an unduly high bank rate; what is more, early in 1934 the bank rate was actually reduced before the application of an all-round cut. Owing to the political conditions prevailing in Italy, and to the illegality of strikes, the cuts were carried out with the minimum of friction or evasion. The result was that, until the end of 1934, the price level in Italy remained approximately in the vicinity of the price level in other Gold Bloc countries, notwithstanding the expansionary effect of her public works scheme.

For a long time it was believed that, while a dictator in a Fascist State was in a position to adopt such measures, it was unthinkable under a system of Parliamentary democracy. During 1935 it was discovered, however, that this is by no means the case. In more than one democratic country consistent deflation was adopted in order to defend the gold parity. Prior to the devaluation of the belga, Belgium adopted, or was about to adopt, measures which amounted to a limited degree of consistent deflation. Her example was followed by other countries in Western Europe.

(3) Consistent Deflation in France and Holland

In connection with his drastic economy measures, M. Laval adopted the same system. In fact, in many ways he went even further than Italy. For, in addition to cutting rents and certain items of the cost of living by decree, he also ordered the reduction of interest on public and certain private indebtedness to the extent of 10 per cent. He did not take the trouble to disguise this reduction under the pretence of voluntary conversions. It was presented as the logical outcome of the necessity for deflationary measures in defence of the franc. The adoption of consistent deflation was not as simple a matter in France as in Italy. It led to disturbances in the naval shipyards and elsewhere, and in more than one instance the Government had to yield to some extent in face of determined resistance to the cuts. There was, moreover, much evasion, and for various reasons the actual effect of the cuts upon the price level or the cost of living was disappointing.

Soon after the publication of M. Laval's economy measures, another democratic State resorted to the same system. Dr. Colijn, in attempting to balance the Dutch Budget, linked up his economy measures with reductions in the interest on mortgage loans and other similar cuts. His scheme was rejected by Parliament. Strangely enough, part of the Opposition parties criticised his measures on the ground that they did not go far enough, and suggested that he should go a step further by cutting down not only the interest but also the principal of mortgage debts. Since the proposed drastic economies met with strong resistance, Dr. Colijn decided to abandon the scheme, confining himself to some relatively moderate cuts without any application of consistent deflation. The idea has not, however, been dropped completely, and sooner or later it will probably be applied.

(4) An Alternative to Devaluation?

Let us now consider the immediate practical aspects of the new system. Is its application likely to be able to save the gold currencies? Can consistent deflation thus provide an alternative to devaluation? Let us take the example of France. It is possible that, by forcing a slight reduction in the cost of living, the budgetary cuts would have been made somewhat less unbearable. Indeed, anticipation of this result probably explains why the cuts did not meet with more violent opposition. As, however, M. Laval's cuts were followed by an increase in the cost of living, those who suffered the cuts are worse off than they were before. If the cuts are to be repeated, the position of these classes might easily become unbearable. And the cuts would have to be repeated should France persist in her effort to restore equilibrium between French prices and world prices without devaluing the franc. Judging from past experience, it may be taken for granted that all-round cuts in Government expenditure, interest, etc., inevitably lead to a fall in revenue.

Before very long the budget would once again be hopelessly unbalanced, and to reduce the deficit the cuts would have to be repeated. As certain items such as expenditure on national defence would not be touched, the cuts on the remaining items would have to be made all the heavier. The direct victims of the cuts would derive some compensation from a reduction in the cost of living, but once again it would be impossible to make the scaling down in every sphere. There would be growing discontent among victims of the cuts if the operation were repeated over and over again. What is more, it would establish a vicious circle in which cuts, reductions in the cost of living, lower purchasing power, falling prices and profits, and a decline in budgetary revenue would chase one another endlessly.

It is doubtful whether it is politically possible to carry out consistent deflation indefinitely. As far as France is concerned, it is evident that a second all-round cut would lead to grave political disturbances, and it is doubtful whether any Government would run the risk of facing the consequences of such a fateful decision. Even in Italy, where the iron rule of Signor Mussolini precludes the possibility of such political repercussions, it was considered inexpedient to resort to measures of consistent deflation too frequently. Throughout the crisis there were only two all-round cuts of approximately 10 per cent each, even though several more would have been required to bring about a complete adjustment. After his second all-round cut, Signor Mussolini evidently reached the conclusion that, after all, *le jeu ne vaut pas la chandelle.*

(5) Demoralising Effect of Consistent Deflation

There is another danger which might upset the operation of the system. If carried far the application of consistent deflation, not only to interest charges, but also to capital burdens, would be unavoidable. In fact, the Dutch opposition has already made proposals to that effect. In order to save debtors from insolvency, through the effects of deflation on their earnings and on the value of their assets, it would become necessary to reduce their liabilities. The result would be that the banks would suffer heavy losses. To be consistent, they would have to be indemnified through an extension of the cuts to deposits. Any such attempt, however, would result in wholesale withdrawals by depositors and would lead to financial collapse. Thus, in addition to leading to a budgetary deadlock, consistent deflation would also provoke a banking crisis. Consistent deflation, if carried to its logical conclusion, thus tends to undermine credit and confidence. Debtors in general, and the largest debtor of all, the Government itself, would in the long run have to pay a heavy price for the relief provided by consistent deflation. While creditors and investors may be willing to put up with one cut in their claims in the hope that it will settle the problem for good, if the cuts are expected to be repeated, holders of claims that are likely to be affected by the cuts may easily become panicky and may throw their holdings on the market. The capital depreciation thus caused would preclude the possibility of contracting new loans on acceptable terms. Indeed, it is doubtful whether the Government, having repeatedly cut its debt service, would be able to borrow at all on any terms for a long time. The reason why the French Treasury finds it almost impossible to borrow in the market is partly that the debt service was cut by 10 per cent; and yet, it was only one cut so far.

Admittedly, consistent deflation will enable the countries of the Gold Bloc to prolong their resistance to devaluation. The fact that it enables their Governments to reduce debt charges leads to a postponement of the moment when deflation reduces itself to absurdity. It will, however, make no difference to the final outcome. Possibly consistent deflation may prolong the life of the gold currencies for twelve months or more, but it will not avert their ultimate fate.

Looking now to the future of consistent deflation, we can conclude that it is most unlikely that the principle will be adopted as the basis of the normal monetary policy of any country. It would be a retrograde move entirely in conflict with the general trend, which points towards the adoption of a less rigid attitude towards gold parities than has prevailed in the past. Far from adopting the principle that gold parities should be maintained at the cost of frequent all-round adjustments of all prices and charges, in all probability there will be more willingness to adjust gold parities in face of strong pressure.

(6) Consistent Inflation in Practice

During the war and post-war inflation many items lagged behind the general trend. The Governments, so far from seeking to enforce uniformity in the rising trend, concentrated much effort upon deliberately delaying or preventing altogether the rise of certain items, such as the prices of essential commodities, rents, etc. In some instances, it was not until long after the stabilisation of the currencies that these items were allowed to adjust themselves to some extent to the new level. There were barely any instances of deliberate action on the part of Governments that could be described as measures of consistent inflation. One of the few exceptions was the valorisation of Government securities and various types of other claims in countries where inflation reached a very advanced stage, and where the depreciation of the monetary unit caused exceptional hardship to the rentier classes.

It was not until the advent of President Roosevelt that the principle implied in consistent inflation found practical application to some degree. One of the basic principles of President Roosevelt's New Deal was that reflation should be accompanied and supported by a reasonable rise in wages. The adoption of various codes under the National Recovery Administration aimed at accelerating the pace at which the wages were adjusted to the reflated price level. The example remained, however, more or less isolated. It created, none the less, an important precedent which may in the course of time produce a profound influence upon the Governmental attitude towards wages.

An attempt was made in the United States to force upon

the Administration the adoption of the principle of consistent inflation for a large section of Government debt and private debt. Had the efforts to uphold the gold clause been successful, the practical result would have been that a substantial section of public and private indebtedness would have kept pace with the degree of inflation expressed in the rise in the price of gold in terms of dollars. As, however, the Supreme Court refused to uphold the gold clause, this effort at consistent inflation failed.

CHAPTER XXXI

NEGATIVE INTEREST RATES

(1) Velocity of Circulation of Money

Most monetary reform proposals are concerned with the physical volume of means of payment available for production or consumption. There is one school, however, which takes relatively little interest in the actual quantity of currency and credit, and concentrates instead upon their velocity of circulation. By velocity of circulation we mean the number of times a given amount of currency or credit changes hands in a given period of time. It is evident that the same amount of currency and credit can do more work if it is turned over more frequently. An increase in the velocity of circulation of money tends, therefore, to produce the same effect as an increase in its quantity. A given volume whose velocity is increased can finance a larger amount of production and consumption. At the same time, compared with an increase in the physical volume of money, it has the advantage that it does not tend to undermine confidence. It is no wonder, then, that many monetary reformers have turned towards this method of expansionism.

There are some very mild methods by which the velocity of circulation can be increased. The "spending" campaign launched by radical economists during the early period of the depression, when they declared it to be the civic duty of everybody to spend as much as he could afford, was in substance an endeavour to speed up the velocity of the circulation of money. An even more moderate device to the same end was the campaign launched in the Press some years ago by which everybody was called upon to pay his bills with the least possible delay. Needless to say, neither of these two campaigns produced any substantial or lasting results.

(2) Negative Interest on Deposits

There are more drastic means by which the velocity of circulation can be increased. These measures can be considered with the proposal for a negative interest rate. If holders of bank notes or of bank balances were threatened, not only with loss of interest, but with the imposition of a negative interest charge as a penalty for keeping their funds idle, they would take good care to keep as little cash or bank balances as possible. Various proposals have been made to this end. The best known amongst them are the proposal made by Mr. Isidore Ostrer for a negative interest rate on bank deposits, and the proposal made by Silvio Gesell for the establishment of " free money ". The idea behind the first proposal is that by penalising idle deposits by a negative interest rate their owner could be compelled to make productive use of the funds either by spending them, thereby increasing employment, or by producing goods themselves or by lending the funds to those engaged in production. In reality, this last is exactly what the banks themselves are doing. They are in a position to lend to industries simply because individuals and firms leave idle funds in their safe custody. Since these funds are re-lent through the intermediary of the banks they cannot be considered " idle " in the real sense of the term. Banks are in a better position to find the right borrowers than the individual holders of balances.

Occasionally it is to the interest of banks to defend themselves against *embarras de richesse* by discouraging new deposits for which they are unable to find lucrative employment. This is what happened in Switzerland, for instance, where the banks, being unable to employ their funds, wanted to defend themselves against an additional influx, and apart from disallowing interest on deposits, they began to charge a small commission. The object of this attitude was not, however, to force funds into productive channels. Indeed, the idea of doing so by means of negative interest rates seems to be altogether impracticable. To carry it to its logical conclusion, it would be necessary for banks to charge negative interest on their loans, in which case there would be no lack of borrowers, though some of us would not use the funds for productive purposes.

(3) Negative Interest on Notes

Many adherents of the negative interest rate school want to apply the idea to cash only, and not also to deposits. Unquestionably, the idea of penalising idle funds has more justification for notes than for deposits. As we have pointed out, deposits are usually employed for productive purposes by the banks. On the other hand, hoarded notes are idle funds in the quite literal sense. So long as they are hoarded, their velocity of circulation is nil, and from the point of view of financing production they may be considered for all practical purposes non-existent.

It was for this very reason that during the war a Hungarian publicist named Edmond Pályi proposed that the Government should issue interest-bearing money, in order to encourage hoarding. During the later stages of the war Hungary, together with other belligerent countries, began to feel the effects of inflation. It was not only that large amounts of currency were issued to finance part of the war expenditure, but, owing to the spending fever caused by the war atmosphere, the velocity of circulation of the increasing quantity of money was also becoming larger and larger. The war loans were not able to mop up the surplus cash to an adequate degree. The rise in commodity prices was popularly attributed to this surplus cash. Mr. Pályi's idea was that by increasing the amount of hoarded notes, the velocity of circulation of the currency would be reduced and therefore these inflationary influences could be partly offset.

The purpose of proposals for a negative interest rate on bank-notes is exactly the opposite of the proposal outlined above. The object of some of those who have put forward similar proposals was to reduce the volume of hoarded notes in the broadest sense of the term. In countries like Great Britain, where the use of current accounts is almost universal and where the hoarding of notes is practically unknown, the significance of these proposals cannot be truly appreciated. After all, if the notes are subject to negative interest, all their holders have to do is to carry the smallest possible amount of them and pay in everything that is not required immediately into their current accounts. The state of affairs is totally different on the Continent, where the habit of keeping current accounts is confined to business firms and to fairly wealthy individuals. In their case, the danger of having to put up with negative interest would induce the holders of notes to get rid of them speedily by paying their bills as quickly as possible and in some instances even by spending more. It is probable, however, that, should the scheme be adopted in such countries, it would lead after a while to the development of the banking habit by large classes of the population. The object of Gesell, the best known of the early advocates of negative interest rate, is, however, much more than that of bringing about a dishoarding of notes. He aims at the abolition of interest rates. To that end Gesell proposes the issue of the so-called "free money" which would deteriorate in value; for this reason its holders would be anxious to use it before it deteriorated. According to Gesell's proposal, the currency notes should be made to depreciate by one-tenth of 1 per cent per week or by approximately 5 per cent per annum. To bring the value of the notes to its nominal figure, stamps would have to be attached to them every week and the cost of these stamps would be equivalent to the depreciation of the notes. On the basis of a depreciation of 5 per cent per annum, it would be necessary to affix to a £1 note stamps to the total value of one shilling within twelve months. To make the process technically easier, at the end of every year the stamped notes would be exchanged for new notes ready for stamping. In Gesell's opinion the fact that to keep notes in idleness would cost money would induce the holders of notes to buy goods, or alternatively, to lend their money free of interest. This latter aspect of the scheme appeals to some of the advanced members of the cheap money school. Mr. Keynes himself in his latest book, *The General Theory of Employment, Interest and Money*, has pronounced himself in favour of the Gesell scheme. He says that the idea behind stamped money is sound and that it is possible that means might be found to apply it in practice on a modest scale. But he points out that Gesell overlooked the possibility of exchanging notes for bank balances, debts at call, foreign money, precious metals, etc., as a means of avoiding the interest penalty as well as the intended alternative of spending on goods or lending for productive purposes. Indeed, it is difficult to see why banks should be expected to accept deposits in depreciating money without charging a negative interest to the depositors. As we have seen in recent years, the mere decline of interest rates on loans to an abnormally low level was sufficient to induce the banks, in effect, to charge a moderate negative interest on deposits. If banks were to be liable to the payment of negative interest on their note supplies, the chances are that they would pass on this expense to their customers in the form of a negative interest charge which would also allow for handling charges over and above the amount spent on the stamps.

(4) The Wörgl Experiment

Carried to its logical conclusion, the " free money " means that the notes would be subject to negative interest even after they had been paid into the banks, and that the banks would, in their turn, be compelled to charge negative interest. Unless this were the case, the significance of the proposed negative interest on notes would be very limited. This is one of the many shortcomings of the pseudo-scientific proposals put forward by Dr. Robert Eisler, who would like to see bank-notes or " current money " depreciated while a constant value were maintained for the so-called " bank-money " or balances with banks. There is nothing whatever in his scheme which justifies the notoriety, however short-lived, it enjoyed. Having fallen into well-deserved oblivion, it is certainly not worth resurrecting.

Those who believe in Gesell's proposals triumphantly point to the example of the free money experiment of the Austrian municipality of Wörgl. It is beyond doubt that on the small scale on which it was applied in the small Austrian township the experiment was, during the limited period of its application, successful. It led to a remarkable increase of the velocity of circulation of money. Arrears of taxes and other outstanding debts were paid off as quickly as possible. Both the municipality and private individuals began to spend more freely so as to avoid losing interest on their bank-notes. Unemployment disappeared, trade became prosperous. It is a pity that the intervention of the Austrian National Bank brought the experiment to an end, for it would have been most interesting to watch its development in the long run, especially if the example had been followed on a larger territory.

While the Wörgl experiment has been quoted to boredom in English economic literature, a much more important experiment, carried out in Germany during a period of years, has almost entirely escaped attention. A group of enthusiasts who call themselves "Physiocrats" formed a company in Berlin for the purpose of issuing notes called "Wäras" on the principles of Silvio Gesell. A mining engineer named Hebecker, anxious to reopen the Schwanenkirchen colliery which had to be closed down for lack of capital, obtained 50,000 Wäras from the Physiocrats. With the aid of these notes—which had to be stamped every month in the same way as the notes issued in Wörgl—he reopened the mine and the district began to enjoy an era of prosperity, owing to the fact that every holder of the Wära notes was anxious to spend them quickly in order to avoid having to pay negative interest in the form of stamps. This was in 1930, but Wära notes have been used in other less well-known instances ever since 1926. In October 1931, however, the issue of these notes was forbidden by the German Government, and the experiment came to an end.

(5) Limitations of Negative Interest Reform

It may well be asked whether the discouragement of saving by means of negative interest is really an unqualified advantage. This question was discussed in detail in Chapter VIII, dealing with the movement favouring cheap money. We pointed out then that an excessive reduction of interest rates has certain disadvantages. Such a reduction discourages saving, and compels those not entitled to a pension to postpone their retirement and "die in harness". What is true of unduly low interest rates is true to a much higher degree of negative interest. It is evidently far-fetched to believe that by reducing or eliminating interest, all the world's ailments can be cured. Inadequate saving can be as harmful as excessive saving. Moreover, a policy of negative interest may lead to evil consequences in the form of over-spending and over-speculation.

The idea that is worth retaining from the negative interest rate proposals of Gesell and others is that monetary management cannot be complete unless it regulates the apportionment of incomes between spending and saving. The ratio between the two should vary according to circumstances. It is difficult, nevertheless, to imagine any method of direct intervention by which this proportion can be regulated. While the Governments can have wide powers to regulate the incomes of the population, only in countries like Soviet Russia, where the amount of goods available is limited, can the limit of spending be influenced by the official policy. Failing any direct method of intervention, the authorities have to fall back upon the old-fashioned method of varying the degree of *inducement* to saving. No hard-and-fast rule can be established in this respect for all times. When a boom seems to threaten, in certain circumstances it is desirable to encourage saving, while during periods of depression spending should be encouraged. To the latter end, the reduction of interest rates allowed on idle funds may not in itself go far enough, and it is conceivable that occasionally negative interest is the right solution. As an auxiliary means of encouraging spending at times when encouragement is needed, the proposed system may be quite useful. It is, however, certainly not the panacea for all our troubles that its advocates claim it to be.

CHAPTER XXXII

DUAL SYSTEMS OF CURRENCY

(1) Object of Dual Systems

The monetary reform schemes which we have dealt with so far have been those based on the principle of the unity of the monetary system. Whether or not these reformers favour the linking of the currency to gold, whether or not they favour the adoption of two metals instead of one as a basis of the system, in each case they advocate a single type of currency for each country. Our next step is to examine those proposals which advocate the adoption of a system of dual currencies, whereby the same country would have two different types of currencies which need not be in fixed relationship to each other, and could, therefore, fluctuate in terms of each other.

The schemes that have been put forward for the adoption of a dual system of currency may be classed in three groups, according to the following objects:

1. Stability of one currency for internal use, with a second variable currency for international purposes.
2. Stability of one currency for international purposes, and elasticity of another currency for internal use.
3. Stability of the unit of account of bank balances, loan contracts, etc., and fluctuation of notes.

These headings cover a variety of proposals differing from one another in many important details. In dealing with them, as with various other reform proposals, it is necessary to distinguish between proposals for temporary solutions and proposals for permanent systems. In many instances, the measures proposed or actually adopted merely aimed at solving temporary difficulties and were not intended to serve as a basis of permanent monetary reform. In other instances, dual currencies developed casually under the force of circumstances and without theoretical foundation. Nobody expected the duality of the currency system to be permanent; in fact, this condition was considered an unmitigated evil, and the authorities endeavoured to restore the unity of the monetary system at the first opportunity. It is, of course, very difficult to draw the line between proposals for provisional palliatives and those for permanent reform. Sometimes, measures which are adopted as palliatives lead to permanent reforms, and vice versa. In any examination of the theoretical basis of the various reform measures, proposed or operating, it is of course the reformer's intention that must be stressed.

(2) Three Types of Dual Currencies

The purpose that underlies various proposals for the establishment of dual currency varies according to the nature of the proposals. In some instances, the reformers realise the difficulty of maintaining the stability of a currency both internally and internationally, and also the disadvantages of wholly sacrificing either the one or the other type of stability. These reformers therefore reached the conclusion that a country should have two different currencies, one of which would be maintained stable in relation to foreign currencies while the other would be adjusted in accordance with internal requirements. Conversely, some reformers seek to maintain a stable currency for internal purposes, while allowing a special external currency to fluctuate in accordance with the requirements of foreign trade.

According to another monetary philosophy—if it can be called a philosophy at all—the need for stable currency and the desire to stimulate trade by means of a depreciating currency should be reconciled through a dual monetary system. Thus, it is argued that, since it is useless to aim at the theoretical ideal of an absolutely stable currency, we should make the best of existing conditions by adopting for certain purposes a special unit of account which would remain stable even if the currency in general use depreciated.

(3) Internal *v.* External Currencies

The idea of having one currency for international purposes and another for internal purposes has tempted many reformers. Such reformers are inspired by one of two considerations. Some of them want to maintain the international stability of the currency without thereby handicapping an internal expansion. Others, again, aim at adjusting the international value of a currency to the requirements of foreign trade without thereby unsettling the internal price level. In both instances, a dual system of currency is suggested as the solution. Mr. Taylor Peddie's idea is to have an internal currency which is inconvertible and an international currency which is based on gold. The former, he contends, could be expanded in accordance with the requirements of trade, irrespective of international considerations, while the latter could be maintained stable in relation to gold and gold currencies irrespective of expansion of the internal currency. The two currencies would of course have to fluctuate in terms of each other and their fluctuation would act as a shock-absorber. Thus, depreciation of the internal currency in terms of the external currency would enable exporters to continue to sell abroad even though the price level had risen in terms of the internal currency. The same result can, however, be achieved much more simply with the aid of a managed currency with a gold backing, provided that the gold backing is sufficiently strong to enable the authorities to disregard a moderate selling pressure. The dual system of stabilisation does not eliminate the evil of exchange fluctuations and it is indeed difficult to see what advantage it possesses over a straightforward inconvertible paper currency.

Another possible dual system is to maintain a stable currency for internal purposes but to provide an elastic or depreciated currency for the purpose of foreign trade. The reason for the desire for such duality is the fear of internal inflation combined with the imperative necessity for increasing exports by means of exchange depreciation. This system has been adopted in practice by a number of countries during the crisis and will be dealt with in detail in the next chapter. It compares unfavourably with an outright devaluation which creates a much neater situation. Fears of internal inflation as a result of the devaluation of a currency are almost invariably grossly exaggerated.

(4) Stable Unit for Loans

Another kind of dual monetary system is the one advocated in the first instance by Dr. Vissering, whose proposals formed the basis of Dr. Eisler's scheme ten years later. According to this scheme, there should be a stable currency for the purpose of long-term contracts and a depreciating currency for the purpose of stimulating business activity. This aim is supposed to be achieved by arranging the deliberate depreciation of bank-notes by means of a negative interest rate, while at the same time maintaining the stability of the monetary unit for bank balances and long-term contracts. It is difficult to discover any valid argument in favour of this over-ingenious scheme. We referred to it in the last chapter, dealing with negative interest rates, and it certainly does not deserve any detailed discussion. At one time it stirred up some interest, but this soon disappeared.

A variation of this kind of dual currency stabilisation scheme is that which proposes the adoption of a stable unit of account for the requirements of long-term contracts, whose stability is independent of the fluctuations of the currency used in practice. This system, like those of the depreciating currencies for foreign trade purposes, has developed almost entirely without theoretical background. It consists of the adoption of a " gold clause " in loan contracts. This proposal will be dealt with in detail in the next chapter. It may well be asked whether the existence of such currencies for the purpose of long-term contracts is desirable. Inasmuch as they are beneficial to one of the contracting parties, they are bound to be damaging to the other party. The assumption is that in the long run most incomes move in sympathy with the changes in the value of the monetary unit. If certain payments over a long period are maintained artificially stable, whether in terms of gold or in terms of commodities, while the current monetary unit undergoes a change in value, then this arrangement is bound to lead to unearned profits or undeserved losses to the contracting parties. The operation of gold clauses in long-term contracts would be equitable and practicable only if it could be assumed that, when a currency appreciates or depreciates in terms of gold, all prices and incomes adjust themselves, completely and within a brief interval, to the change in the price of gold in terms of the current monetary unit. This assumption, however, is entirely false. While usually there is a tendency for prices and incomes to adjust themselves to changes in the price of gold—though there is no such tendency when there is simultaneous devaluation of the principal currencies—the adjustment is never complete, and at best there is a time-lag which in many instances amounts to several years. Many prices and incomes never adjust themselves to the new price of gold.

(5) Commodity Clauses

It is suggested sometimes that the gold clause should be replaced by a commodity clause or a cost of living clause, by virtue of which the index number of commodity prices or of the cost of living would determine the amount payable under contracts. This sort of clause would doubtless be less liable to cause injustices than would a gold clause, since prices and incomes are more likely to adjust themselves to the average level of prices or to the cost of living than to the price of gold. Even so, substantial discrepancies could arise temporarily and even permanently between individual prices or incomes and the various index numbers.

While the fixing of payments under long-term contracts in terms of legal tender money may lead to hardship and unfair results, unless the change in the value of the monetary unit is very substantial it is more often than not a smaller evil than those arising from gold clauses or even commodity clauses. Generally speaking, the systematic adoption of such clauses cannot therefore be regarded as a desirable kind of monetary reform. Evidently, the establishment of absolute justice in face of fluctuating prices and incomes is impossible. From a purely practical point of view, the advantages of the system are more than outweighed by its disadvantages.

It appears that all the dual systems of currency introduce an unnecessary element of complication which would qualify their advantages even if we were to accept the claims made by the advocates of this system. In reality, these claims are for the most part either entirely unfounded or at any rate grossly exaggerated. Most of the dual systems proposed are either " quack " remedies or they can perform only a limited service as temporary makeshift arrangements. It is not in that direction that monetary reform is ever likely to make headway. Nor is it possible to discover in the proposals for a dual currency any important constructive element which is worth retaining as part of a proposal for permanent reform. We shall explain in the next chapter that the adoption of dual currency is sometimes a necessary evil which may fulfil a useful function for a limited period, but its existence is certainly not an ideal state of affairs. Experience has shown that every country with dual currency has taken the first opportunity to restore the unity of its monetary system.

CHAPTER XXXIII

DUAL CURRENCIES IN PRACTICE

(1) The Rentenmark Experiment

The early post-war period provided a number of examples of multiplicity of currencies, in various countries in Central and Eastern Europe. The disintegration of the Austro-Hungarian and Russian empires and the inheritance left behind by the German and Austrian occupation armies resulted in a situation in which two or more currencies were circulating concurrently in the same country. Some of these currencies were more stable—or, shall we say, less unstable—than the others, and they fluctuated in terms of each other. This situation was not, however, the result of deliberate monetary policy, and was not in any way the result of reform measures. It is thus beyond the scope of this book.

The first example of the deliberate adoption of a dual currency was provided by Germany in 1923. The depreciation of the mark had by then reached a very advanced stage and the monetary unit had become utterly useless as a standard of value, medium of exchange, or unit of account. At this moment it was decided to introduce a new currency, the rentenmark, not to supersede the mark immediately, but to circulate concurrently with it for a short while. As this new currency was supposed to be well secured and the amount of its issue was limited, it maintained a stable value in relation to commodities, and duly appreciated in terms of marks as the latter continued to depreciate. The success of the rentenmark experiment was largely responsible for the initial confidence with which the new monetary unit—the reichsmark—was received, a confidence which enabled the German authorities to stabilise. After stabilisation, the rentenmark disappeared as a separate currency and the unity of the monetary system was restored. During its brief period of existence it rendered a very useful service, but as soon as normal conditions returned there was no longer any need for its continued existence.

Germany was not the only country to resort to the expedient of a dual currency system. In other countries where inflation reached an advanced stage a fictitious unit of gold currency developed as a unit of account. The duality of the system was abandoned in each case the moment the legal tender currency was stabilised. While the system operated it rendered a service in tiding the financial mechanism over a period of confusion.

(2) Gold Unit *v.* Paper Unit

The idea of providing a stable monetary unit for the purpose of contracts while the general currency is subject to fluctuations received practical application in several countries during the crisis. In Hungary, among others, the Government in 1932 adopted a fictitious unit, the gold pengö, in terms of which Government loans were issued and bank deposits were accepted. The object of this device was to check the export of capital, by providing capitalists with the means of internally safeguarding themselves against a depreciation of the monetary unit. It is doubtful whether, in the absence of Draconian exchange restrictions, the adoption of the gold pengö could in itself have gone far towards checking the flight from the pengö. In any case, the policy had an adverse effect in that for a long time it discouraged the Government from officially admitting the fact of the depreciation of the pengö. Hungary was thus deprived of the advantages which Austria, among others, enjoyed from her official recognition of the unofficial depreciation of her currency.

The adoption of a fictitious gold unit in co-existence with the legal tender unit had less justification during the big depression than during the post-war currency chaos. During recent years there has been no real chaos such as would justify the introduction of an emergency measure in the form of a dual currency system. Such are the disadvantages of the arrangement that it can be justified only by a state of extreme emergency.

(3) The "Gold Clause"

The systematic adoption of gold clauses by Governments and individual debtors, even if it is not done in pursuit of a monetary policy, in practice creates a system of dual currency. The United States provided a characteristic example of this state of affairs. Ever since the inflation during the Civil War, it had become the custom to include a clause in loan contracts by virtue of which debtors were to discharge their liabilities in gold dollars of the existing weight and fineness. For many decades the gold clause had no practical significance, as the dollar was maintained stable in relation to gold. The clause thus came to be regarded as a mere formality. After 1933, however, the gold clause threatened to be the cause of endless trouble, and theatened to jeopardise the success of President Roosevelt's efforts to bring about trade recovery through allowing the dollar to depreciate. Had the validity of the gold clause been upheld, the depreciation of the dollar, instead of relieving the already unbearable burden of private indebtedness, would have increased it further, simultaneously increasing the burden of the public debt. As President Roosevelt's main object, in allowing the dollar to depreciate, was to bring a much-needed relief to farmers and to other insolvent debtors, it is only natural that soon after he assumed office he had legislation passed by Congress to abolish the gold clause. It was abolished both in Government contracts and in private contracts. It was not, however, until January 1934 that this legal unification of the currency became safely established through its approval by the Supreme Court.

The American experience shows that gold clauses are upheld only when they mean nothing in practice; and the moment that a depreciation of the current monetary unit makes the gold clause operative, practical considerations necessitate its abolition. Its existence simply creates a misleading and false feeling of security.

(4) Currencies for Foreign Trade

The crisis provided an opportunity for experimenting with various other kinds of dual currency systems. In the first place, it gave rise to the development of special currencies for the purpose of foreign trade. In Germany, the transfer moratorium was followed by the accumulation of substantial funds on blocked foreign accounts, and these various types of blocked marks went to a substantial discount compared with the "free" reichsmark, which was retained at par. The

Government authorised the use of the various types of blocked marks for payment for certain exports. Thus, while the reichsmark remained stable there was a depreciating currency —in fact several currencies depreciating to a different degree according to the uses to which they were allowed to be put —for the purpose of foreign trade. Germany thus enjoyed the advantage of a relative stability of her internal prices together with the advantages of the stimulus given to foreign trade by depreciating currency. The same situation developed in a number of other countries in Central and Eastern Europe. In some instances, the degree of the depreciation of the currency for external purposes was regulated according to the various types of imports and exports for whose payment it was used. Roumania, for instance, elaborated a schedule by which the discount of the foreign currencies for the requirements of importers and exporters varied between 10 per cent and 45 per cent according to the class of the commodities concerned.

Unquestionably, the combination of internal stability with international elasticity has its advantages. It is, however, too untidy a compromise to form the basis of a permanent system. In any case, it can work to only a limited degree, for if the use of a substantially depreciated special currency for international purposes assumes large dimensions, in practice it will amount to the unofficial depreciation of the basic currency of the country concerned. If blocked foreign balances are used as a special currency for international trade, the supply of such currency will sooner or later come to an end. The arrangement can, it is true, be prolonged if the Central Bank pays a premium to exporters for their foreign exchange, and if it allots foreign exchange to importers at a premium. This arrangement, however, amounts to an official devaluation of the currency even though the authorities of the countries refuse to call the child by its name.

(5) Stamped Money

Another method of dual currency which found limited and short-lived application during the crisis was the one by which a stable currency and a deliberately depreciated currency existed simultaneously for internal purposes. This is the application of the negative interest rate policy which was dealt with in Chapter XXXI. The small Austrian town of Wörgl, to whose experiment we then briefly referred, adopted a scheme by which it issued notes which decreased in value by 1 per cent every month. Every month holders had to buy from the issuing authorities a stamp amounting to 1 per cent to bring the note up to its face value. Since everybody wanted to avoid having to buy these stamps, the velocity of the note circulation increased considerably. During the first few days of their issue the notes as a whole changed hands several times and within the first month they were paid in and paid out again by the municipal authorities no less than twenty times. As a result, old debts were paid off, more money was spent and employment was created. At the same time, the real legal tender money remained unchanged. As this experiment was discontinued after a short while, and as in any case its sphere of application was very narrow, it is difficult to arrive at any definite conclusion on the basis of these results. It is interesting to note, however, that the crisis which was responsible for much of the progress made towards monetary reform in many other directions also brought into existence the practical application of this particular method of dual currency.

There is very little chance, however, that either this or any other kind of dual currency will be adopted as a permanent measure on an extensive scale. Even the United States, which has been the land of monetary experiments since the advent of President Roosevelt, has fought shy of dual currency. If President Roosevelt did not care to add this to his many other experiments, it was not for lack of advice to do so. Dr. Eisler paid a visit to the United States to persuade the Administration to adopt his scheme, but his agitation was unsuccessful. If President Roosevelt and his " brain trust " were not enterprising enough to experiment with dual currency of any kind—in fact one of President Roosevelt's first acts was to restore unity by abolishing the gold clause—the reformers who advocate such systems stand but little chance of witnessing their adoption.

CHAPTER XXXIV

INTERNATIONAL CO-OPERATION

(1) National v. International Reform

All the monetary reform proposals which have been dealt with in the foregoing chapters are schemes designed for application in particular countries, independently of the attitude of the rest of the world. Most of those who advocate these reform proposals would, of course, favour an international monetary policy based on the adoption of their respective schemes by all countries or at any rate by all important countries. Failing that, however, they advocate various national solutions of the monetary problem. In many instances, however, the would-be reformers have given up hope of international solutions, and their schemes are based on the assumption that their country must work out its salvation independently of the attitude of other countries. They propose, in fact, alternative solutions to international co-operation.

Let us now consider those reform proposals which aim at international solutions based on co-operation between the Governments of all countries, or at any rate between a large number of them, including the three or four leading countries whose co-operation is essential for any solution based on international understanding.

The conception that the monetary system and monetary policy are matters not of national, but of international concern has gained ground considerably since the war. It is now realised that the choice of the monetary system or monetary policy by any one country is bound to affect conditions well beyond its borders, and it is recognised that the more important the country concerned, the larger the extent to which foreign countries are affected by its monetary developments. And yet, in practice, the conception that monetary policy is the internal affair of every country still reigns supreme. International law, whether through treaties or usage, regulates the rights and duties of two countries towards a river which passes through the territory of both. Monetary policy, however, is still considered outside the realm of international law, even though the interests involved are infinitely superior in many cases to those involved in river rights.

(2) Pre-War and Post-War Schemes

The idea that clashes between national monetary policies should be eliminated through international co-operation was practically unknown until after the war. There were many instances of collaboration between monetary authorities of various countries before and during the war, but they were prompted by momentary practical considerations and had no theoretical background. It is true that suggestions for the establishment of an international currency were put forward long before the war, but such suggestions were regarded as purely Utopian, and nobody concerned with the practical application of monetary policy ever gave them serious consideration.

After the war a number of proposals for an international monetary system were put forward, mostly by practical bankers such as Mr. Ter Meulen, Dr. Vissering, Mr. Frank Vanderlip, etc. These proposals varied in detail and most of them were hopelessly impracticable in the then existing conditions of political and economic rivalries. When the currency chaos during which they originated came to an end, there was no further talk about international monetary systems. Interest in an advanced form of international co-operation between monetary authorities remained, however, and attracted many theoretical economists. During the years that preceded the crisis, the evidence of a scarcity and maldistribution of gold aroused much interest in problems of international monetary co-operation. As we shall see in the chapters dealing with monetary internationalism in practice, progress was made between 1923 and 1931 towards the practical application of the principles of international monetary co-operation. This movement suffered a severe reverse during the crisis, when monetary nationalism attained an unprecedented degree all over the world. At the same time, the currency troubles once more gave rise to proposals aiming at the establishment of an international monetary system with the object of preventing the recurrence of the troubles from which the world has been suffering since 1931.

(3) International Currency

The most extreme proposals in that direction aim at the establishment of an international currency backed by an international gold reserve and managed by an international currency board or super-Central Bank. This institution would be established in some neutral country—preferably in Switzerland—where the international gold reserve would be kept. The nations would pool their gold resources and the super-Central Bank would allot them their due proportion of international bank-notes which would be the sole currency all over the civilised world. The respective shares of individual countries, and changes in these shares, would be determined by a committee of impartial experts. The Governments would not be in a position to use the printing press to cover budgetary deficits or to finance excessive expansion. As the whole world would have the same currency, there would be no more exchange fluctuations and the price level all over the world would tend to be uniform. The advocates of the system even go so far as to claim that, thanks to the existence of an international currency, customs barriers would gradually disappear and perpetual peace would be ensured.

It is magnificent—but it is not monetary policy. There have always been and always will be dreamers who regard the world as one large unit and who consider it possible to overcome the barriers of nationalism in the political as well as the economic and financial sphere. It appears unlikely that such an extreme degree of internationalism as is implied in the schemes of international currency will ever become possible. The example of the United States shows that even if a number of States are prepared to merge into a political Union, they retain and jealously safeguard their financial and monetary autonomy. Even if it were possible to establish a European United States—which would be halfway towards the creation of a World State—the member States would want to retain their central banks with note issuing rights, just as the twelve economic districts of the United States have their own Federal Reserve Banks.

(4) Independence of National Monetary Policy

Even under a Communist régime, national differences would remain. The apparent unity of interests and policy of the Union of Socialist and Soviet Republics conceals bitter controversy and jealousies beneath the surface, not only between the various members of the Union, but even between smaller units and spheres of interest. The reason why these conflicts are not allowed to interfere with the outward unity of the system is that one member of the Union is strong enough to suppress any open resistance. The unity established in the Soviet Union is essentially a *Pax Romana* based on the dictatorship of a strong State over weaker States. To secure the requisite conditions for the establishment of world currency, it would be necessary for a strong nation to conquer the whole world and to rule it ruthlessly, suppressing every opposition. Otherwise the system would be impracticable.

So long as independent nations exist, it is simply inconceivable that the Governments would relinquish their sovereign right to determine their monetary system and to direct the broad outlines of their monetary policy. Conceivably, however, they might come to agreements affecting their monetary system and their monetary policy within a limited scope, and subject to termination of the arrangements by one-sided decision, with or without notice. But a surrender of the right of decision to an international body is something simply inconceivable. Experience at Basle and Geneva is not exactly encouraging to hopes that experts will ever forget their nationality and become in the first place impartial experts, instead of being in the first place Englishmen, Frenchmen, Germans or Italians. Even if by some miracle it were possible to find such a set of experts, no nation would ever trust them sufficiently to rely upon their impartiality in distributing the "life-blood" of the nations and in determining thereby their relative and absolute degree of welfare. In any case, the task of allocating correctly a limited amount of international currency between various nations borders on the impossible even from a purely technical point of view. There is no foolproof method by which the system of allotment could be reduced to operations of simple arithmetic. And yet, it is only such simplification of the rules of allotment that could possibly command confidence. Even under such a system, the allotment would be bound to cause grievances in one country or another, and the Governments concerned would sooner or later break away from the arrangement.

(5) Pooling Gold Reserves

Another major obstacle is that countries with large gold stocks would never agree to a pooling of their gold reserves. Even countries with small gold stocks would hesitate to hand over their reserves to an international body. They are aware that in emergency the possession of a national gold reserve may save them from starvation or defeat, and they prefer to depend on the national reserve, however small, rather than on the goodwill of an international committee. The preliminary condition for an international gold reserve is the establishment of perpetual peace between the nations. So long as the possibility of war exists every nation will want to retain a gold reserve for the requirements of national defence.

According to an intermediate proposal, while gold reserves should be pooled in theory, each nation should retain the physical possession of its own contribution to the total. The national gold reserves would be left in the safe custody of the participating nations instead of being transferred to the central gold reserve at Basle or Geneva. From a political point of view, such an arrangement may appear more palatable than the pooling of gold stocks in a neutral country, but it may well be asked whether in such circumstances the various gold reserves would be regarded as security for the international bank notes. In case of war or other major emergency, or even in case of disagreement between the Government and the international committee, some participants would seize the gold stock in their possession and the international notes would to that extent be deprived of their cover. And since the notes would have to be interchangeable if the arrangement were to have any meaning at all, the seceding State would be placed in a position of drawing upon the gold stocks of the other States or buying goods abroad with the aid of its note quota, thereby passing on the liability to the remaining members of the monetary union. It would amount to obtaining something for nothing, and to the less conscientious members it would be a strong temptation to desertion.

(6) Redistribution of Gold

All but the extreme advocates of monetary internationalism realise that the maintenance of national gold reserves is inevitable. This in itself would make it impossible to establish an international currency. Reasonable monetary internationalists consider that an equitable redistribution of the world's monetary gold supplies is the next best thing.

For several years redistribution of gold has been one of the most popular catchwords in monetary literature. Most of those using the term freely have not taken the trouble to define exactly what they mean by it. If redistribution means that some countries must without compensation voluntarily surrender the surpluses they possess, in order to enable other countries to secure an equitable share in the world's gold stock, the idea is if anything even more impracticable than the pooling of gold reserves, when the contributors would at least retain part-ownership of their former gold. To suppose that any of the countries possessing more than their due share of the world's monetary gold stocks would be prepared to become public benefactors is absurd. The mere idea that France and the United States would part with a substantial portion of their gold as charitable gifts to other nations is fantastic. And yet this is what some of those advocating redistribution had vaguely in mind.

Those who were more realistic proposed that the countries possessing a surplus should surrender it to the countries whose stocks were deficient in the form of a loan or in return for bonds bearing some form of international guarantee. Even such a redistribution, however, would provide an extremely difficult problem to solve. Most countries would be reluctant to exchange their solid gold for bonds, however well guaranteed the latter might appear. The experience of the last few years has proved that foreign investments cannot in times of crisis adequately perform their function of being secondary gold reserves.

According to a more practical proposal, instead of exchanging gold for loans by international arrangement, the nations with large holdings would agree to redistribution by admitting the issue of foreign loans in their capital market. Here again the difficulty lies in the limited absorbing capacity of the capital market for foreign loans. Moreover, since foreign lending usually tends to result in a favourable trade balance for the lender, the gold thus disposed of would, like the ring of Polycrates, return to its owner. This is what happened during the period of post-war stability. France was unable to absorb foreign loans, partly because of the unwillingness of her investors to take them up. The United States was lending abroad on a gigantic scale, but as a result of her export surplus her gold came back over and over again, and her stock increased instead of diminishing.

Apart from all this, it would be very difficult to agree upon the basis for the redistribution of the gold by no matter what method. It is doubtful whether holders of large surplus stocks would consent to abide by the decision of an international committee of impartial experts, and failing that, the redistribution would be governed not by scientific considerations but by political compromises.

(7) An International Monetary Policy

Many people who do not believe in the possibility of an international currency, or even in that of the equitable redistribution of gold by agreement, advocate an international understanding upon monetary policy. The extreme form of this proposal is the suggestion of an international bank which would dictate the monetary policy of national Central Banks in the same way as the latter dictate the policy of commercial banks and banking houses in their respective countries. Here again the scheme breaks down on the impossibility of inducing Governments to relinquish their sovereign rights in favour of an international body.

According to a more moderate proposal, the Governments should retain their monetary autonomy but should agree upon a uniform monetary policy. A resolution as to the desirability of that course was actually adopted by the World Economic Conference of 1933. The rigid application of the principle would, however, meet with almost insurmountable difficulties. Even if it were possible to bring about an agreement between fifty or more Governments regarding the monetary policy to be pursued, the application of the policy might differ widely in various countries. It is indeed impossible to apply a uniform rule to countries whose circumstances differ widely and fundamentally. What most advocates of an international monetary policy have in mind is co-operation not between fifty or sixty nations, but between the three or four nations whose policy determines the international monetary tendencies, and whose attitude is in any case followed by dozens of "satellite" States. Even though the reduction of the number of participants would simplify matters, it would by no means eliminate the difficulty caused by the difference in the conditions, requirements and mentality of the leading nations. France is essentially deflationist, while the United States is essentially inflationist. Between them Great Britain holds an intermediate position. How would it be possible for the statesmen of these countries to persuade one another to accept either the other's point of view or at least a compromise? And how would it be possible for them to persuade their Parliaments and electorates that it is worth while to make concessions for the sake of international co-operation? While it might be possible to conclude and maintain such an agreement between countries governed by dictators, it is almost unthinkable in countries with parliamentary democracy. If the majority in Parliament or of the electorate of one of the countries were in favour of a change in the monetary policy, then the Government would have to abide by their wishes even at the cost of having to discontinue the international agreement.

(8) Limited Scope of Co-operation

Moreover, at times the efficient conducting of monetary policy requires swift decisions. It would be difficult if not impossible for fifty or even a much smaller number of Governments to come to a sufficiently prompt understanding when a quick change of policy was essential to avert a crisis. This obstacle could be overcome only by the establishment of a permanent organisation at which the Governments would be represented by plenipotentiary delegates. Even then the difficulty would be that in many instances the Government, Parliament or electorate would not ratify the decision taken.

The extent to which international co-operation can play a part in the sphere of monetary policy is thus limited. In a negative sense it can and should prevent currency wars and even glaringly selfish acts on the part of individual Governments. In a positive sense co-operation could and should assume the form of co-ordination of monetary policies rather than an attempt at rigid uniformity. As it is impossible to enforce decisions by majority vote, the most the Governments can do is to regard one another's special monetary problems with understanding. It is useless for a Government to insist that another Government should restrict credit so as to fall into line with others, when it is evident that such a policy is either politically or economically impracticable in the country concerned. While a uniform monetary policy would be an ideal solution, the next best thing would be an agreement to disagree on the fundamental principles of the monetary policy and an understanding about the attitude to be taken up in face of conflicting policies, so as to mitigate the evil consequences of the inevitable friction.

In a still more limited way international monetary co-operation may assume the form of occasional mutual assistance ; technical collaboration ; exchange of information ; regular personal intercourse. All this has actually been accomplished during the last ten years or more. It will therefore be dealt with in the following chapter on international co-operation in practice.

CHAPTER XXXV

INTERNATIONAL CO-OPERATION IN PRACTICE

(1) Progress since the War

The sphere in which the practical adoption of monetary reform after the war attained the highest degree was that of international co-operation. Admittedly, to the advocates of international currency, the progress made towards monetary internationalism during the period of post-war stability may appear totally inadequate. Viewed from the angle of the pre-war situation, however, the change was almost revolutionary. Co-operation between Central Banks or Governments was not, it is true, altogether a post-war development. In the past arrangements were occasionally made for one Central Bank or Government to assist another in a temporary financial embarrassment. The best known and most frequently quoted instance was that of the Baring crisis in the 'nineties when the Bank of France came to the rescue of the Bank of England. Such cases, however, were only isolated instances. Generally speaking, it may safely be stated that co-operation between the monetary authorities of various countries was the exception and not the rule. Had anybody suggested in 1913 that Central Bank governors should hold monthly meetings to exchange views on the international monetary situation and on the particular situation of each country; that Central Banks should systematically exchange statistical and other information; that they should communicate to one another their impending acts such as bank rate changes or decisions to suspend the gold standard; that they should systematically assist one another technically and support one another financially; that occasionally they would even modify their own monetary policies to suit the convenience of some other country, such a prophet would have been denounced as a Utopian dreamer. Had he dared to suggest that in less than two decades there would be an international bank controlled by Central Banks, the main object of which was to be to endeavour to co-ordinate monetary policies and place international collaboration on a systematic basis, in all probability his sanity would have been called in question. Thus, while we may argue that progress towards monetary internationalism has not been satisfactory, to claim that there has been no progress at all would bring us into conflict with facts.

(2) Co-operation between Central Banks

There was a certain amount of close collaboration between monetary authorities during the war. This was, however, a matter of political necessity and was not expected to survive the termination of hostilities. Indeed, collaboration came to an end after the Armistice both among the Central Banks of the defeated Central Powers and, somewhat later, among the Central Banks of the victorious Allies. From about the middle of 1919, all Central Banks once more began to fend for themselves. Before very long, however, the first signs of a new tendency towards monetary internationalism became noticeable. One of the positive results of the Brussels Conference of 1920 was the adoption of the resolution calling for close collaboration between Central Banks. While other resolutions were shelved by those who approved them, Central Bank co-operation had become a reality.

In practice the first fruit of that collaboration was the *de facto* stabilisation of the Austrian currency as a result of advances obtained by the National Bank of Austria from the Bank of England prior to the conclusion of the League of Nations Loan in 1923. This transaction created an important precedent which was followed on many occasions during the next eight years or so. In the case of Hungary, Germany, the Free City of Danzig, Bulgaria, Greece, Belgium, etc., the currencies were stabilised largely as a result of co-operation between Central Banks. It is true that the League of Nations Finance Committee had the lion's share in providing financial assistance to most of these countries. The attitude of the Finance Committee was in itself, however, largely the result of Mr. Montagu Norman's policy of co-operation. Apart from this, the reconstruction of these countries would have been difficult if not impossible but for the advances granted by the

Bank of England or subsequently by a group of Central Banks. A detailed account of monetary reconstruction through international co-operation between 1922 and 1931 is outside the scope of this book. Those interested in it must be referred to the author's book, *The Bank for International Settlements.* Here we are concerned with the reconstruction movement only in so far as it was achieved by a reform in the shape of international monetary co-operation. The mere fact that assistance was regularly forthcoming to a country with a weak currency undoubtedly constituted an important monetary reform.

(3) Instances and Rules of Co-operation

The technical collaboration between Central Banks, exchange of information, etc., need not necessarily be regarded as being in themselves of sufficient importance to rank as monetary reform measures. On the other hand, the occasional decisions to adapt the monetary policy of one Central Bank to the requirements of another country may be considered as monetary reform measures of foremost importance. For instance, the decision of the Federal Reserve Bank of New York in August 1927 to reduce its bank rate so as to obviate the necessity for an inopportune increase of the British bank rate constituted a revolutionary departure from pre-war principles and practice. Similarly, in a negative sense the undertaking of the French monetary authorities to refrain from withdrawing gold from the Bank of England constituted an important step towards monetary internationalism. This precedent was followed by the adoption of the rule that no Central Bank is to withdraw gold from another without the consent of the Central Bank whose gold is to be withdrawn. But the fact that the French Government considered it expedient to state from time to time that it had given no binding undertaking which would restrict its freedom of action in regard to gold withdrawals duly indicates the political limitations of international monetary co-operation.

Another rule of international monetary co-operation was that gold purchases by Central Banks in the London market were to be co-ordinated by the Bank of England. Yet another change which deserves to be considered as a monetary reform measure was the understanding that Central Banks should not withdraw funds suddenly from each other's markets in circumstances which would cause embarrassment to the country from which funds were to be withdrawn. This principle was applied in particular by the French monetary authorities, who refrained from withdrawing their sterling deposits too suddenly. During the sterling crisis of 1931, it was applied by almost all Central Banks.

(4) The Bank for International Settlements

The post-war movement of co-operation between Central Banks attained its culminating point in the establishment of the Bank for International Settlements. Its creation raised hopes of rapid progress towards monetary internationalism. Unfortunately, these hopes did not materialise. During the brief interval between the establishment of the Bank and the financial crisis of 1931, it had already become apparent that in face of the jealousies between Governments and the ultra-conservatism of Central Banks, the Bank for International Settlements was unable to fulfil the hopes attached to it. Nevertheless, but for the premature advent of the crisis, the Bank might have established itself as an important factor in the international monetary sphere. Its resources were growing rapidly, and while it was far from being the super-bank it had been expected to become, it was in a position to assist and improve matters on a modest scale. Had its evolution continued undisturbed for a decade or so, in all probability it would have assumed first-rate importance as regulator of the international flow of funds and as a source of support in times of adverse pressure. Even though suggestions of international clearing, international gold reserve and other ambitious schemes had been shelved, the Bank would in all probability have strengthened its position within the relatively narrow scope of its activities. As it is, the very existence of such an institution and its activities in the international monetary sphere, however limited these activities were, constituted an important reform measure. It was the first attempt, feeble but systematic, at creating order in the place of anarchy in the international monetary sphere. The very fact of the Bank's establishment was a great encouragement to monetary internationalists, and to would-be reformers in general. After all, it was the world's most conservative and orthodox quarters that embarked, however timidly, upon this particular monetary experiment.

(5) Effect of the Crisis

The advent of the crisis brought about a reversal of monetary internationalism and caused a severe setback in the co-operation between Central Banks. Admittedly, after the Creditanstalt crisis some feeble efforts were made to support the Central European countries which were suffering from monetary difficulties. The attitude of most Central Banks during the run on the pound that led to the suspension of the gold standard in Great Britain was also inspired by a spirit of co-operation. After the suspension of the gold standard in Great Britain, however, all efforts at co-operation were discontinued. Economic nationalism flared up all over the world and manifested itself to a particularly large extent in the monetary sphere. All pretence of trying to adjust monetary policies to the interests of other countries was abandoned. The ruthless repatriation of Central Bank balances from London was largely responsible for the heavy slump of sterling at the end of 1931, and the ruthless withdrawal of official French dollar balances was the first blow that shattered confidence in the dollar. President Roosevelt's policy of deliberate depreciation of the dollar in 1933 dealt another fatal blow to monetary internationalism.

It is nevertheless a mistake to imagine that the crisis has altogether wiped out the progress made towards monetary reform through international co-operation. There is still a high degree of technical co-operation between Central Banks such as never existed before the war. The Bank for International Settlements is still in existence even though its resources have dwindled and its activities have become severely curtailed. What was meant to be a super-bank is now little more than a Club for Central Bank Governors with an efficient organisation for collecting information, but the mere existence of such an institution constitutes progress undreamed-of in pre-war days.

The fact that monetary co-operation, in form if not in substance, survived the crisis is of great significance from the point of view of the future of monetary internationalism. It provides the technical channels through which monetary reform in the shape of international co-operation can make progress once the circumstances that have caused the setback in the movement have ceased to exist. Once the world has recovered from its present depression, and once stable monetary conditions have been restored on the basis of relative equilibrium, monetary internationalism will stand a chance of resuming its progress.

It would be idle, however, to expect that international co-operation will ever attain a sufficiently advanced stage to provide the whole solution of the monetary problem. To-day the very idea may seem to us absurd, and yet during the period of post-war stability a number of experts, both theoretical and practical, seriously believed that co-operation in itself would be capable of curing the world's monetary evils. This conception is dangerous in that it diverts attention from other more realistic and more practicable methods of monetary reform. Indeed, it is advisable for realistic monetary planners to leave international co-operation out of their reckoning and to work out the solution of the monetary problems of their respective countries on a national basis. If and when conditions become suitable for international co-operation, any results obtained should be regarded as sheer windfalls which might cease at a moment's notice when political or economic influences bring about another wave of economic nationalism.

(6) Sterling Bloc and Gold Bloc

During the crisis, attempts were made to establish international co-operation in limited spheres. The Ottawa Agreement of 1932 sought to establish a uniform monetary policy within the British Empire with the possibility of extending it over a number of other countries. The group thus created is known by the name of the Sterling Bloc. The degree of collaboration is so far very small. It has amounted merely to the maintenance of the currencies of the Sterling Bloc relatively stable in relation to sterling. This in itself can hardly be said to constitute monetary reform. The idea, however, that a group of inconvertible paper currencies should be maintained stable in relation to one another, while they should be allowed to fluctuate in terms of gold, may be regarded as a reform measure provided that it is a permanent arrangement. There is no reason to suppose, however, that any of the authors of the Sterling Bloc regard the arrangement as anything but a makeshift. The countries of the Sterling Bloc may well find it gratifying to be able to use the gold currencies as shock-absorbers, and thus to be able to maintain their internal stability at the expense of the countries with gold currencies. The gold countries, however, may not be able or willing to put up with this arrangement indefinitely. In any case, the Governments of the Sterling Bloc themselves hope to return to the gold standard in due course.

The collaboration established between the countries of the Gold Bloc provided another example of monetary internationalism within a limited geographic sphere. Its results have been definitely disappointing. The existence of the Gold Bloc did not prevent Belgium from devaluing her currency when she realised it was to her interest to do so. All the collaboration in the Gold Bloc amounts to is that its members declare that they will pursue that monetary policy which they intend to pursue in any case. The moment they change their policy they are at liberty to break away from the group. There is no mutual assistance, or even undertaking as to uniformity of monetary policy, either within the Gold Bloc or within the Sterling Bloc. In any case, as both groups are essentially temporary formations, they cannot be regarded as a stage towards monetary reform in the form of monetary internationalism.

CHAPTER XXXVI

THE EXCHANGE CLEARING SYSTEM

(1) Practice Ahead of Theory

We have seen that in the case of consistent deflation practical experience moved faster than theory. The same is true, only to a much higher degree, of exchange clearing. The system in its rudimentary form of bilateral clearing agreements was in operation in many countries before any theoretical basis had been created for it. Under the stress of practical necessity, practical statesmen tumbled upon this solution before they were advised to do so by economists. Dozens of bilateral exchange clearing agreements were adopted before the economists began to take notice of the system. Indeed, it was the London Chamber of Commerce, a body consisting of practical business men, that was the first to realise the broader implications of the exchange clearing system. In its memorandum published in 1932 it advocated the adoption of exchange clearing as the fundamental point in its general monetary and economic reform scheme.

In substance the proposals put forward by the London Chamber of Commerce and other supporters of the exchange clearing system amounted to a scheme for the substitution of international clearing for the foreign exchange market. According to this scheme, every nation should establish a clearing office through which all transfers abroad would have to pass. The nationals of all countries would pay the amounts due, or their equivalent in their national currency, to their national clearing office. Out of the balances thus accumulated, the payments due from abroad, the equivalent of which had been paid in by the debtors to the clearing offices of the debtor countries, would be paid to the creditors. Foreign exchange operations would be replaced by simple book-keeping entries arranged between the clearing offices of the countries concerned. There would be an international clearing office which would act as intermediary for offsetting the debit and credit balances which were not offset in the ordinary course by reciprocal payments.

(2) Temporary or Permanent Solution?

Those in favour of exchange clearing may be divided into two categories. A number of them—mostly statesmen and Government officials but also some bankers and business men—are in favour of exchange clearing as a temporary makeshift by means of which they hope to bring the international monetary deadlock to an end. They regard it as a means of surmounting the difficulties caused by restrictions on foreign trade and exchanges, as a means by which they can avoid defaults on external debt and can obtain the unfreezing of frozen commercial or financial claims. The conclusion of a number of exchange clearing agreements was due to such considerations. If exchange clearing were nothing more than a temporary arrangement in face of a temporary abnormal situation, it could hardly be classed among reforms. There is, however, a small but growing group of supporters of the system, who advocate exchange clearing not as a temporary measure but as a permanent solution.

Exchange clearing is generally proposed as an alternative to the gold standard. According to these proposals, the currency should be inconvertible and scientifically managed with the object of securing the largest volume of employment, while at the same time keeping the price level in each country as far as possible at equilibrium with the world level. Between various currencies there would be fixed exchange rates on the basis of which transfers from one country to another would be made. All transfers would go through the international clearing office, and there would be no private traffic in exchanges. Instead of relying on speculation to fill the gap between supply and demand in any particular currency at a given moment, the differences would simply appear as debit or credit balances on the clearing accounts. The international clearing office would be instrumental in the clearing of debit and credit balances against each other. If country A has a debit balance against country B, country B has a debit balance against country C, and country C has a debit balance against country A, then the situation can be adjusted by simple book-keeping entries. The clearance of international claims and counterclaims, which at present takes place in a haphazard way through the working of the foreign exchange market, would take place through the exchange clearing system by means of controlled and regulated channels. Various methods of arranging international clearing have been proposed, but, while they differ from one another in matters of detail, they all aim at the clearing of international transfer items in substantially the same way as internal transfer items are cleared by the bankers' clearing houses.

(3) Advantages of the System

The exchange clearing system presents a number of obvious advantages.

1. It introduces a reasonable spirit in foreign trade relations. As things are, every country aims at exporting as much as possible and importing as little as possible. Under the exchange clearing system the export of goods can be paid for only by import of goods: thus it is not to the interest of any country to try to obtain a huge export surplus by means of dumping or by means of prohibitive import restrictions. Under the exchange clearing system, the Governments would be just as keen on increasing their imports as they are on increasing their exports. The Governments will have to realise that the exporters and creditors can expect to be paid only if the country concerned is prepared to take a corresponding amount of goods.

2. It substitutes a scientifically regulated system for the existing haphazard method of international transfers. Under exchange clearing the inevitable discrepancies between debit and credit items of a country at a given moment do not disturb the international or internal monetary situation. Instead of causing an unwanted depreciation of the exchange with all its unfavourable consequences, an adverse trend merely causes an accumulation of debit balances on clearing accounts. The mere fact that a country has debit balances does not in itself interfere with the stability of its currency. It does not lead to an outflow of gold which would automatically contract credit. Should the adverse tendency be persistent, it is for the authorities of the country concerned to make up their

minds whether to correct the situation by deflation or by the adjustment of their parities. In no case will their hand be forced by a sweeping speculative exchange movement as under the régime of free exchanges.

3. Exchange clearing safeguards the stability of the currency not only against the effect of an adverse trade balance, but also against speculative attacks and international movements of capital. It provides the most effective and least inconvenient form of exchange restriction. While under any other form of exchange restriction the foreign importer who assists the exporters of the country concerned by leaving part of the profits of exports abroad does not offend the law of his own country, under the exchange clearing system any attempt to circumvent the clearing arrangement by such means would be an offence against the laws of both countries concerned.

(4) Scientific Management

4. Exchange clearing would enable statesmen, economists, bankers, etc., to know exactly every day the balance of payments of their own country and of foreign countries. Under the existing system those responsible for the monetary policy of the country and those who grant credit to foreign countries or do business with them are completely in the dark about the exact or even the approximate position of their own country and of foreign countries. In the absence of the statistical material which would enable them to form a reasoned judgment, they have to follow their instinct, which as often as not is wrong. As, under the exchange clearing system, every international payment goes through the hands of the authorities, the system enables them to ascertain the exact position and to act accordingly.

5. Exchange clearing is an inevitable part of any system of efficient monetary management or economic planning. Scientific management of a currency and rational planning of production, distribution and consumption are simply unthinkable unless a rational method is adopted for international transfers. A reasonably planned internal expansion can be undertaken more safely under exchange clearing than under a system of free exchanges. This does not, of course, mean that under exchange clearing a country can spend indefinitely without its foreign trade being affected. The degree to which it can

expand with impunity is, however, much larger than under a system of free foreign exchanges.

6. Exchange clearing is the one form of international monetary co-operation which does not presuppose either the elimination of political or financial rivalries, or the restoration of confidence between the nations. It can therefore be established and can operate successfully even in the existing atmosphere of distrust and rivalry. For this reason, it is more practicable than any other form of co-operation, since there is but little chance of achieving the ideal state of affairs in international relations, without which other methods of co-operation could not work satisfactorily.

(5) Interference with Freedom of Trade

The exchange clearing system is subjected to much criticism, mainly on the ground that it interferes with the freedom of international transfers and trade. It is denounced on the ground that it would kill the foreign exchange market; that it tends to reduce the volume of foreign trade; that it constitutes the most irksome form of exchange restriction; and that it is detrimental to the interests of countries which do not adopt the system. There can be no doubt that exchange clearing interferes with the freedom of foreign trade, but it does so in the same way as traffic regulations interfere with the freedom of traffic. Yet intervention is necessary to regulate both traffic and international trade, in the interests both of those directly concerned and of those of the community as a whole. According to some supporters of the system, it is the main advantage of exchange clearing that it diverts foreign trade into safe and sound channels by increasing the bilateral character of international commercial relations. There is much to be said for this conception if it is not driven to extremes. The triangular and multilateral character of existing trade relations is to a large extent overdone, and to that extent its conversion into bilateral trade would be an advantage. On the other hand, a certain amount of triangular and multilateral trade is inevitable and advantageous and should be retained. There is no reason why it should not be retained under an exchange clearing system provided that the system develops into international clearing, or at any rate into regular triangular and multilateral clearing.

Exchange clearing is sometimes accused of being nothing but barter. In reality, under exchange clearing individual importers of all countries concerned can choose their goods freely and need not at the same time trouble to find somebody who is prepared to accept goods in exchange. Most of those who regard exchange clearing as barter confuse it with the system of compensation, under which goods are actually exchanged against goods. In any case, even trade by means of barter is better than no trade at all.

(6) The End of the Foreign Exchange Market

Unquestionably, exchange clearing, if adopted universally and extended over every kind of international transfer item, would mean the end of the foreign exchange market. There is no reason, however, to deplore such a development. The foreign exchange market is not nearly so admirable a system as opponents of exchange clearing represent it to be. Indeed, it may be said to contain all the vices of the system of *laissez-faire*. It provides endless opportunity for using private property to the detriment of the community through shifting funds from one centre to another. It cannot function without international speculators who are thus given the dignified rôle of performing an indispensable social function. It provides opportunity for speculators to exceed this rôle and embark upon reckless and mischievous activities. Indeed, if there were no other arguments in favour of the exchange clearing system, the mere fact that its adoption would do away with the foreign exchange market would in itself be amply sufficient to make a strong case in its favour. Any of the reform schemes discussed in the preceding chapters would stand but a poor chance of succeeding if the freedom of international transfers were retained. That freedom worked more or less satisfactorily in pre-war days, amidst conditions of relative political and economic stability. To-day, however, the world's economic system, and especially its financial superstructure, has become far too sensitive to be exposed to the shocks that inevitably occur under a system of free transfers. The strength and frequency of shocks, too, has undergone a considerable increase since pre-war days, owing to the increase in the volume of fictitious wealth, which makes it possible to shift from country to country amounts of a magnitude undreamed of a generation ago. To safeguard the hypersensitive against the increased danger of shock, it is necessary to sacrifice the system of free international transfers and replace it by the exchange clearing system.

(7) Exchange Clearing and Foreign Trade

Probably the most effective of all arguments against exchange clearing is the accusation that it tends to reduce the volume of international trade. In reality, this is by no means necessarily the case. On the contrary, it is the disturbing effect of anarchy in international trade and finance that from time to time tends to create a situation in which foreign trade is inevitably reduced. Under the régime of freedom, foreign trade can be expanded only to the detriment of internal economic expansion. The necessity of maintaining conditions under which it is possible to increase exports constitutes a severe handicap to the improvement of the standard of living. As a result, there is a growing tendency in favour of a high degree of economic isolation in which each nation can work out its own salvation internally. And yet, an expansion of foreign trade is not incompatible with an expansion of home trade provided that foreign transfers pass through the channels of exchange clearing. Under that system, both for the individuals engaged in foreign trade and for the community as a whole, it becomes safe to import or to export. This does not, of course, mean that under exchange clearing a country can over-export or over-import indefinitely. A country which insists on having favourable trade balances, without being able or willing to consolidate the surplus in the form of long-term investments, would find that all it gets for its exports is a number of credit balances on clearing accounts, which do not even bear interest. A country which over-imports systematically and is unable to obtain the consolidation of its debit balances will find sooner or later that its creditor countries will restrict their exports so as to be able to liquidate their frozen clearing balances. It is only in such cases—which will be the exception and not the rule—that the working of exchange clearing may occasionally lead to the contraction of foreign trade. As a general rule, the creditor countries, before restricting their sales to the debtor country, will do their utmost to increase their purchases from it.

(8) Exchange Clearing and Restrictions

Unquestionably, the exchange clearing system entails a certain amount of red tape. It necessitates the filling in of forms and in some cases the procuring of certificates or origin, etc. For this reason alone it is unpopular with part of the business community. Naturally enough, if the choice lies between transacting the same amount of business with or without these irksome formalities, the decision is not difficult. If, however, exporters find that they can sell goods and obtain payment for them only on the basis of exchange clearing, they will probably be quite willing to put up with relatively slight inconveniences. It is not correct to regard exchange clearing as an exchange restriction—not, at any rate, where foreign trade and legitimate foreign financial transactions are concerned. On the contrary, exchange clearing does away with the necessity of exchange restrictions in that sphere, since it enables importers and debtors to make payment in their own national currency. It is only for unwanted transfers of funds, which in the ordinary course would produce a disturbing effect, that exchange clearing operates as an exchange restriction.

The existence of exchange clearing would enable the countries to remove or relax various forms of restrictions imposed on international trade, such as quotas or prohibitive tariffs. Exchange clearing can effectively fulfil most of the functions for the sake of which such trade restrictions have been adopted. From this point of view, the adoption of exchange clearing constitutes a move towards greater freedom in the international interchange of goods.

Finally, exchange clearing is often attacked on the ground that it is detrimental to the countries which are not prepared to adopt the system. Unquestionably this is so, but surely the fault lies not with the system but with the countries which are unwilling to fall into line. The remedy lies in their own hands and they have only themselves to blame if they refuse to apply it.

(9) Exchange Clearing and Gold Standard

There is only one point at which the exchange clearing system, in the form it is proposed by the London Chamber of Commerce and others, lays itself open to justifiable criticism. It is a mistake to regard the system as being incompatible with the gold standard. There is no reason whatsoever why exchange clearing should not be combined with a modified form of gold standard, under which gold could, at the option of debtors, be used for the settlement of debit balances on clearing accounts. This arrangement would facilitate the working of the exchange clearing system, as it would provide a shock-absorber and would enable countries to carry on normally for a while in spite of an adverse trend in their foreign trade. There would be no free conversion of notes or free withdrawal of gold by the creditors, so that there would be no inducement to over-export for the sake of accumulating a huge gold reserve. On the other hand, countries desirous of importing in excess of their exports would be in a position to do so by drawing upon their gold stock. With the aid of such a limited gold standard, it would be possible to postpone the day when countries with credit balances would feel compelled to stop exporting to the countries with debit balances.

International lending in the form of cash loans, which are essential for the progress of undeveloped countries, would be impossible under the exchange clearing system unless it were combined with the gold standard. The creditor countries would be in a position to consolidate their clearing balances in relation to debtor countries, or to grant loans which would create credit balances on the clearing account of debtor countries, enabling the latter to increase their imports. When, however, it comes to lending in the form of cash to countries which are unable to procure sufficient capital in their home market, the transfer of gold is the only possible way of doing it under exchange clearing. The ideal system would be universal exchange clearing combined with a limited gold standard, for in that case the nations could possess reserves to fall back upon on rainy days. Those who are rigidly opposed to combining exchange clearing with the gold standard are guilty of the same degree of doctrinairism which they rightly denounce in their opponents.

CHAPTER XXXVII

EXCHANGE CLEARING IN PRACTICE

(1) Origin of the System

Many of the monetary reform schemes which we have discussed are dismissed by the orthodox school, and also by less-prejudiced quarters, as Utopian dreams. The exchange clearing system cannot, however, be disposed of so lightly. For, although little is known about it in English-speaking countries, the system is actually operating to a more or less limited degree in twenty-five countries, including such important countries as France, Germany, Italy, Holland, Belgium, Switzerland and, since January 13, 1936, also in Great Britain. The first exchange clearing agreement was concluded in November 1931, so that the system has been applied in practice for some years. At the time of writing, there are seventy-seven exchange clearing agreements in operation. In face of these facts it is difficult to denounce the system as impracticable. Its existence cannot be denied. The question is whether it can be extended and improved in accordance with the schemes put forward by those who believe in international clearing. From this point of view, the progress of the system has been most encouraging.

The system was adopted, not as a result of any proposals made by theoretical economists, but under the inexorable pressure of circumstances. As a result of the financial crisis of 1931, it appeared that the financially weak countries would soon be unable to maintain that indispensable minimum amount of imports which was required to satisfy the primary necessities of their populations. Their gold reserves were dwindling rapidly, despite exchange restrictions, for these were far from watertight. It is true that the restrictions checked superfluous imports, but as practically every other country had imposed similar restrictions, as fast as each sought to strengthen its technical position by reducing imports or by not paying for them, so it suffered a disadvantage because its exports in turn were excluded from other countries or were not paid for.

(2) The Deadlock of 1931

The absurdity of this deadlock was only too obvious. Every one of the Danubian and Balkan States closed its frontiers to the exports of the others and blocked payments to them. As a result, none of them appeared to be better off than it would have been if no such precautions had been taken. And yet the imposition of restrictions by these countries was inevitable. Given the weakness of their gold resources, they could not possibly trust to luck that under a régime of freedom they would not become the victims of an adverse trade balance and an outflow of funds which would eventually reduce them to starvation and chaos.

The result was a deadlock which threatened to strangle international commercial intercourse with the weak countries completely. The only obvious way to break this deadlock, in the absence of means of overcoming its fundamental causes, was to achieve an agreement for the interchange of goods in such a way as to preclude the possibility that the interchange would deplete currency reserves. This solution was arrived at through the conclusion of exchange clearing agreements.

The necessity for such a solution—the obvious one—was not confined to relations between weak countries. There was an equal necessity for its application in the relations between strong countries and weak countries. The latter were unable to pay cash for their imports from the strong countries. The arrears of overdue commercial debts as a result of transfer moratoria were accumulating, and exporters of the financially strong countries were faced with the alternative of taking the risk of having to wait indefinitely for payment, or of losing their market. Evidently, the solution was to use the proceeds of the exports of weak countries to strong countries to meet the payments for the imports of weak countries from strong countries. This is what actually happened in many instances. In fact, the first exchange clearing agreement was concluded not between two weak countries, but between a strong and a weak country.

(3) The First Clearing Agreement

On November 14, 1931, the Swiss and Hungarian Governments concluded the first exchange clearing agreement. By virtue of this agreement, payment for trade between the two countries was to be made through the intermediary of the two Central Banks. There was no longer any need for Swiss and Hungarian importers and exporters to buy and sell exchanges in connection with their dealings between each other. The substance of the agreement was that Swiss importers of Hungarian goods would pay the purchase price in Swiss francs into a special account kept by the Swiss National Bank, and that Hungarian importers of Swiss goods would pay the purchase price in pengös into a special account kept by the Hungarian National Bank. Swiss exporters to Hungary were to be paid out of the amounts paid in by Swiss importers from Hungary, while Hungarian exporters to Switzerland were to be paid out of the amounts paid in by Hungarian importers from Switzerland.

At the time of its conclusion, the agreement attracted barely any attention even in the countries directly concerned, much less in other countries. Most people regarded it as "just another form of irksome exchange restriction". Even the originators of the scheme themselves appear not to have realised the true significance of their innovation. They thought they had adopted a new palliative when in reality they had created a new system which may become the forerunner of a new era.

When the first exchange clearing agreement was concluded it had no theoretical background. As is so often the case, practical statesmen and administrators stole a march on economists. The inauguration of the new system was not preceded by any theoretical discussions between experts. Indeed, for long after its establishment, economists failed to take any particular notice of it. They simply considered it an additional variety of restriction, an additional manifestation of economic nationalism. As we pointed out in the last chapter, it is to the credit of the London Chamber of Commerce that it was the first to recognise the broader implications of the exchange clearing system.

(4) Opposition to the System

In the countries where the system was actually in operation, its broader implications were not recognised. The Press duly reported every new exchange clearing agreement and every change in the existing agreements, and gave publicity to the complaints arising from their working. The Universities condemned exchange clearing as they condemned blocked accounts, transfer restrictions and other similar interferences with freedom. The statesmen responsible for the conclusion of exchange clearing agreements never missed an opportunity to apologise for them as measures dictated by inevitable necessity, and never failed to pledge their word that they would be removed, together with other restrictions, as soon as conditions made removal possible.

When the author of this book published his book on *Exchange Control*, in which he presented exchange clearing as a permanent and rational solution in keeping with the general tendency towards planning, his attitude was subjected to sharp criticism by many reviewers of the book. M. Lamoureux, the then French Minister of Commerce, recognised, however, the significance of the new trend of thought, which began to receive support also in Continental economic literature. On M. Lamoureux's initiative the League of Nations appointed in September 1934 a special committee to enquire into the clearing and compensation systems. It was not until three years after the conclusion of the first exchange clearing agreement that most of its supporters and opponents began to realise the true significance of the new system, and the necessity for closer investigation of its nature and possibilities. Although the League Committee performed its task most inadequately, its enquiry certainly has the merit of having drawn attention to the problem, and of providing material concerning the various clearing agreements.

(5) Progress of the System

The first clearing agreements were remarkably primitive. In some instances they covered only a narrow group of imports and exports. For instance, in the first clearing agreement between Italy and Bulgaria, Italian purchases from the Bulgarian tobacco monopoly were offset by Bulgarian purchases of certain Italian industrial products through the intermediary of a clearing account. Some of the early clearing agreements were wider in scope. They covered the entire visible trade of the countries concerned. They also made provisions for repayment of commercial arrears. It was only gradually, however, that exchange clearing agreements began to embrace other international transfer items, besides those arising from visible trade. In the course of experience it has been found necessary and desirable to extend exchange clearing to cover various invisible items such as tourist traffic, shipping freights, insurance premiums and interest on debts, and to certain capital items such as loan repayments, transfer of legacies, etc. Some of the more recent exchange clearing agreements cover practically the whole range of international transfer items between two countries, so that the foreign exchange market has ceased to exist in the reciprocal relations between the countries concerned.

Simultaneously with the extension of their scope, the exchange clearing agreements have also undergone considerable technical improvement. The initial mistakes were gradually eliminated through trial and error; loopholes which had at first given ample opportunities for evasion were discovered and stopped; provisions were made against the abuse of the system by countries who sought to use it for running up a huge debit balance; arrangements were made to reduce as far as possible the delays in receiving payment through exchange clearing. In the course of four years the system has improved beyond recognition. Although still far from being watertight—indeed it cannot be so unless and until every country has adopted it—it now provides much less opportunity for abuses on the part of individuals or Governments than it did in its primitive form.

(6) Extended Application of Clearing

While the scope of exchange clearing agreements was extended and their facilities improved, the geographical sphere of their application also underwent gradual if not uninterrupted expansion. From time to time, exchange clearing agreements which did not work satisfactorily were discontinued. The fact, however, that the same countries which terminated some of their exchange clearing agreements subsequently concluded others shows that their decision to suspend agreements was not due to any inherent defect of the system, but to circumstances which prevented certain agreements from giving satisfaction. The endeavour of the German Government to finance its trade deficit by means of exchange clearing agreements led to the termination of the German-Belgian exchange clearing agreement, and France also gave notice to terminate her agreement with Germany. On the other hand, the application of economic sanctions led to the adoption of additional exchange clearing arrangements. The British Government, breaking with its persistent opposition to the system, decided in November 1935, in connection with economic sanctions, to make the existing voluntary clearing arrangements with Italy compulsory. It was agreed at Geneva that Switzerland, owing to her status as a neutral country, should not participate in the embargo on Italian goods, but should take steps to ensure that no cash payment should be made, and to that end exchange clearing arrangements were to be established. Finally, in January 1936 the British Government concluded its first bilateral exchange clearing agreement—with Spain. While the Italian clearing arrangement was semi-political, the Spanish arrangement was prompted by purely commercial and financial motives. Thus was the acceptance of the principle of exchange clearing initiated by the country which had hitherto stubbornly refused to depart from the doctrine of the freedom of international transfers. In spite of her free-trade traditions—which subconsciously survived after the protective duties were adopted—Great Britain realised the necessity for replacing the free foreign exchange market by exchange clearing. Admittedly, the arrangement was declared to be purely temporary. Its adoption constituted none the less an important landmark in the progress towards the universal adoption of the system.

(7) League's Opposition Fails

The replies to the questionnaire sent out by the League of Nations Secretariat to the Governments which concluded exchange clearing agreements make it plain that while there is much criticism of the details of the system, practically all Governments have found that it has achieved the purpose for which it was concluded. For this reason, the efforts of the League authorities to induce the Governments to discontinue the system were of no avail. While most Governments regarded it as a necessary evil and would be only too pleased to do away with it at the earliest possible moment, circumstances were such as to make it impossible for the time being to revert to the old system in international transfers.

The desperate effort of the League of Nations to oppose the development of exchange clearing proved a complete failure. Although the League Committee in charge of the investigations did its utmost to make out the strongest possible case against exchange clearing, and although its efforts to that end received the endorsement of the League Assembly in September 1935, the result was entirely negative. Not only has no progress been made towards the liquidation of the system since the publication of the Report in May 1935, but, as we have pointed out, the system received a strong stimulus in consequence of the change of the British official attitude towards it. It is significant that the opposition of the League Committee to exchange clearing was largely inspired by the British members, and at the time their attitude represented the official British standpoint. In the course of a few months, however, the British Government itself had to admit that the adoption of exchange clearing was inevitable.

(8) Triangular and International Clearing

Hitherto we have been dealing with exchange clearing in its most primitive form, that of bilateral clearing agreements. In many instances, however, the system has moved beyond that stage. Triangular clearing arrangements have been concluded in a number of instances. Although such cases are still the exception and not the rule, the very fact that such arrangements have been reached foreshadows important developments in that direction. In several instances, especially in Central and Southern Europe, triangular arrangements enabled creditor countries to liquidate clearing balances which would otherwise have become frozen. The fact that it was possible to reach such agreements shows that exchange clearing does not exclude the possibility of triangular trade. Admittedly, the progress towards the adoption of triangular clearing has been very slow and there has so far been no instance of multilateral clearing. If, however, every country were to have bilateral clearing agreements with every other country there would be much more opportunity for swapping debit and credit balances triangularly or multilaterally. In the existing circumstances, what is surprising is not that triangular and multilateral clearing has not made more rapid progress, but that it has made any progress at all.

It is to be hoped that a time will arrive when triangular and multilateral exchange clearing arrangements will become the rule and not the exception. This can be made possible through the establishment of an international organisation to act as intermediary between various countries engaged in exchange clearing. Even though the League of Nations, the Bank for International Settlements, all Central Banks and most Governments are at present strongly opposed to the idea, it is nevertheless gaining ground, and international clearing is beginning to be considered the system of the future.

(9) Future of Exchange Clearing

If, as is expected, the countries of the Gold Bloc should have to devalue in the not too distant future, the resulting currency confusion will undoubtedly lead to the adoption of exchange clearing to an increasing degree. It is conceivable that within the next year or two the number of bilateral agreements will increase considerably, in which case the opportunity for triangular and multilateral arrangements will also increase. At the same time, pressure in favour of some central organisation to co-ordinate the various bilateral agreements and to provide better opportunities for triangular and multilateral transactions will increase, and may even overcome the resistance of orthodox quarters. The establishment of international clearing is thus within the realm of practical politics. Even if this end is not attained in the course of the next few years, the adoption of international clearing can be only a question of time.

Doubtless, with the improvement of economic conditions most Governments will revert to *laissez-faire* in international transfers. When, however, the next international crisis occurs, they will undoubtedly resort once more to exchange clearing. This time they will be in a position to apply the system in its more advanced form. While in 1931 and subsequent years, lack of experience was largely responsible for the deficiencies of the system, there is reason to believe that when, on the occasion of the next crisis, its improved version is applied it will give more satisfaction, all the more so as in the meantime an adequate theoretical background will have been created for it and its shortcomings will be duly examined and discussed. The chances are, therefore, that on the occasion of the next crisis there will be less dissatisfaction with, and opposition to, the exchange clearing system and it will progress to its more advanced stage. Conceivably, it may then come to stay, or if not, it may be adopted as a permanent institution on the occasion of some future crisis. Sooner or later, the world will learn by costly experience that exchange clearing is the rational system of international transfers, and that its adoption is in accordance with the requirements of both progress and stability.

CHAPTER XXXVIII

MONETARY ISOLATION

(1) Monetary *v.* Economic Isolation

While a number of reformers seek the world's salvation in monetary internationalism, others believe that the solution of our problems lies in monetary isolationism. In fact, sometimes the same reformers advocate both, that is, they are whole-heartedly in favour of monetary internationalism but add that, should distrust and jealousy between the nations make this course impossible, the alternative is extreme monetary isolation. The isolationist school maintains that it is to the interest of the individual countries and in the long run even of mankind in general that the world should be broken up into communities entirely independent from a monetary point of view. They consider this desirable in order that each country should be free to work out its own salvation independently of other countries. It is pointed out that under an international monetary system the progress of the world as a whole depends upon the pace dictated by the least progressive of countries, just as the speed of a fleet depends upon the speed of its slowest unit. If one of the important countries refuses to expand credit for the sake of improving the welfare of her population, then other countries which dare to expand will have to pay the penalty as a result of adverse international pressure caused by the difference in their relative degrees of expansion. If one of the major countries, prompted by a deflationary mentality, chooses to restrict, then in order to avoid economic depression and financial crisis the other countries will have to follow it, however reluctantly, and however much they might wish to proceed in the opposite direction.

Monetary isolation could be achieved by means of severing all monetary links between one country and the others. Should this aim be achieved, there would no longer be an international price level, and there would be no exchange rates between the various currencies. Prices, production and consumption, monetary policy, interest rates, etc., would in each country be entirely independent of monetary influences from other countries.

On the surface this system appears to imply the highest possible degree of economic isolation in addition to monetary isolation. This, however, is not necessarily the case. There would be no need for a country which adopted monetary isolation to grow rubber in hothouses or to confine its consumption to goods which could be produced entirely out of home-produced materials. Monetary isolation is not incompatible with a certain degree of commercial intercourse between the nations. Indeed, it is essential for the maintenance and increase of their standard of living that they should interchange goods, so as to acquire those goods which either cannot be produced at home at all or can be produced only at prohibitive cost. Such an interchange, however, would have to be barter in form or in substance.

(2) Exports under Monetary Isolation

Under an inter-dependent international monetary system, an internal expansion of production brought about by monetary expansion carries with it the germ of its own destruction in that a substantial rise in internal commodity prices threatens the international stability of the currency and necessitates measures for its defence. Under the system of monetary isolation, however, there is nothing to prevent a well-planned and carefully executed internal expansion from going ahead indefinitely, provided that it does not exceed the limit beyond which it would undermine internal confidence. Such effect as a reasonable expansion may produce on the internal price level would not influence the foreign trade of the country concerned. Goods would be exported, not for the sake of commercial profits but, if necessary, even at a loss, in order to enable the country to obtain in exchange the indispensable foreign goods which it requires. From this point of view, the discrepancy between the internal and international price level would be a matter of small importance. The Government would have to subsidise exports to the extent that was necessary to enable its exporters to compete with their foreign rivals in spite of the higher cost of production. The wider the gap between internal and international prices the more costly this process would necessarily be. At the same time, provided that the internal expansion that caused the rise of internal prices were well planned, it would result in a large increase of the nation's wealth. As a result, the nation could well afford to subsidise its exports out of its surplus wealth, especially as the volume of exports would be only a small percentage of the volume of national production.

Let us assume, for the sake of argument, that an expansion of credit led to an increase of the national output by 10 per cent, and that it also caused a rise in the price level by 10 per cent. If exports represent, say, 20 per cent of the value of national output, and they have to be subsidised to the extent of 10 per cent, then the cost is 2 per cent of the national income. The community could well afford this 2 per cent, considering that expansion would have increased its total income by 10 per cent. Needless to say, such a system would presuppose a high degree of economic planning, though those opponents of the system who denounce it as Communism are guilty of mild exaggeration. Doubtless, the system would work most smoothly in a Communist State, where production for home consumption and for export is the concern of the same authority. The position of the Communist State can best be compared with those of a huge privately owned vertical trust which has to run some of its departments at a loss in order to secure the profitable working of the combine as a whole. It is, however, conceivable that the system of a monetary isolation could be adopted under the régime of private property, provided that a high degree of planning of production and distribution were adopted. Otherwise the additional taxation necessitated by the subsidising of exports would lead to a contraction of purchasing power which would result in depression, or at any rate would check expansion. The detailed discussion of this problem falls within the realm of economic planning, and thus is beyond the scope of this book.

(3) "Unlimited Expansion"

Monetary isolationists claim that this is the only method by which it would be possible to take full advantage of technical inventions, efficient methods of production and economic planning in general. They are convinced that, once it were detached from the disturbing international influences, a country could raise the standard of living of its population almost indefinitely. Housing conditions could be improved, roads, schools and hospitals could be built, the output of capital goods as well as consumption goods would be limited only by the technical limits of productive capacity—limits which would tend to widen with further inventions and the improvement of industrial and agricultural methods—instead of being limited by monetary considerations. It is impossible to deny that the temptation held out by monetary isolationists is very strong. If all this could be achieved by scrapping the international monetary machinery and reverting to barter in international trade, then unquestionably the price paid would be very small in proportion to the result. But can all this really be achieved at the cost of monetary isolation, and again, could it not be achieved by any other methods?

The reply to the first part of the question is in the affirmative. Although foreign trade with the aid of subsidies as described above and in the absence of the international monetary machinery might in normal times work much less smoothly than does the system of free competition, the isolationist system is none the less feasible. It could be greatly facilitated by the adoption of international compensation or barter, through which the country with the higher price level might reduce its losses on its export trade. After all, the country with the lower price level is also anxious to export, and might be willing to bear part of the burden which under normal trading conditions would fall entirely on the shoulders of the country with the higher price level. The extension of international compensation transactions since 1931 bears witness to the possibility of doing foreign trade on a large scale even with the complete exclusion of money. Such trading would become even easier if some international centre could be established which would act as an intermediary for international barter. Assuming that gold were used in these transactions, not as a monetary unit but as a commodity which everybody is willing to accept, there would be no insurmountable obstacle to monetary isolation.

We do not propose to discuss in this volume whether or not internal economic planning could produce all or most of what we expect of it. There can be no doubt that, relieved of the necessity of having to watch the gold reserve, exchange rate, transfer of funds, etc., the authorities could concentrate entirely upon the requirements of internal trade; and if the system of economic planning stands a chance of ever succeeding, then it would be bound to succeed in such ideal circumstances.

(4) Alternative Solutions

Is it not, however, possible to achieve the same end without having to sacrifice the international monetary apparatus? There are indeed two other schemes which tend to produce similar results to those of economic isolationism. The one is the system of inconvertible paper currencies, the exchange rates between which are constantly adjusted to correspond to the changed economic parities, and the other system is that of international exchange clearing.

In theory, the system of inconvertible paper currencies and fluctuating exchanges compares favourably with monetary isolation. It may well be that a bad international monetary apparatus is better than no apparatus at all, provided that it does not interfere with the internal monetary policy of the countries concerned. In practice, however, it is difficult to imagine that the fluctuation of exchanges would not react upon the internal monetary situation. As we pointed out in an earlier chapter, it is a mistake to imagine that the exchange rate is always a passive factor which will adjust itself to the purchasing power parities between the countries. In many instances, the movements of the exchanges themselves influence the purchasing power parities. Let us suppose for the sake of argument that, as a result of monetary expansion in country A, its price level in relation to country B increases by 10 per cent. In theory, a depreciation of its exchange by 10 per cent would restore the equilibrium. In practice, however, the rise in country A may cause a rising tendency in country B, contrary to the monetary policy of that country. Or a depreciation of the exchange of country A may cause a further rise in the price level of A. For, in addition to the rise caused by the monetary expansion, the prices of imported commodities would become more expensive. Moreover, assuming that the freedom of the foreign exchange market were retained, a depreciating tendency in the currency of A would bring forth a flight of funds from A to B, and this together with speculation would accentuate the depreciation far beyond the 10 per cent represented by the change in the purchasing power parity. So long as there is a free foreign exchange market and a comparatively free international interchange of goods, prices and interest rates, the whole monetary policy of a country is exposed to international influences.

(5) Exchange Clearing

The other alternative to monetary isolation is the adoption of international exchange clearing. We discussed this system fully in the last two chapters, and here we need recall only that the system combines the advantages of an international monetary apparatus with those of monetary isolation. Under such a system there would be no need to revert to barter in order to procure the indispensable necessities that cannot be produced at home. The cumbersome methods of compensation could be avoided. Goods would be bought and sold across the frontiers in terms of money even though book-keeping entries would replace transfer through the foreign exchange market. It would be possible to transfer funds for approved purposes, to lend and borrow abroad. Nothwithstanding this, the country could remain aloof from international influences to a much larger extent than in the case of inconvertible paper currencies with fluctuating exchanges, and almost to the same extent as in the case of monetary isolation.

Under exchange clearing a rise in internal prices caused by monetary expansion could either be offset by a corresponding deliberate adjustment of the exchange rate, or, at the Government's option, it could be ignored and the debit balance that would develop in consequence could be offset by subsidising exports.

Since it would be to the interest of countries with the lower price level that they should liquidate their credit balances on clearing account with the country with a higher price level, they might be prepared, as under the system of compensation, to take part of the loss by accepting the goods of their debtor at prices above the world level. Thus the cost of subsidising exports would be no higher than it would be under the system of monetary isolation combined with compensation agreements.

It may be argued that exchange clearing is nothing more

and nothing less than monetary isolation. Whether this is so is a matter of opinion. If it is monetary isolation, it is certainly the most efficient and least inconvenient form of that system. Through its adoption the influence of international developments on the internal situation is reduced and it can in any case be regulated by the authorities of the countries themselves. Harmful shifting of funds and speculation in exchanges are ruled out and the exchange rate can be altered whenever alteration is deemed desirable, and altered with the least possible disturbance to the situation of the country itself and of other countries.

The difference between exchange clearing and monetary isolation proper is that, under the former, commercial and financial transfers of most kinds would continue, only they would have to go through the channels of clearing accounts. Under monetary isolation, on the other hand, one currency would become virtually unsaleable in terms of other currencies, and such transfers as would take place would constitute a Government monopoly.

There is thus no need to adopt the extreme course of monetary isolation in order to safeguard monetary management and economic planning from disturbing international influences. The same result can be achieved with the aid of international exchange clearing. That system, coupled with a limited gold standard, is the ideal solution of the international aspect of the monetary problem.

CHAPTER XXXIX

MONETARY ISOLATION IN PRACTICE

(1) THE EXAMPLE OF SOVIET RUSSIA

THERE is only one country which in recent years has put the idea of monetary isolation fully into practice. That country is the Soviet Union. From an economic point of view, Soviet Russia is far from being isolated. She has maintained a substantial volume of import and export trade; she has obtained credits abroad, has kept substantial accounts with foreign banks, and has opened overseas branches of her banking and trading organisation. All this is contrary to the principle of economic isolation such as was adopted, for instance, in Paraguay for a while during the last century, or in Japan prior to the European penetration. The monetary isolation of Soviet Russia was not the result of any preconceived scheme but of the sequence of developments. To begin with, the Soviet rouble had the same relation to other monetary systems as had any other currency, even though the disturbed political and economic conditions in Russia during the first few years of the Soviet régime interfered with the reciprocal monetary influences between that country and the rest of the world. Even after the Soviet currency was stabilised, it was not the Government's intention to isolate its monetary system from international influences. The tchervonetz was quoted in foreign markets. After her inflationary experience, it appeared on the surface that Soviet Russia would revert to the orthodox monetary system.

In reality, the complete absence of free commerce continued to prevent prices in the Soviet Union and abroad from affecting each other. Thus, in fact if not in law, monetary isolation of the Soviet Union was complete. The prices of goods exported from Soviet Russia were not determined by the internal price level and by the exchange rate, but by the degree of the necessity for the Soviet Union to export in order to be able to import. Independently of their internal prices, wheat, timber, oil, etc., were sold at prices which were competitive enough to enable the Soviet Union to sell abroad a sufficient quantity of goods. Indeed, the price level ceased to have any meaning in the Soviet Union, for the price of goods obtainable by means of ration tickets was controlled, while prices in the " black " market were vague and difficult to ascertain.

(2) Embargo on Soviet Note Imports

In 1925, the Soviet Government took deliberate steps to make its monetary isolation complete. It prohibited the repatriation of its own notes. This was done in order to make the notes unsaleable abroad, so as to prevent a flight of capital. Although the embargo was not altogether effective—smuggling continued on a large scale via Persia and other Near Eastern countries—for the purposes of legitimate business the quotation of the Soviet notes on the continental Bourses was purely nominal.

With the prohibition of the export and import of Soviet notes, the monetary isolation of the Soviet Union became complete in law as well as in fact. These notes were issued purely for internal purposes. They ceased to play any part in international commercial or financial intercourse. Indeed, such intercourse has become the monopoly of the official foreign trade and banking organisation. The official rate of exchange has practically ceased to have any meaning at all, for exportable products are quoted in terms of foreign currencies by the foreign trade organisation. From the point of view of the Soviet Government, the technical disconnection of the monetary system of the Soviet Union from the world system had the advantage of disguising from the world the extent of the inner depreciation of the currency. It is true that foreign travellers in Soviet Russia came back with amazing stories about the fantastic " black " rates paid for their pound or dollar notes. There was, however, no " black " quotation of the tchervonetz in foreign centres, where the Press continued to quote the official rate as a matter of form long after that rate ceased to have any meaning in practice.

In the case of Soviet Russia monetary isolation was due not so much to any deliberate monetary policy as to the planned economic system adopted by the Soviet Union. This is not the place to consider the merits and demerits of the Communist Five Years Plan compared with the liberal capitalist system. Given the fact that Soviet Russia adopted planning as the basis of her economic system, the only possible way in which she was able to safeguard her planned production from the caprices of international influences was by the adoption of monetary isolation. A free foreign exchange market with facilities for transferring funds abroad and for speculating in the national currency would inevitably have frustrated all estimates.

(3) Partial Isolation in Italy and Germany

The fact that free international transfers and a planned economic system are incompatible with each other is not adequately realised by the majority of planners who, while anxious to subordinate production, distribution and even consumption to Government planning, consider it possible to maintain the orthodox system of transfers. While Soviet Russia adequately realised the necessity of combining planning with monetary isolation, it was some time before this fact was realised in countries where economic planning attained a less advanced state. Both Italy and Germany resorted gradually to a high degree of monetary isolation, but this solution was not adopted in connection with their policy of economic interventionism. It was simply the consequence of an overvalued exchange and of a stubborn determination to maintain, nominally at any rate, the old parity. To that end, long before the pursuit of National Socialist economic policy led to the adoption of a certain degree of planning, Germany adopted exchange restrictions which went far towards achieving monetary isolation. To a large extent monetary isolation in Germany assumed the form of a controlled exchange, and a large part of her foreign trade and transfers was based on exchange clearing agreements. It was not until 1935 that it became evident that the German price level had broken away from the world level. As a result of internal expansion due to rearmament and public works, prices in Germany rose well above those of the Gold Bloc countries, not to speak of the prices of the Sterling Bloc or the United States. It became necessary to place German foreign trade on an essentially artificial basis. Exports received substantial subsidies out of the proceeds of levies imposed upon those industries which were benefiting by the internal boom.

In Italy, the same stage was reached in 1935 as a result of the Abyssinian conflict and the economic sanctions. The internal price level rose well above the world level and this rise, together with the embargo on Italian exports, induced the Government to resort to the system of heavy subsidies. Difficulties in the way of releasing foreign lira balances led to the virtual suspension of the quotation of the lira in foreign exchange markets. Italian foreign trade is no longer governed by considerations of price and profits. Imports have been reduced to the requirements of the fighting forces and the barest necessities of the civilian population, while exports are being stimulated artificially by Government subsidies, to overcome not only the discrepancy between Italian prices and the world level, but also the League embargo on Italian goods.

(4) Isolation and Expansion

While Soviet Russia adopted a clear-cut system of monetary isolation, in both Germany and Italy that system is combined with exchange clearing, compensation and with the survival of the outward form of the orthodox system of exchanges. In both cases, the limited degree of monetary isolation has gone a long way towards enabling the two countries to expand internal production independently of international influences. This is not the place to discuss whether the purpose of this expansion—rearmament in the case of Germany and war in the case of Italy—can be justified from a national point of view. The fact we are concerned with is that if a country decides, rightly or wrongly, to embark upon a policy of internal expansion, monetary isolation can go a long way towards enabling it to do so. The fact that both Germany and Italy adopted the system in order to pursue destructive ends should not create prejudice on ethical grounds against the system itself. After all, it is not the fault of a system if it is used for destructive purposes. The fact that Italy and Germany were able, as a result of their resort to a high degree of monetary isolation, to manufacture lethal weapons, explosives and poison gas, proves that by the same means it would be possible also to increase national production for constructive purposes.

Both Germany and Italy would have been able to achieve much better results if they had not chosen to handicap themselves by principles of monetary orthodoxy. As a result of the defence of the reichsmark and the lira at overvalued levels, both countries sacrificed a large part of the benefit derived from partial monetary isolation.

Whether or not monetary isolation will be resorted to in future by a larger number of countries and to a larger degree than it has so far been adopted, depends upon developments in the sphere of international politics as well as finance. Should a suspension of the gold standard by France lead to an unprecedented degree of currency chaos, it might induce many countries to scrap the international monetary machinery and resort to monetary isolation. Political developments may also tend to work in the same direction. In particular, the adoption of economic sanctions against Italy will encourage the tendency towards economic isolation, which if it materialises will doubtless be accompanied by a high degree of monetary isolation. On the whole, however, it seems more probable that the future lies with the other alternative to monetary isolation—the more subtle and more efficient method of exchange clearing. As we have pointed out in earlier chapters, that system is likely to be generally adopted in the long run. In that event, it will obviate the necessity for crude monetary isolation.

CHAPTER XL

CO-ORDINATION OF REFORM SCHEMES

(1) Need for Co-ordination

We have now reached the most difficult part of our task. Having dealt with a number of reform schemes, we must now attempt to extract from them the points that in our view are worth retaining, and to co-ordinate them into a combined reform scheme. The task is both difficult and thankless. Monetary reformers, enthusiastic about the particular scheme which they regard as a hundred per cent solution of the problem, have every reason to resent an attempt to reduce the importance of their proposal to, say, 10 per cent or 20 per cent of the total. Indeed, coming as it does from quarters which are in sympathy with their ideas, they probably resent the attempt more than they would the total rejection of their schemes by their orthodox opponents. Even those would-be reformers who are broadminded enough to consider it necessary to adopt more than one remedy usually lay too much emphasis on their own favourite idea. And yet it is a mistake to imagine that there is one simple patent medicine that could possibly cure all the ailments of our highly complicated economic system. If only all serious would-be reformers could be brought together and induced to see their own favourite schemes in true perspective, the result of such a conference would be the elaboration of a truly constructive and comprehensive reform scheme supported by the whole united force of the monetary reform movement. As it is, the reform movement is hopelessly divided and its influence is diminished by rivalries between the various schools and the various factions of each school.

Since the possibility of such reconciliation of various reform schools is very remote, it is for those who are in sympathy with reform movements in a general way, without having thrown themselves whole-heartedly into any one particular camp, to try to suggest a co-ordination of the reform schemes. In this respect it is essential to distinguish between the ideal and the practicable.

(2) The Policy of Cheap Money

A policy of cheap money is unquestionably essential in the interest of progress. It is more essential now than it was before the war owing to the increase of fictitious wealth since 1914, an increase which saddled the productive classes with an unduly heavy interest burden. If it should be possible to reduce the burden of deadweight debt by drastic devaluation and by a substantial increase of production, the relative importance of the cheap money policy would undoubtedly decline. It would nevertheless remain essential for the purpose of safeguarding trade from time to time from the constriction of unduly high interest rates. Under the liberal system, high interest rates were an inevitable weapon for the defence of the currency against international influences, and for the discouragement of boom and over-speculation. Under a managed system, however, more rational means could be employed to the same end. There is no need to penalise legitimate and sound trade for the excesses of over-expanded branches of production or of reckless speculation.

One solution which has been suggested is a reduction of interest rates to a level at which they simply cover the risk and the clerical work involved, without including a bonus arising from the scarcity of capital. This, however, would be possible only under a planned economic system, when over-production, both general and particular, could be cured by direct intervention instead of by the slow counteraction of high interest rates. Assuming that it will be a long time before a planned economic system will be adopted, it will remain necessary to raise interest rates occasionally. What is essential is that each country should be in a position to regulate its interest rates in accordance with its internal requirements, independently of international influences. To that end universal international exchange clearing would be the best solution. That system, however, is not likely to be adopted for some time at any rate, and meanwhile the technical devices put forward by Mr. Keynes—the Central Banks' intervention in the forward exchange market and the widening of the gold points—constitute the best practicable solution.

(3) Credit Expansion

Credit expansion is indispensable for the increase of production, and those who think that the world cannot afford to wait for the expansion to take place as and when the monetary stock of gold increases, are justified in their impatience. In the interest of the improvement of the standard of living through an increase of production it is essential that cheap and plentiful funds should be at the disposal of production. It would be a mistake, however, to overrate the importance of credit expansion unless it is accompanied by an increase of purchasing power and unless the consumers are prepared to utilise the increase. Moreover, production must at times be encouraged by other means than credit expansion, in particular by means of public works. In given circumstances, efforts to increase the velocity of circulation of money are likely to produce better results than an expansion of its quantity. To that end the occasional use of negative interest may come into consideration.

Expansion in itself is an unscientific device unless it is regulated in pursuance of a certain object. This object may be to raise or maintain the price level in face of an expanding production, or it may be to increase employment. It is also necessary that in case of need the expanding tendency should be reversed. Monetary management should not consist of perpetual expansion, but of periods of expansion alternated with periods of consolidation. In the absence of a planned economy, credit expansion will from time to time have to give way to contraction. Here again, as in the case of the policy of cheap money, it is essential that if and when it is necessary to reverse expansion, it should be done solely from the point of view of internal trade and not under the influence of international factors.

(4) Managed Currency

Unquestionably, it is desirable that the automatic character of the monetary system should be abolished and that a managed currency should be adopted. The choice lies between managed paper currency and managed currency with a gold backing. The author definitely favours the latter system. In his opinion, it is possible to combine a managed currency with a limited gold standard, by which gold is used for the settlement of international indebtedness on the initiative of the debtor. In the author's opinion, such a system combines the advantages of the gold standard with those of the managed monetary system, without having the disadvantages of either. The fact that the monetary authorities possess gold reserves should not prevent them from managing their currency as if it were an inconvertible paper currency.

The idea of elastic parities does not appeal to the author. On the other hand, he is opposed to a return to the system of absolutely rigid parities. He believes that Governments should reserve the right to alter parities when their maintenance appears to involve sacrifices that are out of proportion to the advantages of stable parities. In this respect at any rate the desiderata of would-be reformers are within the realm of practical politics. While there is a wide gap between the ideal and the practicable regarding the policy of cheap money and credit expansion, there is no reason why a high degree of monetary management should not be adopted or the principle of alterable parities accepted. In this respect the remedy lies to a large extent in our own hands.

(5) Drastic Devaluation and Strong Reserves

In order to avoid the necessity of over-frequent changes in parities, it is necessary to carry out a drastic devaluation of all currencies, as a result of which the commodity value of gold would increase considerably and the margins of gold reserves would become adequately large. If the world had a surplus of gold instead of a scarcity, it would be easier to resist adverse pressure without the need for alteration in parities. It would also provide a fair scope for credit expansion without the risk that expansion would undermine confidence.

Indeed, the author attaches much importance to the provision of the strongest possible backing for the currency and credit system. In addition to an increase in the book-keeping value of gold reserves through drastic devaluation, he favours the admission of silver to a limited degree as note cover. Moreover, he advocates the admission of commodity reserves as supplementary note cover. In any case, the necessity will doubtless be duly realised for Governments to keep substantial reserves in some non-perishable commodities required for the national defence or for the nations' food supply in case of war or blockade. Assuming that the Governments do construct such reserves, it would clearly be advantageous if they were also regarded as secondary reserves of the note issue, and indirectly of the credit structure. In this respect, too, the ideal solution may be regarded as entirely practicable. It would not even necessitate any fundamental change in the prevailing conceptions. Indeed some of the reforms actually carried out during the past two decades have been at least as revolutionary as those suggested above.

The author is not in favour of over-complicating the monetary system by means of dual currencies. Nor, generally speaking, is he in favour of negative interest rates except during brief periods when production or consumption needs stimulation by an increase in the velocity of circulation of money.

(6) International Co-operation

The author believes in the advantages of closer international collaboration in the monetary sphere; but he considers as purely Utopian those proposals for a central gold reserve, for a uniform monetary policy or for the issue of international currency. In this respect, the ideal and the practicable are miles apart. In the author's opinion, monetary internationalism should assume a form which is not dependent upon the realisation of the dream of removing rivalry and distrust between Governments. The apparently paradoxical suggestion of international monetary co-operation without political or economic internationalism can however be realised by the establishment of international exchange clearing. In this respect, the author holds very strong views, and cannot regard himself as an impartial judge. He considers that international exchange clearing is the ideal solution of the problem of international transfers and trade. He is convinced that with the aid of exchange clearing the advantages of relatively free trade could be preserved, while at the same time internal monetary management could be safeguarded against disturbing influences to just the same extent as it would be safeguarded under the system of monetary isolation. Exchange clearing is indispensable to complete monetary management and economic planning.

The author is anxious not to fall into the error for which he criticises other monetary reformers. In spite of his enthusiasm for exchange clearing he realises that it can provide only a partial solution and that it can form only a part of a more comprehensive scheme of monetary reform. He does not even believe that exchange clearing can and should replace the gold standard. Just as a managed currency is not incompatible with the maintenance of a limited gold standard, the combination of the latter with exchange clearing is also a feasible and desirable solution. It has the great advantage that it obviates the necessity for monetary isolation, which, in the absence of such a solution, would be resorted to by all countries who were particularly anxious to expand internally without being exposed to disturbing international influences.

(7) The Ideal Currency

Thus, internally the ideal currency should be a managed currency with ample gold backing and possibly with subsidiary silver and commodity backing. The object of its management should be to maintain, if possible, the stability of money in terms of both commodities and gold, but this should be regarded only as a means to the end of improving the standard of living. If that end could be better served by sacrificing either internal or international stability, those responsible for the management of the currency should not hesitate to make the sacrifice. Money should be kept reasonably cheap and the manipulation of interest rates should not be used extensively as a means of monetary management. It is preferable to resort to contraction or expansion, aiming directly at the particular branch of production which is out of equilibrium. To go a step further, it is even more desirable to resort to direct control of production than to attempt its regulation through credit restrictions, for in given circumstances these are both unfair and unwise. The authorities should if necessary be prepared to contract credit or purchasing power for the purpose of consolidating a position after a too rapid or an uneven advance. They should also be prepared to resort to artificial means of stimulating production or consumption, whether through public works, the creation of artificial purchasing power, negative interest rates or other devices.

Given the fact that a uniform monetary policy by all

countries is unattainable, from time to time disequilibrium will inevitably arise between the price levels in various countries. The object of monetary management should be to minimise the disturbing effect of such disequilibrium upon internal monetary management. One of the chief shortcomings of the automatic gold standard is the extent to which it allows or compels international disequilibrium to react upon internal trade. No reform can be regarded as satisfactory unless it improves matters in this respect.

(8) International Aspects

A solution by which disequilibrium would lead to perpetual exchange fluctuations could not be regarded as satisfactory. It is essential to avoid falling from the error of over-estimating the importance of international monetary stability, and under-estimating that of internal monetary stability, into the opposite error of over-estimating the importance of internal monetary stability and under-estimating that of international stability. While it is an unpardonable mistake to defend international parities to the last drop of blood, it would be equally wrong to refrain altogether from maintaining a reasonable degree of international stability so long as this could be done without undue sacrifices.

A system preferable to that of free exchanges, whose persistent effort to reach economic parities involves constant fluctuations, is that of exchange clearing. This system should be combined with a complete control over all kinds of transfers, whether current items or capital items. The elimination of unnecessary and harmful international transfers of funds and of international exchange speculation would in itself go a long way towards safeguarding internal monetary management from unpleasant shocks. Exchange clearing would to a large extent also safeguard internal monetary management from the disturbing effects of temporary adverse trade balances. In addition to exchange clearing, monetary internationalism should assume the form of closer collaboration as far as possible. It is necessary, however, to avoid the repetition of the mistake of post-war stabilisation, for that was based to an excessive degree upon international co-operation.

These are the broad outlines of the monetary reform scheme, combining parts of the various proposals made in recent years, which the author considers the best solution of the monetary problem. The new monetary policy should be characterised by a high degree of elasticity and adaptability. It should not allow the new rules to become too rigid and should avoid at all costs the development of a new doctrinairism. It should be prepared at any time to discard any part of the reform scheme which is found unworkable or disadvantageous in the course of experience. Above all, it should maintain its sense of proportion regarding the relative importance of monetary policy as part of the general economic and social policy of the community.

CHAPTER XLI

MONETARY *v.* ECONOMIC REFORM

(1) Danger of New Dogmatism

Having examined all the important monetary reform proposals, and having sought to reconcile them with one another, it remains for us to examine the place which monetary reform occupies, or should occupy, in the economic system. Evidently, monetary reform is not, or should not be, an end in itself. It is to be regarded as a means to the ends of accelerating progress, eliminating setbacks and improving the standard of living. The main criticism against the orthodox monetary school is that it is prepared to sacrifice progress for the sake of upholding its monetary doctrines. Would-be reformers should avoid this particular error at all costs. It would be deplorable if all that monetary reform could achieve were the substitution of one kind of monetary doctrinairism for another kind of monetary doctrinairism.

And yet, there is a strong tendency for monetary reformers to fall into the very error which they are the first to denounce in their opponents' schemes. Many of them are inclined to mistake the means for the end. Possibly because they are so firmly convinced that the reform measures they propose are to the interest of the progress and welfare of mankind, they are inclined to develop a new type of dogmatism which may become as dangerous as the dogmatism of the orthodox school. Like the latter, they can see the world only through the spectacles of their monetary doctrines. Above all, they imagine that if only the Governments were to adopt their special monetary reform scheme the community could be assured of progress, prosperity and everlasting happiness.

(2) Monetary Reforms in themselves not Sufficient

In the foregoing chapters we have done our best to denounce this one-sidedness of most monetary proposals, a one-sidedness which deprives the proposals of much of their constructive value. We have endeavoured to reconcile the apparently conflicting reform schemes by discriminating between their constructive points and their one-sided exaggeration. Even the combination of various reform measures—whether in the form suggested in the last chapter or in some other form—could not possibly be in itself an adequate solution. While it would not rely upon the miraculous effect of one particular remedy, it would still have the shortcoming of trying to solve economic problems by purely monetary means. This is a grave shortcoming, for while it would be idle to deny the importance of money in the general scheme of things, there are other factors of equal importance.

Monetary reform in itself cannot solve the world's economic problem unless it is combined with economic planning. It is of vital importance that production and distribution, and to some extent even consumption, should be subjected to scientific organisation and planning. The majority of monetary reformers either ignore the necessity for doing anything outside the monetary sphere or they think that the desired degree of economic planning can easily be achieved by means of monetary management. To the minds of the one-sided type of monetary reformer, it is sufficient to make money cheaper or to go on increasing its quantity, whether in the form of producers' credits or consumers' purchasing power, or to apply the various patent devices they propose. Once this is done, they believe that economic life may be allowed to take care of itself and that all will then work out for the best. Those who hold such views ignore the true character of the economic system and even the fundamental rules of human nature.

(3) Monetary Planning and Human Nature

In the absence of economic planning, the favourable effects of monetary planning are bound to lead to the development of disequilibria and over-speculation. Human nature being what it is, if conditions remain only moderately prosperous or even stable for several years, most people take it for granted that they will remain so for ever. There will be reckless over-production in various directions on the assumption that in a stable and improving world all goods produced will be bought. There will be over-spending on the part of consumers on the assumption that their incomes will at least be safe, though probably in the belief that they will increase. There will be over-speculation in every imaginable commodity and security. The experience of 1929 has proved that in face of reckless optimism of the public the authorities are powerless to check a credit expansion which in such circumstances tends to feed itself. Indeed, the managed currency which becomes unmanageable may best be compared with an avalanche which may grow rapidly for a while, but which ends by destroying life and property and itself.

In order to ensure that the good effects of monetary reform should be lasting, it is necessary to divert them into well-controlled channels. This is duly realised by serious monetary reformers. They do not regard their schemes as one-way streets, but as influences which can work in both directions. Their schemes can stimulate trade and consumption where such stimulus is needed, but they can also check production and consumption where they tend to develop in unwanted directions and to an unwanted degree. The essential difference between mere expansionism and monetary management lies in the realisation of the necessity of controlling the development brought about by monetary reform. Most advocates of a managed currency are firmly convinced that they are capable of achieving such control by means of monetary management. They assume that, as money is the medium through which producers and consumers can fulfil their function, the regulation of the quantity of money is sufficient to regulate the whole economic system. The tap through which producers' credit or consumers' purchasing power flows can and should be turned in either direction whenever necessary.

(4) Limitations of Monetary Reform

It is deplorable that would-be monetary reformers, even the most intelligent among them, are so obsessed by the monetary aspects of the problems that they utterly fail to see any other aspects of them. Even those who are vaguely aware that something more is required than mere monetary manipulations confine themselves to ill-defined and inadequate proposals for the adoption of planning in some non-monetary spheres. Many of them favour the control of investment at home and abroad and some of them are even aware of the need for general economic planning. Usually, however, they make only passing references to the subject and their readers may well form the impression that economic reform is insignificant compared with monetary reform. In reality, the truth lies in the opposite direction. The importance of economic reform is vastly greater than that of monetary reform, which should be a small part of the broader economic measures.

It would be idle to deny that the adoption of a managed monetary system would constitute a very important step in the right direction. It would be much more satisfactory than the system by which producers' credits and consumers' purchasing power are allowed to take care of themselves and are at the mercy of influences which escape control. Our criticism is that monetary management does not in itself go far enough in controlling economic forces. Those who imagine that monetary management can achieve economic planning have the great failing of thinking in terms of totals and averages while ignoring or under-rating the importance of any development within those totals or averages. They think that in order to regulate production and consumption, it is sufficient to regulate the total volume of credit or the total purchasing power. They do not seem to be particularly concerned about regulating distribution at all. They imagine that, by managing the average price level, they can control the economic system. In reality, the control of the average and of the totals would not prevent development of grave disequilibria in various directions. Over-production would easily develop in various branches of production, while the maldistribution of purchasing power might easily lead to under-consumption. To eliminate or mitigate these evils would require more than monetary management. It would indeed be easy to solve the problem of mankind if the solution amounted only to the adoption of the right kind of currency and to manipulation of the volume of currency.

(5) To Avoid Disequilibrium

In order to achieve the desired end it is necessary to control not only the total production and total purchasing power but also the distribution of this total over various categories and classes. This cannot be achieved by mere monetary manipulations. A high degree of economic planning is required to prevent the over-production, over-speculation and over-consumption which, as we pointed out above, is the natural consequence of a few years of relative prosperity and stability. A high degree of direct control of production—not only of its total but also of its particular branches—and of prices, wages and the distribution of purchasing power would be required to prevent the development of local disequilibria which might easily develop into a general disequilibrium and a first-rate crisis.

Several monetary reformers—Mr. Keynes in the first place—are aware that something more is required than an endeavour to control total production and consumption. They realise the necessity for distinguishing between certain types of consumption. Mr. Keynes lays much stress upon discrimination between capital goods and consumption goods. This is unquestionably an important step, but it may well be asked whether it goes far enough. Even if monetary management were successful in maintaining equilibrium between capital goods and consumption goods, disequilibria may easily develop within these two large categories.

Admittedly, it is possible to control production to a large degree through the intermediary of the banking organisation by extending or withholding credit to certain branches of production. If this is done under the guidance of a central authority, it amounts to economic planning executed with the aid of the banks. It is doubtful whether in itself this regulation would go far enough. After all, many producers are to a large extent independent of bank credits and need not necessarily contract their output merely because bank credit to their branch of production is curtailed. Consequently, it would become necessary to curtail credit to those who depend upon it to a very large degree, and that would be neither fair nor expedient. On the whole, it is desirable to control production by non-monetary means, and to adjust the monetary apparatus to the changing conditions brought about by the non-monetary control.

(6) Distribution and Consumption

Distribution and consumption are independent of monetary control to a much larger degree than is production. It is true that additional purchasing power can be created by monetary means, but the distribution of purchasing power is essentially a non-monetary function. Monetary policy in itself is unable to prevent a maldistribution of purchasing power in various ways. To prevent profit inflation, or other tendencies of a similar adverse effect, the adoption of some kind of New Deal is necessary.

The discussion of details of economic planning is beyond the scope of this volume. In the author's opinion, the tendency towards a higher degree of planning, which has become evident all over the civilised world, has come to stay. It may assume a different form and it may attain different degrees in various countries. It is also possible that from time to time there may be a reaction in favour of freedom and anarchy. In the long run, however, the trend of evolution can only move towards a more rational and controlled system. It is essential that monetary planning should proceed hand in hand with economic planning. This is to the interest of monetary reform and reformers, for the failure of monetary planning owing to the absence of economic planning is calculated to discredit progressive monetary ideas. Excessive confidence of monetary reformers in the infallibility of their schemes may easily lead to the under-estimation of the non-monetary factors. While unquestionably economic planning cannot be complete without monetary management, on the other hand, monetary management cannot do justice to itself unless it is associated with economic planning.

CHAPTER XLII

POLITICAL ASPECTS OF MONETARY REFORM

(1) Reciprocal Effects of Finance and Politics

A volume dealing with various aspects of monetary reform could not be regarded as complete if it ignored the political aspects. Politics and finance are to a very large extent interrelated. It is a commonplace popular with leader writers that while in France finance is determined by political considerations, in Great Britain politics are guided by considerations of the financial interests of the nation. This formula oversimplifies the situation, as formulæ usually do. Politics and finance affect each other reciprocally in every country and in every age, though their relative degree of influence may vary according to country and according to period.

In dealing with the political aspects of monetary reform, we must examine how far the monetary reform movement is affected by political considerations and how far the political situation can be affected by monetary reform. The examination of both questions is of importance since the interrelation between politics and monetary policy has developed to a large extent subconsciously.

We have pointed out in earlier chapters that the increasing influence of the masses of the electorate and the increasing interest which the public is taking in matters of monetary policy work towards the adoption of monetary reform measures. The orthodox system of the gold standard eminently suited the " ruling classes " that controlled the Governments in most countries during the nineteenth century. The cult of stability at the cost of progress is an essentially conservative principle. As at the same time it is in accordance with the teachings of the classical school, it thus received the support of liberals as well as conservatives. This was for the most part tacit support. In the absence of any popular agitation in favour of radical changes in the monetary system, it was taken for granted that the general public desired no such changes. Thus assumption was not far wrong. It is only since the working classes have begun to make themselves felt as a political factor that the chances that the radical monetary reform movement may obtain popular support in its fight against monetary orthodoxy have begun to improve.

(2) Electorate's Lack of Interest in Monetary Reform

Even the adoption of universal suffrage was not in itself sufficient to lead to the acceleration of the progress of monetary reform, for the majority of the electorate did not take any interest in questions of monetary policy. Few elections have yet been fought on the issue of "monetary reform *v.* monetary orthodoxy". The great masses failed to realise the extent to which the improvement of their standard of living was hampered by orthodox monetary policy and by the orthodox system itself. Even the political parties which relied upon the working classes preferred to adopt clear-cut issues such as nationalisation of certain branches of production, or increased social expenditure, rather than to include obscure radical monetary reform proposals in their programme. Strangely enough, the radical monetary reform movement before the crisis found more ready support among essentially conservative classes, such as retired colonels, disgruntled industrialists and grumbling farmers, than among the industrial workmen whose welfare was in reality at stake. Indeed, in Great Britain at any rate, many Socialists viewed some of the radical monetary reform movements with suspicion as a "Fascist" attempt to divert support from Socialism. The Marxian conception of Socialism has very little use for monetary reform. Modern Socialism has begun to take an academic interest in monetary reform problems as and when it began to emancipate itself from the dogmatism of nineteenth-century Marxism.

(3) Effect of the Crisis of 1931

The world crisis of 1931 provided an excellent eye-opener. It made the general public realise, more than innumerable articles, books and speeches could do, the extent to which monetary policy could affect their welfare. The fact that countries which have departed from orthodoxy have recovered to a very large extent, while those which continued to follow the orthodox creed have in consequence suffered to an increasing degree, spoke for itself. It is true that in some countries, such as France or Switzerland, the majority of the public has so far failed to understand the teachings of the experience of the last few years. Yet even in those countries progressive monetary ideas have received an increasing degree of popular support. In 1935 a referendum in Switzerland concerning the proposals of the de Mann Scheme resulted in a strong minority —42 per cent of the votes—in favour of the reform. Considering the extreme conservatism of the Swiss people and their sentimental attachment to orthodox monetary principles, the extent of the minority was significant. In France the successive Governments abstained from devaluing the franc even though their experts realised that devaluation was inevitable, simply because they assumed that the predominant majority of the electorate would be against such steps and indeed against every kind of radical monetary reform. In the author's view, a French referendum similar to the one carried out in Switzerland would in all probability result in a very strong minority in favour of monetary reform. As far as the majority of the public in these countries is concerned, they are undoubtedly guilty of having learnt nothing and forgotten nothing since 1931.

In the Anglo-Saxon countries and in the countries of the Sterling Bloc in general, however, the lesson of the crisis was not wasted, and the public has become conscious of the vital importance of a progressive monetary policy upon their welfare. For this reason, it is unthinkable that in these countries the Governments should be able to switch back to orthodoxy even if they wished to do so. While before 1925 the idea that sterling simply must be restored to its pre-war parity inspired enthusiasm, or at any rate met with tacit approval, on the part of the British public, any British Government which now dared to put forward such an idea would soon be swept away by popular indignation. To-day, the British public knows more about these things than it did ten years ago. Any reactionary attempt in the monetary sphere would meet with determined opposition.

The same may be said to be true in the United States,

though there the excesses of the monetary reform movement may have strengthened the tendency towards orthodoxy in some quarters. Nevertheless, the majority of the public is not likely ever to approve a policy which in the past increased unemployment in the United States to fifteen millions and drove the whole banking system to the verge of bankruptcy. In the British Dominions, too, deflationary orthodoxy would never again be tolerated. The essentially democratic communities of Australia, New Zealand and Canada would never put up with victimisation for the sake of reactionary monetary principles. Even South Africa, with her dependence upon gold production, would reject the orthodox policy which in 1932 threatened to reduce the country to bankruptcy.

(4) Democracy and Monetary Reform

In a negative sense the political factor will thus tend to prevent a retrograde movement in the monetary sphere. In a positive sense it is likely to encourage progressive monetary reform. It is being realised to an increasing degree that monetary reform can go a long way towards increasing the standard of living of the masses. In some countries substantial sections of political opinion have gone so far as to support extremist movements, such as the Douglas credit scheme, as a means of escape from the fetters of monetary orthodoxy. In all probability, we shall encounter such misguided movements in various countries in future, especially if their authorities display a rigid resistance to moderate reform. Just as in the social sphere reform can go a long way towards disarming revolution, so in the monetary sphere a progressive attitude is the best way to prevent the development of extremism.

There can be no doubt that an enlightened democratic community will tend to adopt reasonable monetary reform measures, which, without endangering the financial stability of the country, will make it possible for the population to benefit by technical progress. It is probable that, in future, questions of monetary policy will play a much more important part in general elections than they have done in the past. From this point of view, it is gratifying to note the increase in the interest of the general public in monetary questions. To some extent this increase may be the passing result of the depression which, as we said above, drew attention to the monetary factor. To a very large extent, however, the desire of the public to know more about vital money matters is likely to survive the depression. It is essential that those in favour of progressive reform should do their best to keep the interest of the public alive by discussing their problems in language that is understandable to the man in the street.

(5) How Monetary Reform affects Politics

Let us now examine the question of the effect of monetary reform upon politics. Monetary policy can certainly produce profound effect both on home politics and on international politics. Internally, the adoption of progressive monetary reform can go a long way towards allaying the discontent which is the hotbed of extremist movements, whether Communism or Fascism. It is only amidst conditions of acute depression or violent crisis that political extremists stand a chance of assuming power. But for the fact that unemployment in Germany had increased to six millions by 1933 as a result of deflationary monetary policy, Hitler would never have assumed control. In France, the Croix de Feu movement owes its *raison d'être* to the depressed conditions created by the orthodox monetary policy pursued by successive Governments.

The discontent which threatens to overthrow the constitutions and plunge the countries into the horrors of civil war could easily be disarmed by the adoption of a reasonable progressive monetary policy. In all probability, this will be done in some countries. A policy of expansionism aiming at reducing unemployment to normal proportions will in all probability be adopted where unemployment threatens to lead to political troubles. Indeed, monetary reform is likely to be used to an increasing degree as a political lightning conductor. In democratic countries monetary reform will probably provide the means for the rival parties to make a bid for the support of the electorate. Since the adoption of universal suffrage, the competition between Conservative and Socialist parties in Great Britain, and between their equivalents in other countries, has largely assumed the form of outbidding each other on social expenditure. It is on account of this policy that diehard Tories have accused the British Conservative party of pursuing a Socialist policy. Owing to the large amount of the public debt and the inevitable necessity for rearmament expenditure, a further increase of social expenditure would necessitate the adoption of a more radical monetary policy. In all probability, some Conservatives and Socialists will in future compete with each other in this respect. The monetary policy of the National Government under Mr. Chamberlain has gradually become much more radical than it was in the past, and there is no lack of criticism from reactionary quarters on the ground that the Conservative Government is putting into practice radical monetary principles.

(6) International Politics and Monetary Reform

From an international political point of view, the influence of monetary reform is at last beginning to be realised. It is now evident that monetary orthodoxy is one of the sources of armed conflict. It was because of an orthodox monetary policy that the lira became overvalued and Italy became unable to export a sufficient amount to cover her import requirements, and it was these developments which led Signor Mussolini to the conclusion that it was essential for Italy to acquire colonies with raw material resources. The Abyssinian War was to a large extent the alternative chosen in preference to monetary reform. In the case of Japan, the orthodox policy of restoring the yen to its pre-war parity was largely responsible for the economic conditions which led to the adoption of an expansive foreign policy, culminating in the conquest of Manchukuo. In the case of Germany, Dr. Schacht's monetary orthodoxy is largely responsible for the tendency in German foreign policy towards demanding the restoration of her colonies. Monetary orthodoxy is thus, actually or potentially, an important cause of war. Consequently there is immense scope for monetary reform to serve the cause of true pacifism. It is not adequately realised that the problem of raw material is largely a problem of monetary policy. In time of peace there is no need whatsoever for every country to possess its own raw material resources in order to secure continuity of supply. Provided that it is prepared to adopt a monetary system that enables it to sell as well as to buy abroad, it is a matter of comparatively small importance whether or not it produces its raw materials in its own colonies. Moreover, in time of war the possession of colonies does not in itself secure the continuity of supplies, as was shown by the case of Germany after 1914.

If the world adopts a monetary philosophy which no longer regards as a matter of honour the maintenance of the stability of parities through deflation, then one of the important causes of war can be removed. In that case, a country whose currency is grossly overvalued would not need to embark upon a war of conquest in order to be able to import her food and raw material requirements. All that she would have to do would be to adopt the conception of alterable parities, by which the value of the national currency can be adjusted to a level at which the country concerned can export and can therefore import, and to adopt exchange clearing by means of which goods can be exchanged on a rational basis that is satisfactory to both parties.

(7) Internal Prosperity and International Peace

Monetary reform can also serve the cause of peace by enabling the Governments to increase internal prosperity without having to adopt an aggressive foreign policy in order to secure markets abroad. The nineteenth-century free-trade conception led to the belief that prosperity could be achieved only by the expansion of foreign markets. For this reason undue importance was attached to foreign trade, and the logical outcome was a clash between the conflicting interests of rival nations. It is to the credit of Mr. J. M. Keynes that he has drawn attention to this all-important political aspect of monetary reform. In his book, *The General Theory of Employment, Interest and Money*, he points out that under the old gold standard a favourable balance of payments was necessary to make possible a reduction of interest rates and thus an increase in employment; that since the favourable balance of one country meant an unfavourable balance of another country, internal prosperity could be achieved only by shifting the burden of unemployment to other countries; and that consequently the interests of countries under the gold standard were sharply conflicting with one another. Mr. Keynes is convinced that the pursuance of independent monetary policies by all countries aiming at an increase of their internal prosperity is the right way towards securing a more satisfactory basis for international commercial intercourse between them. For this reason, monetary reform could serve the cause of peace better than the old system of the gold standard.

The importance of the political aspects of monetary reform, whether as an active or a passive factor, cannot be sufficiently emphasised. In particular, it is essential that the public should realise the international political implications of monetary management. Once it is realised sufficiently to what extent pacifism can be served by monetary reform, there can be no doubt that the reform movement will easily overcome the resistance which is now hampering its course in most countries.

CHAPTER XLIII

MORAL ASPECTS OF MONETARY REFORM

(1) The End justifies the Means

The main object of the monetary reform movement is to enable mankind to enjoy the maximum benefit from technical progress. This end is of paramount importance for the welfare of the great masses. It therefore justifies any means by which it can be achieved. If the author is opposed to some of the extreme reform proposals it is not because he is reluctant to break with traditions or time-honoured principles. He believes that all the self-imposed rules and restrictions should be scrapped without hesitation for the sake of the progress of mankind. But in answering the question whether or not it is morally justifiable to sacrifice traditions, law and existing practice, it is always necessary to examine whether any particular proposal is in the long run a step in the direction of progress. In the author's view, extreme proposals endanger the continuity of progress and entail the risk of a setback in consequence of their failure. It is only on such ground that we are morally justified in rejecting reform proposals. Admittedly, it is a matter of opinion where to draw the line between sound and unsound reform schemes. The discussion between advocates and opponents of reform should confine itself to their divergences of views about the whereabouts of this border line.

Unfortunately, reform proposals are frequently opposed, not on the ground that the desired end cannot be achieved through the means suggested, but on the ground that it is not desirable to attain the end by such means. By the nature of things, the orthodox camp is tradition-ridden. It is too anxious to return to the "good old days" to consider other solutions, even though their adoption would mean a material improvement in the welfare of the majority of mankind. Throughout this book we have taken it for granted that the improvement of the standard of living of the masses is more important than anything this extreme wing of the orthodox school stands for. While it may be open to argument whether the means recommended in this volume are suitable to achieve the supreme end, in the author's view it is inadmissible to contest the desirability of the end itself.

(2) Negative and Positive Object of Monetary Reform

It cannot, of course, be emphasised sufficiently that monetary reform alone would be unable to achieve the desired end. We have pointed out on many occasions in earlier chapters that monetary reform should be adopted as part of a general scheme of economic planning. In the absence of economic management, monetary management in itself may lead to disappointing and even disastrous results. Economic planning, however, is unthinkable without monetary management, and without a thorough-going all-round monetary reform. The object of monetary reform is not merely to accelerate the pace of technical progress but also to enable the widest possible range of classes to benefit by the progress. Unquestionably, progress was also made under the orthodox system during the nineteenth century. This progress was at times, and in many ways, remarkable. It was, however, mainly the so-called upper classes that benefited by it, while the standard of living of the great masses was not affected to a sufficient degree. Monetary reform coupled with economic planning should enable producers to increase their output on a very large scale and to sell the surplus to the largest possible number of consumers.

In a negative sense the object of monetary reform is to remove the main obstacle to progress, which is the excessive sensitiveness of the orthodox system and the excessive timidity of its application. In a positive sense the object of monetary reform is to provide the means for an expansion of production and consumption. Evidently the monetary reform movement is inspired by essentially humane considerations. Its good intentions deserve recognition even by those who disapprove of the methods by which various reformers seek to achieve their object. Because of its humane character the monetary reform movement carries immense moral strength. Its supporters have every right to claim to be the standard-bearers of progress and of the improvement of the welfare of mankind. If they are ignored, misunderstood or abused—as they often are—they may comfort themselves with the knowledge that throughout history those who have sought to improve the moral or material welfare of mankind by attempts to change the old order have always met with a similar reception.

(3) Progress *v.* Vested Interests

The struggle of the monetary reform movement is the struggle of humanitarianism against legalism, of progress against conservatism and vested interests. Human nature being what it is, it is only natural that those who have every reason to be satisfied with their degree of welfare under the existing system are opposed to radical changes. Believing that they have a great deal to lose and relatively little to gain through any change, they are naturally in favour of maintaining the existing state of affairs. In reality it is as much in the interest of the wealthy classes as in that of the poorer classes that economic progress should be achieved by means of monetary reform. As we pointed out in the previous chapter, monetary reform can perform a valuable function as the lightning-conductor of revolutionary tension. Evidently it is to the interest of the wealthy classes to support any endeavour calculated peaceably to improve the standard of living of the masses even if in doing so they were to risk losing part of their own wealth. The financial risk involved in monetary reform is incomparably smaller than the political risk involved in stubborn resistance to monetary reform. The opposition of vested interests to monetary reform is, therefore, not only selfish but also short-sighted. It is the task of the monetary reform movement to overcome this resistance and to carry out changes provided that the risk involved in the experiment appears to be justified from the point of view of the possible results to the community as a whole. Since the welfare of mankind means the welfare of the majority it is unjustifiable to abstain from experimenting merely because a minority is satisfied with the existing state of affairs.

The crusaders of monetary reform have by no means an easy task. Monetary orthodoxy has built up an intimidating array of legal and moral defences. It has surrounded itself by laws which are calculated to safeguard vested interests. Any Government which finds it impossible or inexpedient to carry out the letter of monetary legislation is branded as a defaulter. A change of the existing legislation by means of devaluation, an abolition of the gold clause, etc., is denounced as an act of repudiation. It is the task of the monetary reform movement to obtain the demolition of these legal defences and to enact monetary legislation more in keeping with the requirements of progress.

(4) Fight against Orthodox Conception

In addition to its legal defences, monetary orthodoxy has also built a strong line of moral defences by the establishment through generations of the belief that the maintenance of the existing system is a matter of honesty. Systematic repetition through many generations has led many to the view that it is a matter of honour for a nation to defend its parity at no matter what cost. Orthodox economists have, so to speak, established a monopoly of morality. Anyone who contravenes the rules which they approve is denounced as being dishonest or immoral. A quasi-religious element has also been introduced by rejecting monetary expansion with the indignation of the puritans who condemn spending. Indeed, to believe the teachings of the arch-deflationary wing of orthodox economists, it is altogether immoral to seek to improve the welfare of mankind by monetary manipulations. The puritans of orthodox economics actually believe that the aim should be to maintain mankind on a bare subsistence level in the hope that for a lean time in this world mankind will get due reward in the next. It is the duty of the monetary reform movement to overcome this absurd conception.

The underlying truth is that everything is justified if it is in accordance with the interests of mankind. Progress cannot be strangled by self-imposed restrictions adopted in conditions which no longer exist. All systems, legal or monetary, exist to serve the supreme end of improving the welfare of mankind. They have a *raison d'être* only so long as they serve that end. The moment they cease to serve it and become an obstacle to progress they must go overboard. Progress cannot be checked for the sake of upholding a system which no longer serves its purpose.

(5) Too Much "Safety First"

The pace of progress through monetary management should be limited only by essentially practical considerations. Expansion should continue up to the limit beyond which it might endanger confidence and thus might defeat its object. The difference between scientific and moderate reformers on the one hand and reckless reformers on the other is that the latter propose to go beyond the safety limits, and, if their schemes were adopted, they might endanger progress instead of assisting it. At the other extreme the constant preaching of "Safety First" by the orthodox school tends to undermine confidence in and inspire distrust towards even the most moderate of reform schemes. As the extent to which monetary reform may safely proceed towards expansion depends largely upon the attitude of the public to it, the orthodox school possesses considerable power to check progress, even if it should be unable ultimately to prevent the reform movement from overcoming its resistance. There can be such a thing as an overdose of "safety first". Every change from existing and known conditions to hitherto unknown conditions involves a certain amount of risk, but if throughout history mankind had been afraid to take such risks, the world would not be at the stage of progress that it is to-day.

It would be a mistake to imagine that monetary reform in itself necessarily tends to inspire distrust in the mind of the public. On the contrary, unless confidence is undermined by the defeatism of orthodox critics, the adoption of moderate and reasonable reforms should actually inspire confidences. Such an adoption might even lead to a national regeneration similar to that which may follow the adoption of a new religion or a new political creed. The feeling that with the adoption of a new system the community has turned over a new leaf may in itself go a long way towards bringing about an all-round regeneration even outside the monetary sphere. It may introduce an entirely new spirit into the whole economic and political life of the community. Such a spirit would in itself go a long way towards securing the success of the monetary reform.

CHAPTER XLIV

THE FUTURE OF MONETARY REFORM

(1) Orthodoxy fighting a Losing Battle

We have seen in earlier chapters how far monetary reform has proceeded since the war. In a number of directions it has made remarkable progress, but in others it has made little headway, or has failed altogether. It now remains to examine the prospects of the further progress of monetary reform. In Chapter XL we examined the precise directions in which, in the author's view, future monetary reform ought to proceed. Is there any likelihood of such developments, or, indeed, of any progress in general towards the adoption of some form of advanced monetary reform?

One thing is certain. The experience of the last few years has done much to prepare the ground for monetary reform. Under the weight of facts, the orthodox monetary system has become utterly discredited in the eyes of the general public in every country and also in the eyes of the predominant majority of experts. It is true that the orthodox school continues to put up a desperate fight, resisting to the utmost every inch of progress towards reform. It is, however, fighting a losing battle and the number of its supporters is diminishing. This is only natural. The orthodox arguments are defeated by inescapable evidence that since 1931 every country which has relaxed the orthodoxy of its monetary policy has gone a long way towards recovery, while every country which has stubbornly adhered to orthodoxy has suffered heavy disadvantages in consequence.

There is reason to believe that before very long orthodox monetary opinion will suffer a further major reverse through the collapse of the resistance of the Gold Bloc. The devaluation or depreciation of the franc and the other gold currencies would conclusively prove that even the utmost sacrifices for orthodox principles are unable to preserve those principles in the face of grim reality. The more the desperate resistance to the inexorable pressure is prolonged, the more the countries concerned will suffer and the more the need for a more rational monetary conception will be realised.

(2) Central Banks' Advice Disregarded

It is true that in quarters which are most closely concerned with monetary reform, such as Central Banks and the Bank for International Settlements, the lessons of the last few years' experience are still deliberately ignored. The wisdom of these quarters can be summed up in one sentence: "Go back to the gold standard at once and all will be well." They have only one idea which they repeat to boredom on every possible occasion. According to them, those countries which are still on gold should retain their old parities and those which are off gold should stabilise at the highest possible parities. This is the long and the short of the advice they can give to their respective Governments. They do not even make an effort to work out the rules of the new gold standard which is to be adopted Apparently they think that they can resume where they left off at the advent of the *débâcle*, just as the representatives of the *ancien régime* believed before them. They have learnt nothing and forgotten nothing.

Fortunately, the Governments—or at any rate most of them—are inspired by a much more progressive spirit. Since they consist of politicians they cannot afford to be too dogmatic, and have to swim with the tide of public opinion. They are not in a position to follow the examples of Central Banks—even if they should wish to do so—in isolating themselves from the current of the *Zeitgeist*. The statesmen and Government officials have had to realise the necessity for monetary reform. While in the past most Governments allowed themselves to be guided in their monetary policy to a large extent by Central Banks, many of them have come to disregard the advice given from those ultra-orthodox quarters. Even in the countries of the Gold Bloc, where the Governments have not yet gathered sufficient courage to take the plunge in breaking away from orthodoxy, the advice of the Central Banks is followed with increasing reluctance. In France there is a widening gap between the viewpoint of the Bank of France and that of the Government, and there is a sharp conflict between the Treasury's point of view and that of the bank of issue.

(3) Monetary Reform in the United States

The change in the attitude of Governments is particularly evident in the Anglo-Saxon countries. In fact, in the United States there was a sudden and spectacular change in 1933 from monetary orthodoxy to a very advanced degree of monetary radicalism. Unfortunately, the country was the scene of a number of badly planned and badly executed monetary experiments, carried out simultaneously and in circumstances that were anything but favourable to their success. This orgy of monetary reform inevitably led to a certain degree of reaction in favour of a more orthodox monetary policy. At the time of writing the official American policy aims at the liquidation of some of its bold experiments. Notwithstanding this, the official American monetary philosophy is still characterised by a radical spirit. It continues to aim at a managed monetary system backed by a substantial metallic reserve. The spirit of expansion still predominates.

Whether or not this tendency in the United States towards a progressive monetary policy will continue depends mainly upon the result of the next presidential election. Should President Roosevelt be returned, it is certain that he will pursue a bold and ambitious monetary policy without, however, committing the excesses which lack of experience made him commit during the earlier part of his term of office. There will be no more experimenting with the "rubber dollar", no more "flirting" with extreme inflation, and perhaps no more efforts at raising and maintaining the world price of silver at an absurd level. On the other hand, there will be a managed monetary expansion, an ambitious policy of public works and a policy aiming at the creation and correct distribution of purchasing power. During a second term of office, President Roosevelt might stabilise the dollar definitely, but in all probability it would be on the understanding that, on any recurrence of strong adverse pressure, the parity could be changed or the gold standard could be suspended.

(4) Neville Chamberlain *v.* Montagu Norman

In Great Britain there has been no spectacular change in the Government's monetary policy. There has been, however, an evolution so gradual that the fundamental change which has taken place has almost completely escaped attention. In 1931, the Government's monetary policy was as orthodox as that of the Bank of England. After the suspension of the gold standard, a deflationary policy was adopted to prevent sterling from depreciating too much. None but the fanatics of monetary orthodoxy could have found fault with the Government's policy. Indeed, Mr. Neville Chamberlain was in 1931 about as orthodox as Mr. Montagu Norman. To-day, however, he is definitely an expansionist. He favours a policy of cheap money and is against an early return to the gold standard mainly because it would make for dearer money. He believes in maintaining, for the time being at any rate, an elastic international value for sterling in order to avoid drastic changes in its internal value. Indeed, in many ways Mr. Neville Chamberlain is to-day more radical than some of the radical economists—such as Messrs. Keynes, Henderson and Sir Arthur Salter—for they would be prepared to commit themselves to the immediate stabilisation of sterling under certain conditions.

The British Treasury is definitely in favour of monetary expansion. It is alleged that when in February 1935 Mr. Norman, alarmed by what he considered boom-like symptoms in the markets, suggested an increase in the bank rate, the Treasury vetoed this proposal. Monetary expansion in the form of a larger note issue, and increases in bank deposits and in the gold reserve, etc., is proceeding unhampered. Indeed, it may be said that the Treasury has almost fallen into line with Mr. Hawtrey's expansionist ideas, which only a few years ago were considered to be hopelessly out of touch with the Treasury's official view. Also, when eventually the value of sterling is fixed, the Government is in favour of fixing it at a relatively low level, and to avoid international disequilibrium the Treasury favours a devaluation of the currencies of the Gold Bloc. Instead of bringing about an international readjustment in the upward direction, the Government prefers the adjustment to take place in a downward direction.

(5) Progress in Britain and U.S. Compared

It would be difficult if not impossible to fix a date when the change of policy took place. Indeed, in accordance with British traditions, it has taken place so gradually that even those responsible for the change have barely noticed it. For this reason, the trend towards radicalism and reform is on much safer foundations in Great Britain than it is in the United States. Should President Roosevelt be defeated by his Republican opponent at the presidential election, the result will almost inevitably be a spectacular reaction in favour of monetary orthodoxy. The fanatics of sound money will come back with a vengeance and the movement towards reform will be reversed. Dogmatism will once more dictate the pace of drastic deflation, and Professor Sprague's gospel of low wages will become the official religion.

No such change is likely to take place in Great Britain through internal political developments. Should the next election—which in any case is in the distant future—bring in a Socialist Government, the chances are that the progress towards reform would become accentuated and accelerated. As far as the present Government's term of office is concerned, Mr. Neville Chamberlain can be relied upon as a believer in a progressive monetary policy. Although a new convert to the progressive camp, he has evidently discarded the orthodox prejudices which during his first years of office handicapped the progress of British monetary policy. While he is not likely to lend himself to rash experimenting, he will in all probability do his utmost to maintain cheap money and expansion, at any rate until unemployment has been reduced to normal proportions. It is also conceivable that among other progressive monetary measures, the British Government will adopt exchange clearing on a large scale, as a temporary expedient at any rate, if not as a permanent system.

(6) World-wide Tendency towards Reform

Progressive monetary mentality has taken deep root also in the other countries of the Sterling Bloc. It is simply unthinkable that countries such as Sweden or the British Dominions would deliberately return to the chains of monetary orthodoxy now that they have tasted the advantages of an unorthodox policy. The same may be said of countries, such as Belgium, which have depreciated their currencies without actually joining the Sterling Bloc. M. van Zeeland's progressive spirit is likely to continue to inspire the monetary policy of Belgium. As for Japan, political considerations alone would make it impossible for her to revert to orthodoxy. Being engaged in an extremely ambitious task, she is most unlikely to handicap herself by the self-imposed restrictions of monetary orthodoxy.

As for the Gold Bloc and its satellites, the inconvenience caused by the stubborn orthodoxy of their monetary policy since 1931 is likely to bring forth a reaction in the opposite direction. Once the spell is broken through the devaluation or depreciation of their currencies, those in favour of monetary reform will have fair scope.

It is impossible to generalise upon the form which in each country the progress towards monetary reform is likely to assume. In most countries the policy of cheap money will receive widespread encouragement from its success in Great Britain. It is likely to be accompanied by a policy of expansion, though its form and extent, and the degree to which it is managed scientifically, will vary from country to country. It is probable that, when the gold standard is re-established in the leading countries, it will be a system totally different from the one that operated before the war or even before the crisis. It will be much less automatic and much more managed. The theory that parities ought to be absolutely unalterable will in all probability be discarded and replaced by the conception that internal as well as international stability should be maintained as a matter of expediency so long as it pays to maintain them.

Conceivably, however, once stability is restored, there may be a reversal to the old-fashioned orthodox spirit in monetary affairs. In that case, the world will need another severe lesson to teach it the disadvantages of monetary orthodoxy. Taking a long view, the monetary conception can only progress towards a higher degree of rationalism.

INDEX

For Product Safety Concerns and Information please contact our EU representative GPSR@taylorandfrancis.com
Taylor & Francis Verlag GmbH, Kaufingerstraße 24, 80331 München, Germany

www.ingramcontent.com/pod-product-compliance
Lightning Source LLC
LaVergne TN
LVHW011109300926
849160LV00008B/326
* 9 7 8 0 4 1 5 8 1 9 4 0 4 *